Same Difference
and Other Stories

by
Derek Kirk Kim

Top Shelf Productions

Published by Top Shelf Productions,
PO Box 1282, Marietta, GA 30061-1282, USA.
Publishers: Brett Warnock and Chris Staros.
Top Shelf Productions® and the Top Shelf Logo are
registered trademarks of Top Shelf Productions, Inc.
Visit our online catalog at www.topshelfcomix.com.

Indy Rock Pete's appearance in *Emo Rock Hyung* is
courtesy of R. Stevens. Indy Rock Pete is © by R. Stevens.
He appears regularly at www.dieselsweeties.com.

Most of the stories in this collection were first serialized at
www.lowbright.com over the course of 2000-2003.

This is a Lowbright collection.
www.lowbright.com
e-mail: lowbright@hotmail.com
mail: Derek Kirk Kim, PO Box 541, Pacifica, CA 94044

First edition: May 2003
First Top Shelf edition: May 2004
ISBN: ISBN1-891830-57-0

1 2 3 4 5 6 7 8 9 10
Printed in Canada.

This book is dedicated
with great love and respect
to my friends and family.

CONTENTS

Same
Difference

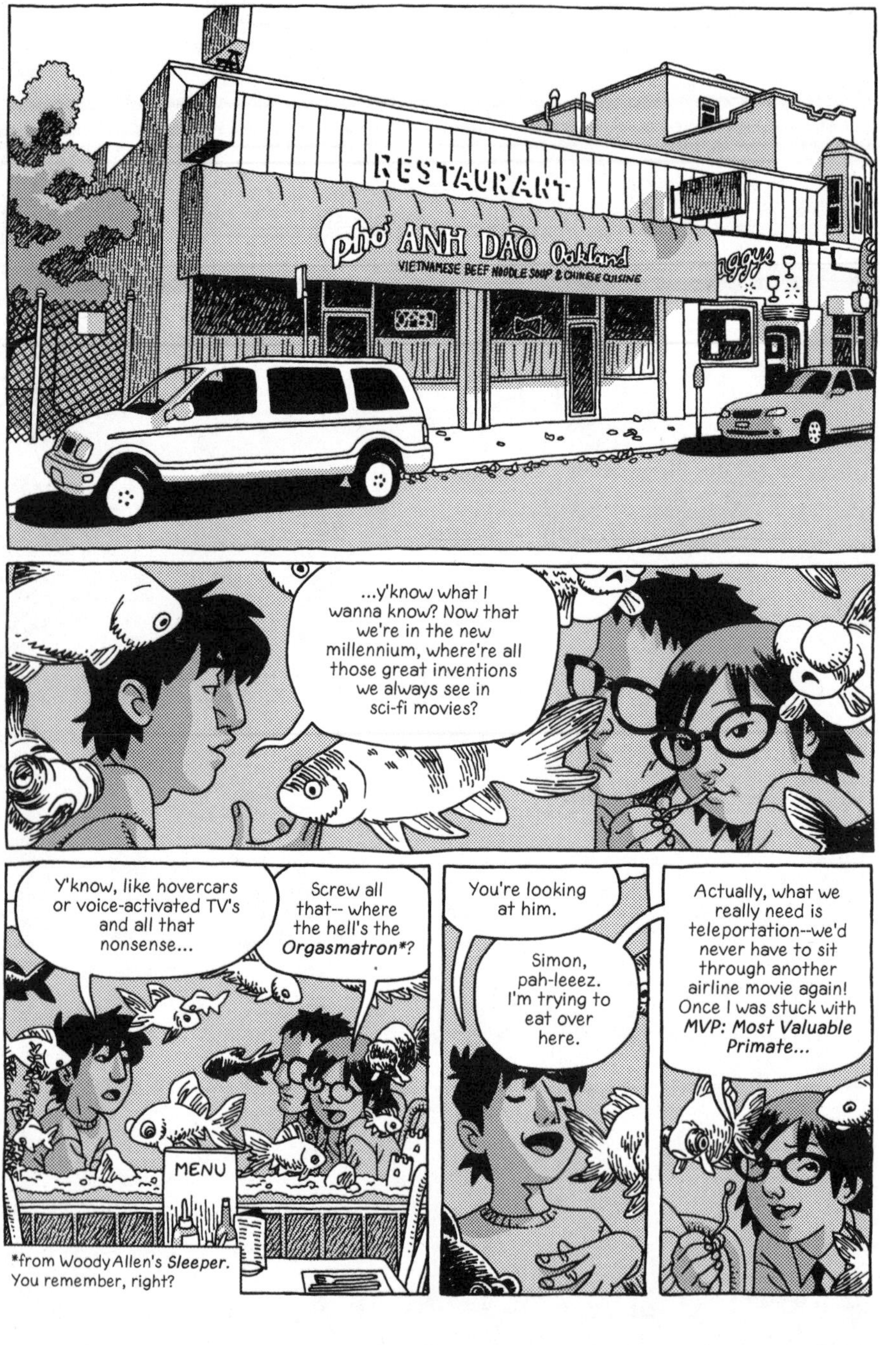
RESTAURANT
phở ANH DAO Oakland
VIETNAMESE BEEF NOODLE SOUP & CHINESE CUISINE
...y'know what I wanna know? Now that we're in the new millennium, where're all those great inventions we always see in sci-fi movies?
Y'know, like hovercars or voice-activated TV's and all that nonsense...
Screw all that-- where the hell's the *Orgasmatron**?
MENU
You're looking at him.
Simon, pah-leeez. I'm trying to eat over here.
Actually, what we really need is teleportation--we'd never have to sit through another airline movie again! Once I was stuck with ***MVP: Most Valuable Primate...***

*from Woody Allen's *Sleeper*. You remember, right?

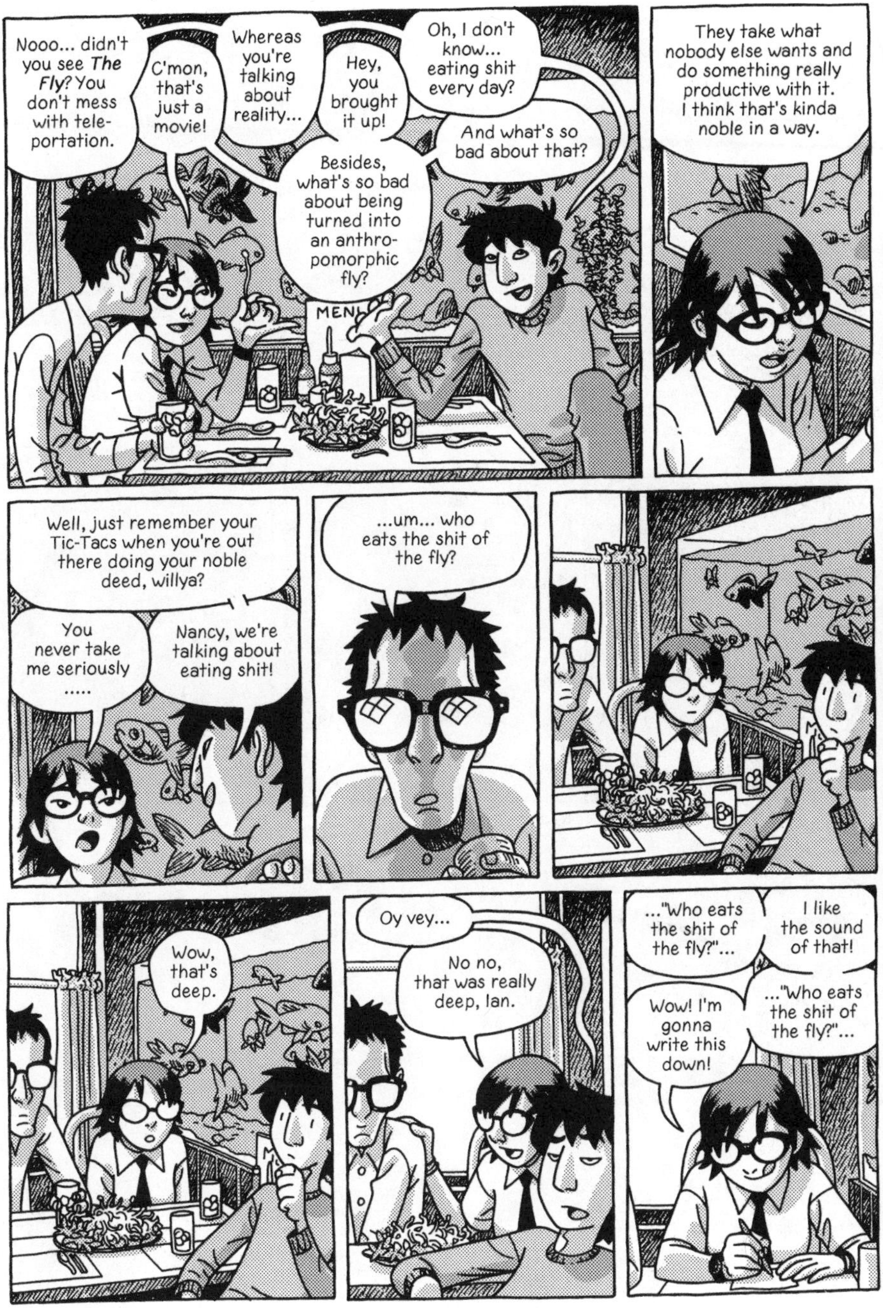

Nooo... didn't you see *The Fly*? You don't mess with tele-portation.
C'mon, that's just a movie!
Whereas you're talking about reality...
Hey, you brought it up!
Oh, I don't know... eating shit every day?
And what's so bad about that?
Besides, what's so bad about being turned into an anthro-pomorphic fly?
MENU
They take what nobody else wants and do something really productive with it. I think that's kinda noble in a way.
Well, just remember your Tic-Tacs when you're out there doing your noble deed, willya?
You never take me seriously .....
Nancy, we're talking about eating shit!
...um... who eats the shit of the fly?
Wow, that's deep.
Oy vey...
No no, that was really deep, Ian.
..."Who eats the shit of the fly?"...
I like the sound of that!
Wow! I'm gonna write this down!
..."Who eats the shit of the fly?"...

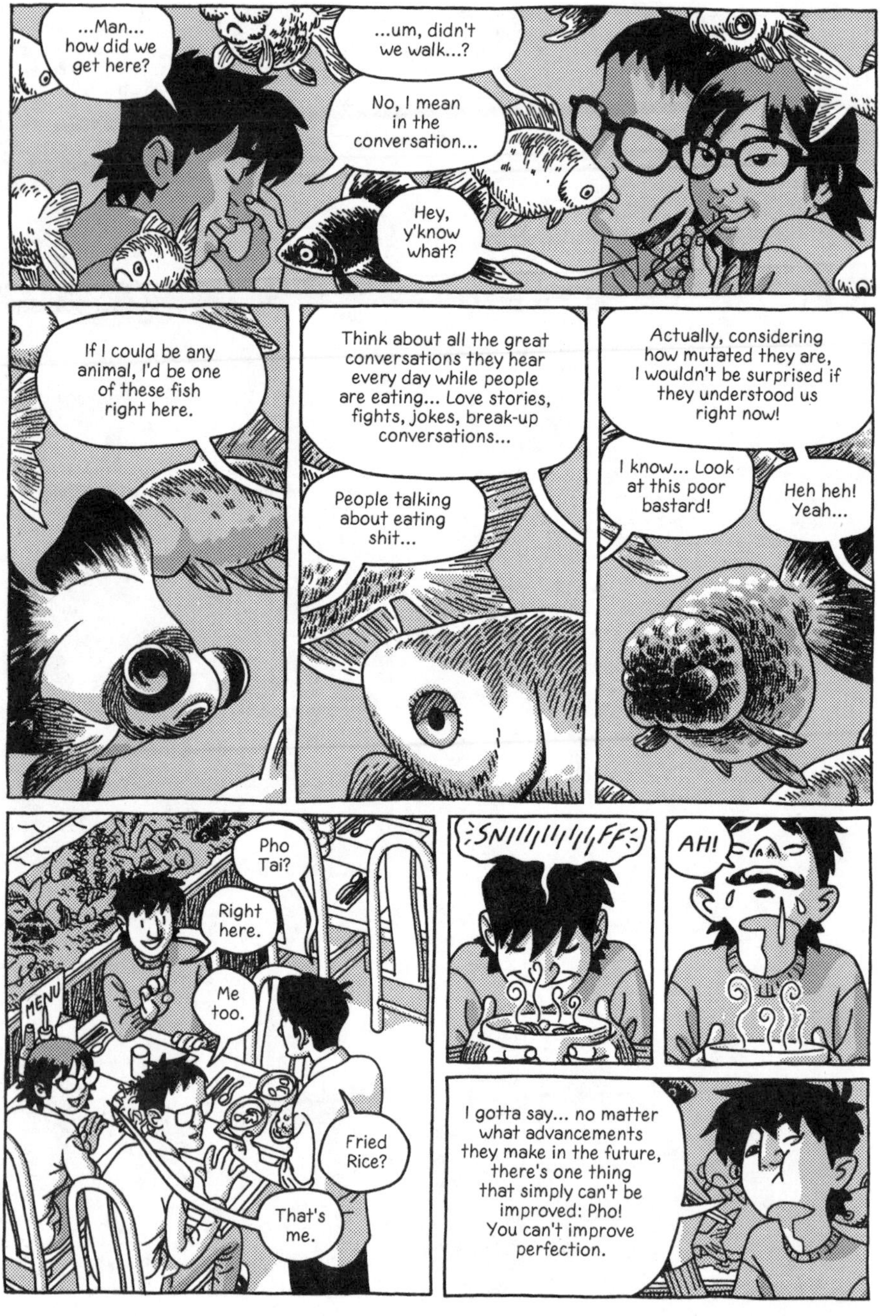
...Man... how did we get here?
...um, didn't we walk...?
No, I mean in the conversation...
Hey, y'know what?
If I could be any animal, I'd be one of these fish right here.
Think about all the great conversations they hear every day while people are eating... Love stories, fights, jokes, break-up conversations...
People talking about eating shit...
Actually, considering how mutated they are, I wouldn't be surprised if they understood us right now!
I know... Look at this poor bastard!
Heh heh! Yeah...
MENU
Pho Tai?
Right here.
Me too.
Fried Rice?
That's me.
SNIIIIIIIFF
AH!
I gotta say... no matter what advancements they make in the future, there's one thing that simply can't be improved: Pho! You can't improve perfection.

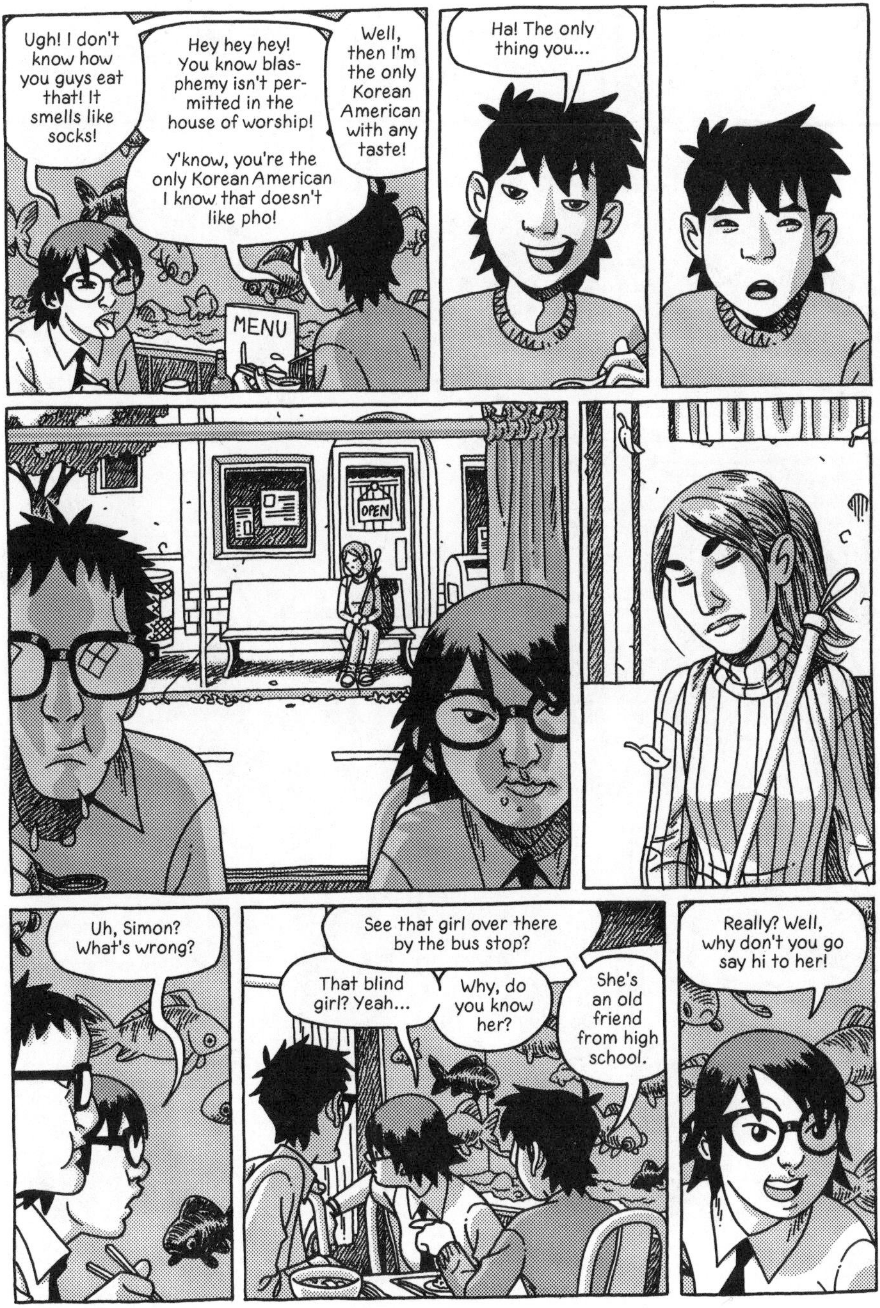

Ugh! I don't know how you guys eat that! It smells like socks!
Hey hey hey! You know blasphemy isn't permitted in the house of worship!
Y'know, you're the only Korean American I know that doesn't like pho!
MENU
Well, then I'm the only Korean American with any taste!
Ha! The only thing you...
OPEN
Uh, Simon? What's wrong?
See that girl over there by the bus stop?
That blind girl? Yeah...
Why, do you know her?
She's an old friend from high school.
Really? Well, why don't you go say hi to her!

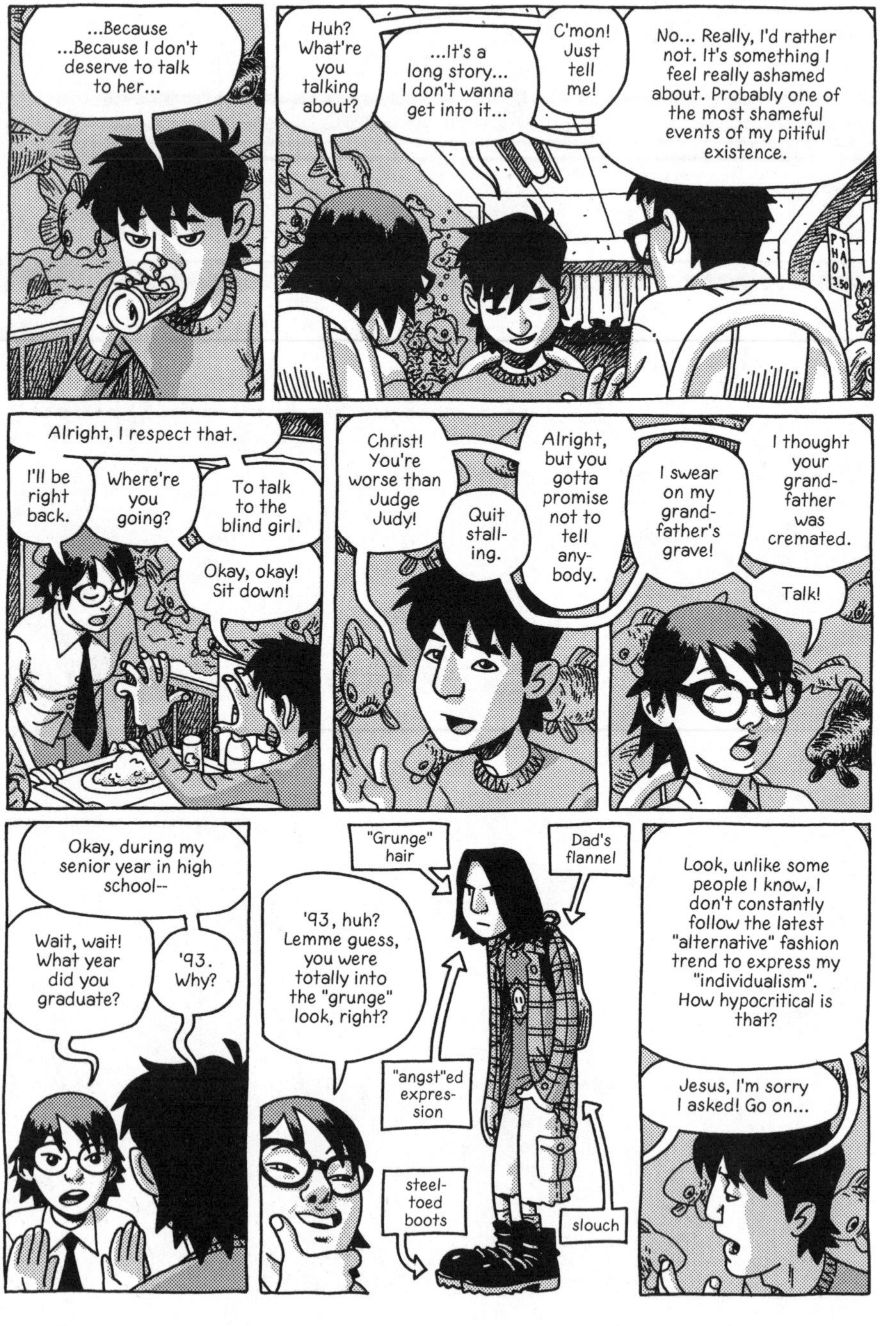
...Because ...Because I don't deserve to talk to her...
Huh? What're you talking about?
...It's a long story... I don't wanna get into it...
C'mon! Just tell me!
No... Really, I'd rather not. It's something I feel really ashamed about. Probably one of the most shameful events of my pitiful existence.
Alright, I respect that.
I'll be right back.
Where're you going?
To talk to the blind girl.
Okay, okay! Sit down!
Christ! You're worse than Judge Judy!
Quit stall-ing.
Alright, but you gotta promise not to tell any-body.
I swear on my grand-father's grave!
I thought your grand-father was cremated.
Talk!
Okay, during my senior year in high school--
Wait, wait! What year did you graduate?
'93. Why?
'93, huh? Lemme guess, you were totally into the "grunge" look, right?
"Grunge" hair
Dad's flannel
"angst"ed expres-sion
steel-toed boots
slouch
Look, unlike some people I know, I don't constantly follow the latest "alternative" fashion trend to express my "individualism". How hypocritical is that?
Jesus, I'm sorry I asked! Go on...

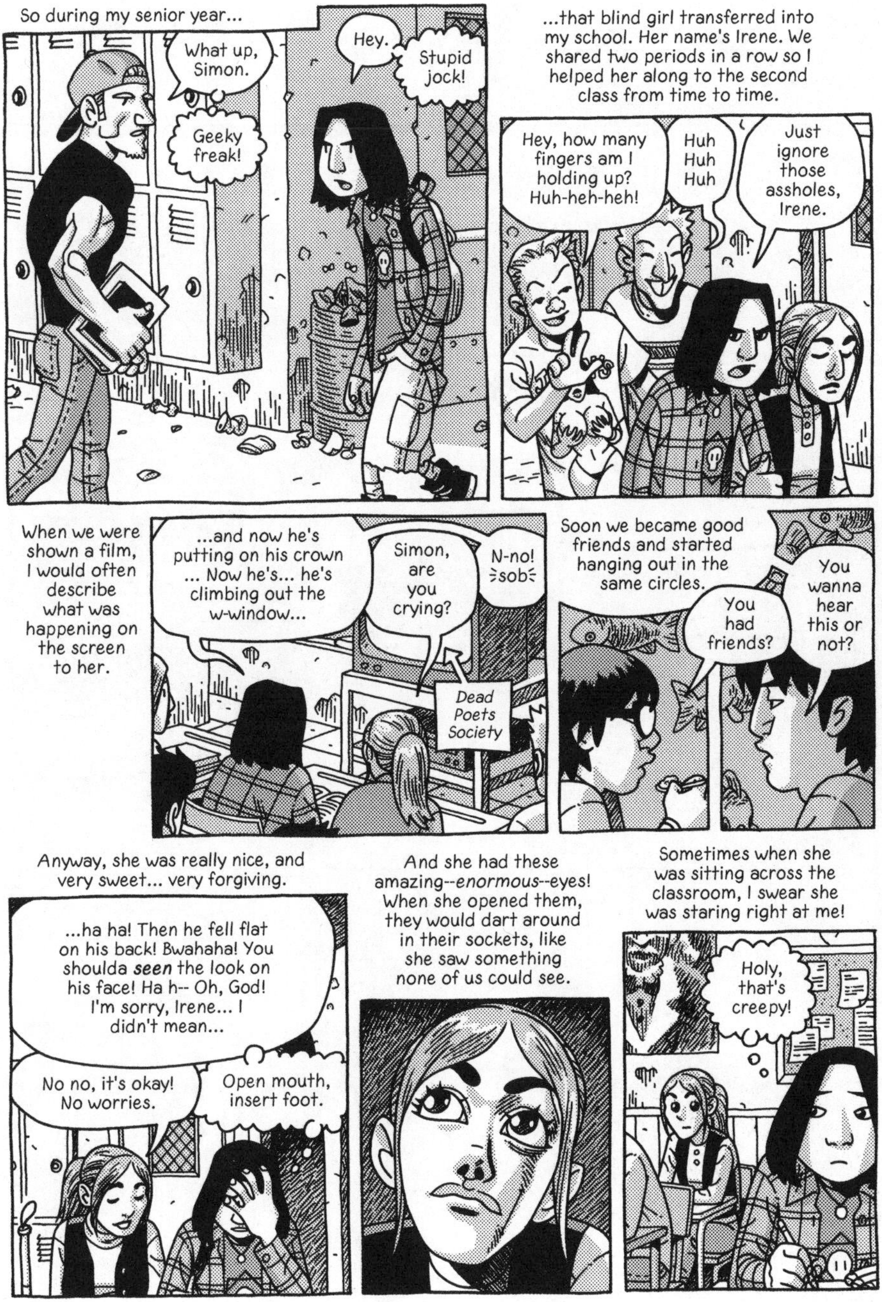
So during my senior year...
What up, Simon.
Geeky freak!
Hey.
Stupid jock!
...that blind girl transferred into my school. Her name's Irene. We shared two periods in a row so I helped her along to the second class from time to time.
Hey, how many fingers am I holding up? Huh-heh-heh!
Huh Huh Huh
Just ignore those assholes, Irene.
When we were shown a film, I would often describe what was happening on the screen to her.
...and now he's putting on his crown ... Now he's... he's climbing out the w-window...
Simon, are you crying?
N-no! sob
Dead Poets Society
Soon we became good friends and started hanging out in the same circles.
You had friends?
You wanna hear this or not?
Anyway, she was really nice, and very sweet... very forgiving.
...ha ha! Then he fell flat on his back! Bwahaha! You shoulda *seen* the look on his face! Ha h-- Oh, God! I'm sorry, Irene... I didn't mean...
No no, it's okay! No worries.
Open mouth, insert foot.
And she had these amazing--*enormous*--eyes! When she opened them, they would dart around in their sockets, like she saw something none of us could see.
Sometimes when she was sitting across the classroom, I swear she was staring right at me!
Holy, that's creepy!

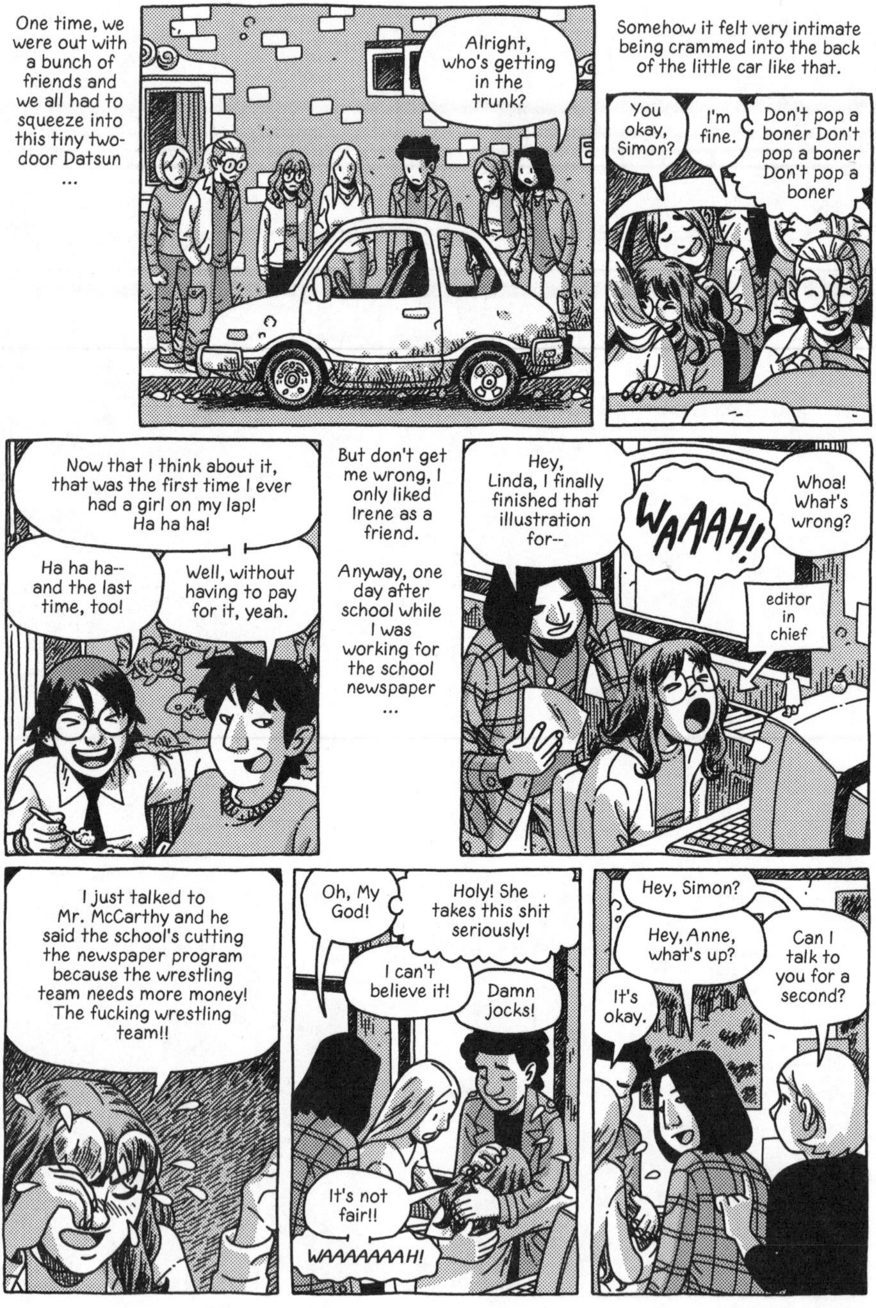
One time, we were out with a bunch of friends and we all had to squeeze into this tiny two-door Datsun ...
Alright, who's getting in the trunk?
Somehow it felt very intimate being crammed into the back of the little car like that.
You okay, Simon?
I'm fine.
Don't pop a boner Don't pop a boner Don't pop a boner
Now that I think about it, that was the first time I ever had a girl on my lap! Ha ha ha!
Ha ha ha-- and the last time, too!
Well, without having to pay for it, yeah.
But don't get me wrong, I only liked Irene as a friend.
Anyway, one day after school while I was working for the school newspaper ...
Hey, Linda, I finally finished that illustration for--
WAAAH!
Whoa! What's wrong?
editor in chief
I just talked to Mr. McCarthy and he said the school's cutting the newspaper program because the wrestling team needs more money! The fucking wrestling team!!
Oh, My God!
Holy! She takes this shit seriously!
I can't believe it!
Damn jocks!
It's not fair!!
WAAAAAAAH!
Hey, Simon?
Hey, Anne, what's up?
Can I talk to you for a second?
It's okay.

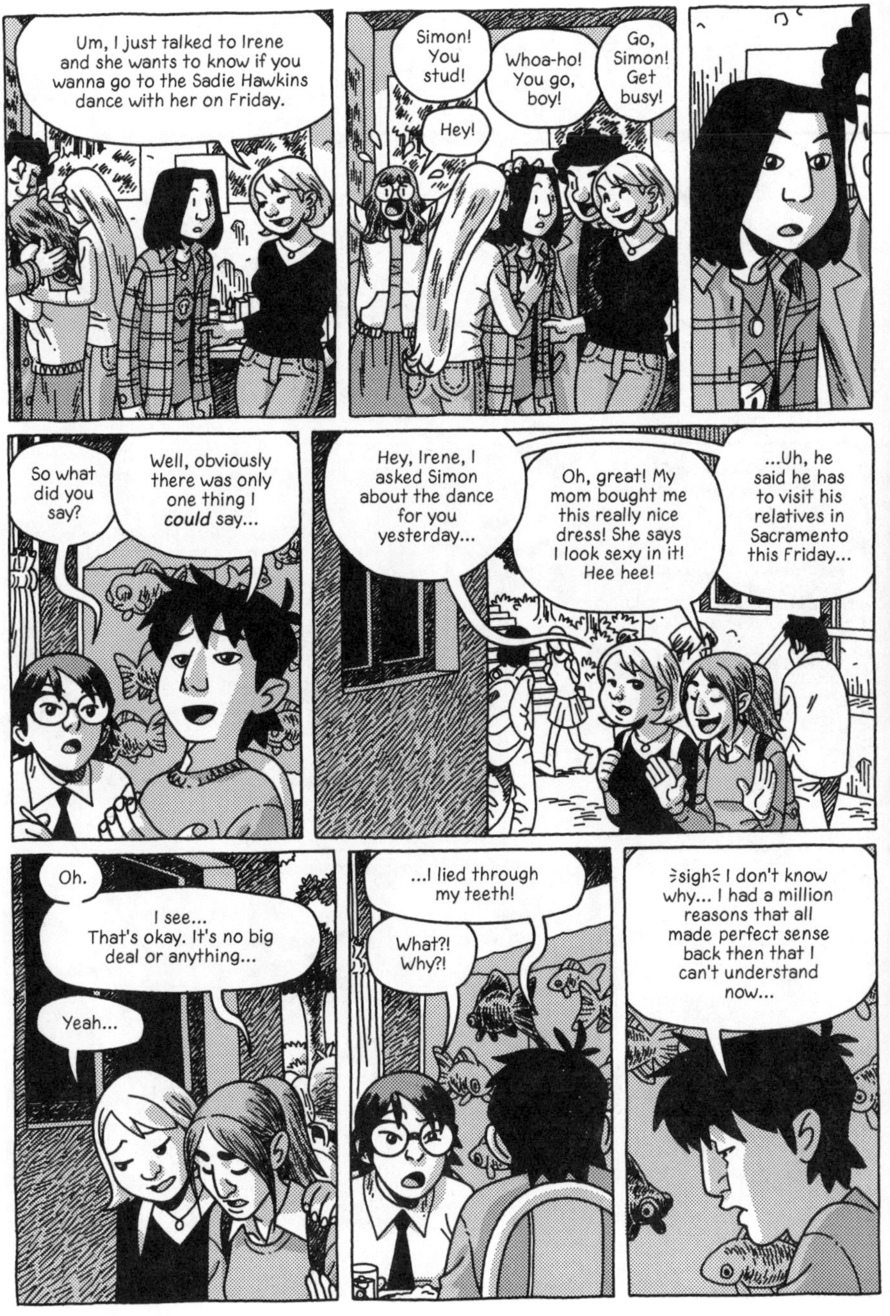
Um, I just talked to Irene and she wants to know if you wanna go to the Sadie Hawkins dance with her on Friday.
Simon! You stud!
Hey!
Whoa-ho! You go, boy!
Go, Simon! Get busy!
So what did you say?
Well, obviously there was only one thing I *could* say...
Hey, Irene, I asked Simon about the dance for you yesterday...
Oh, great! My mom bought me this really nice dress! She says I look sexy in it! Hee hee!
...Uh, he said he has to visit his relatives in Sacramento this Friday...
Oh.
I see... That's okay. It's no big deal or anything...
Yeah...
...I lied through my teeth!
What?! Why?!
≷sigh≶ I don't know why... I had a million reasons that all made perfect sense back then that I can't understand now...

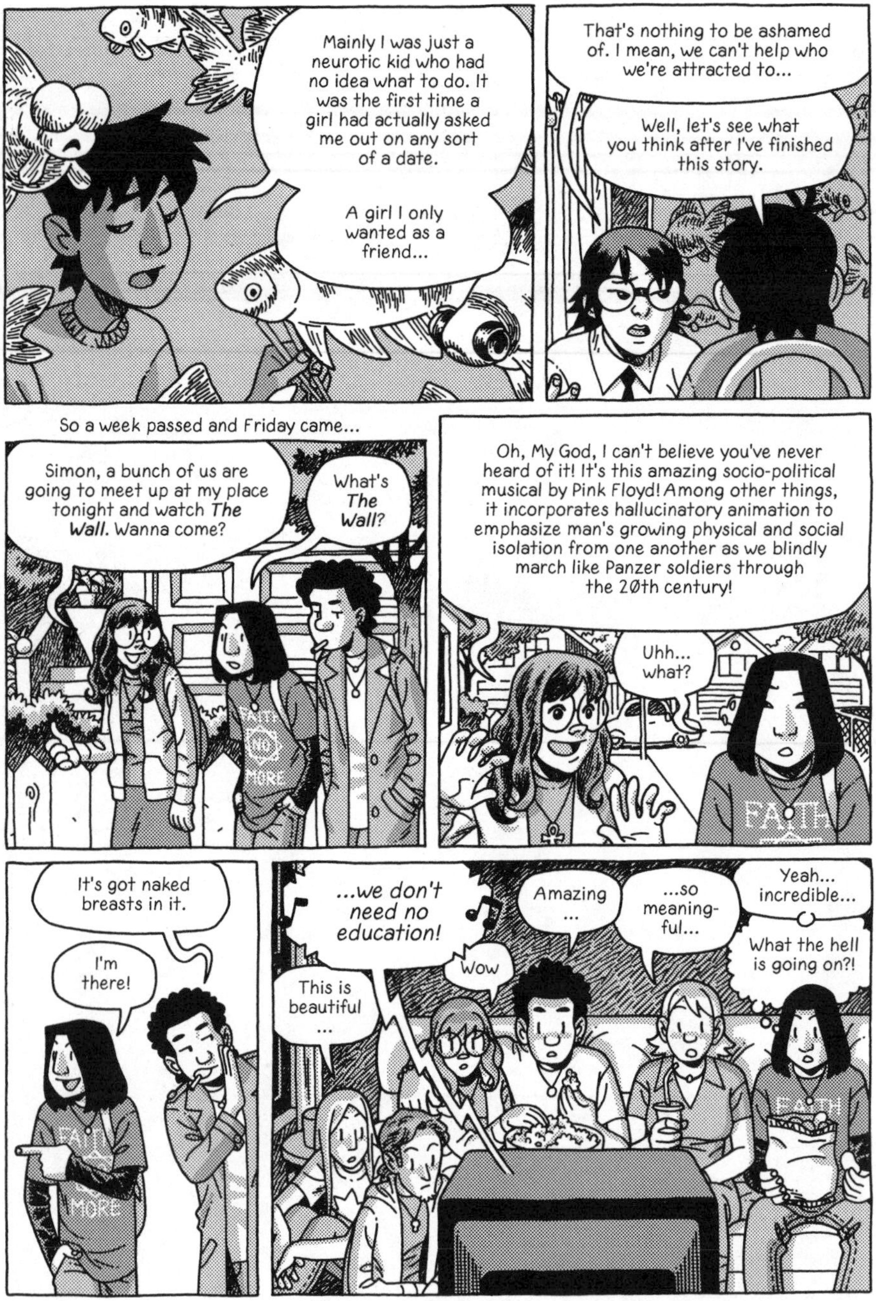

Mainly I was just a neurotic kid who had no idea what to do. It was the first time a girl had actually asked me out on any sort of a date.
A girl I only wanted as a friend...
That's nothing to be ashamed of. I mean, we can't help who we're attracted to...
Well, let's see what you think after I've finished this story.
So a week passed and Friday came...
Simon, a bunch of us are going to meet up at my place tonight and watch *The Wall.* Wanna come?
What's *The Wall*?
Oh, My God, I can't believe you've never heard of it! It's this amazing socio-political musical by Pink Floyd! Among other things, it incorporates hallucinatory animation to emphasize man's growing physical and social isolation from one another as we blindly march like Panzer soldiers through the 20th century!
Uhh... what?
It's got naked breasts in it.
I'm there!
...we don't need no education!
This is beautiful ...
Wow
Amazing ...
...so meaning-ful...
Yeah... incredible...
What the hell is going on?!

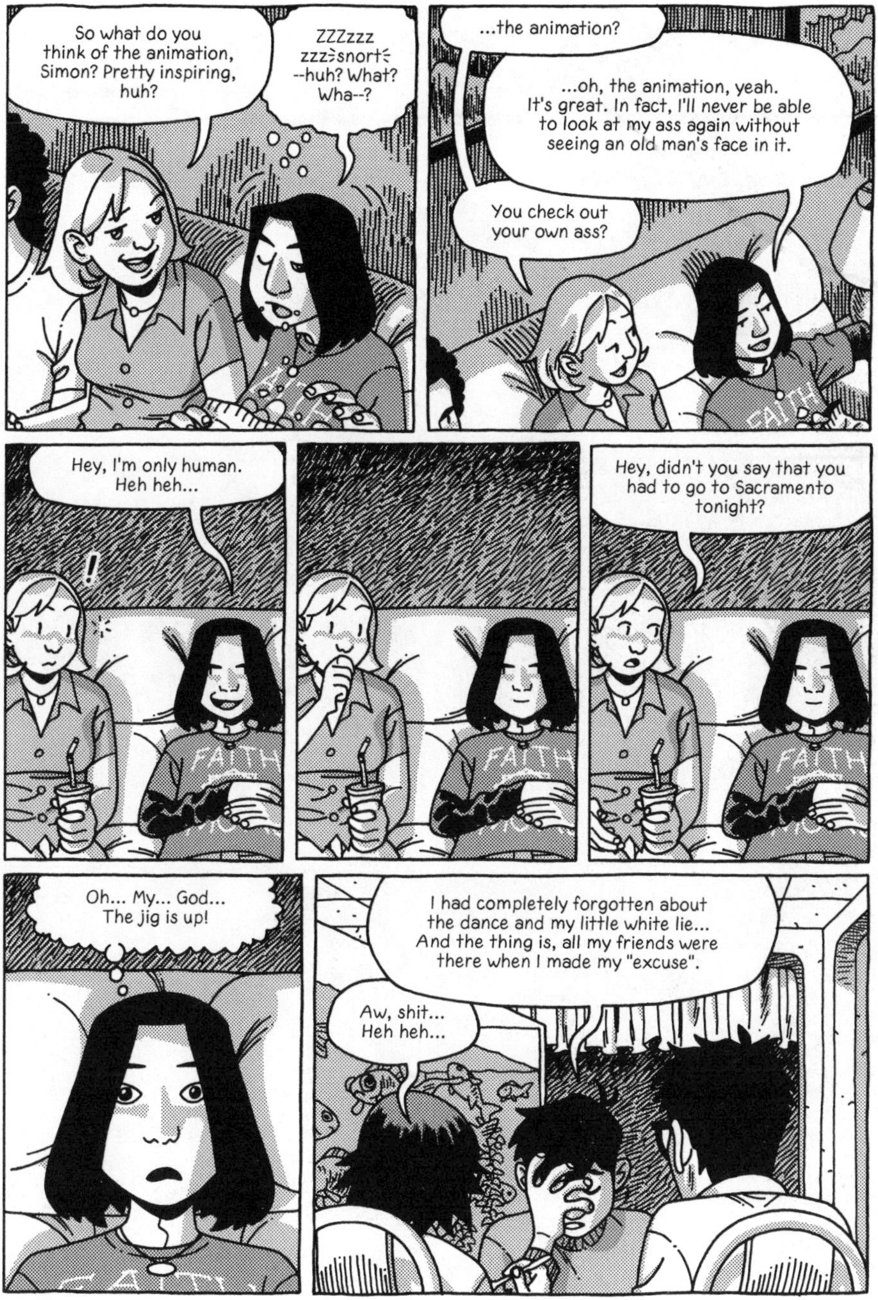
So what do you think of the animation, Simon? Pretty inspiring, huh?
ZZZzzz zzz≶snort≶ --huh? What? Wha--?
...the animation?
...oh, the animation, yeah. It's great. In fact, I'll never be able to look at my ass again without seeing an old man's face in it.
You check out your own ass?
Hey, I'm only human. Heh heh...
!
Hey, didn't you say that you had to go to Sacramento tonight?
Oh... My... God... The jig is up!
I had completely forgotten about the dance and my little white lie... And the thing is, all my friends were there when I made my "excuse".
Aw, shit... Heh heh...

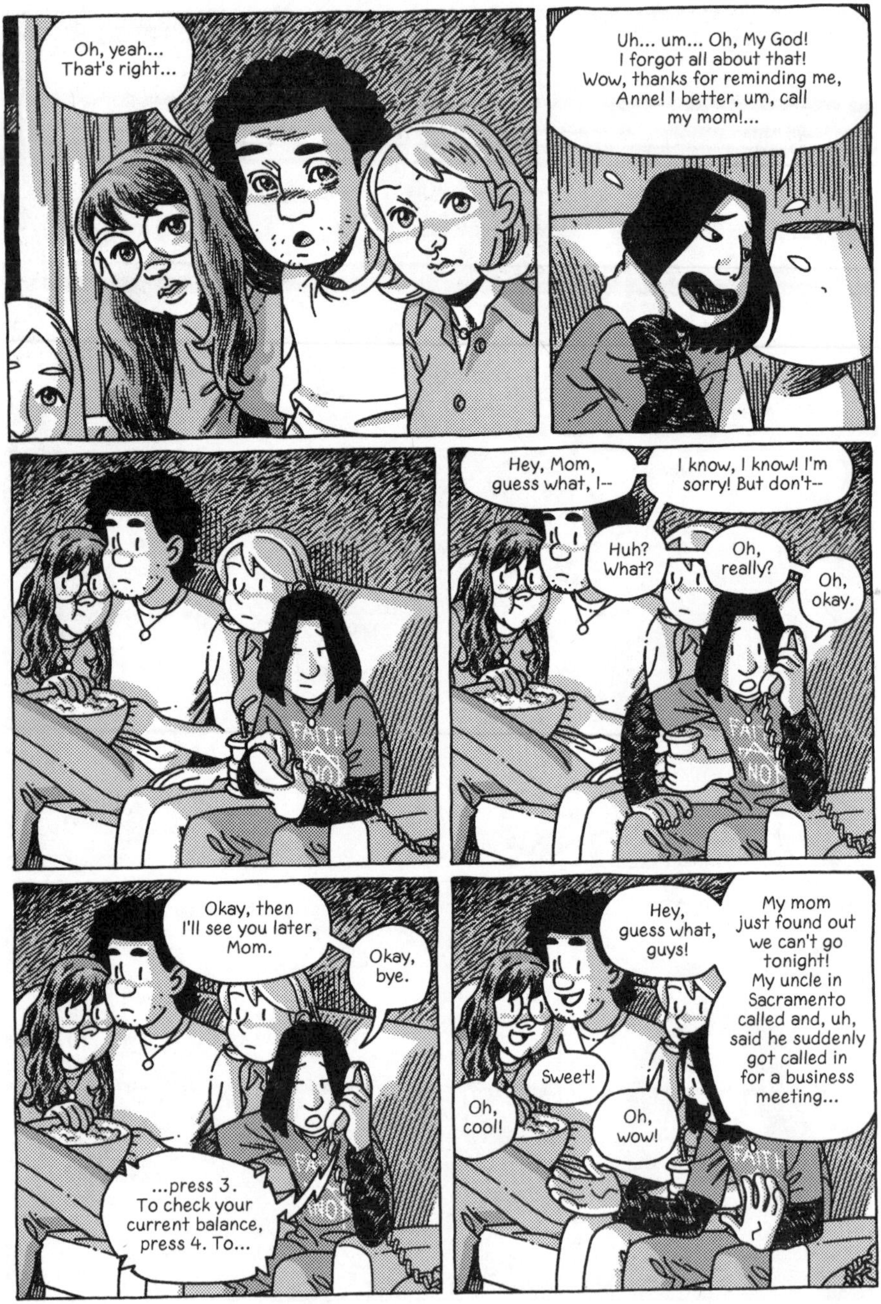
Oh, yeah... That's right...
Uh... um... Oh, My God! I forgot all about that! Wow, thanks for reminding me, Anne! I better, um, call my mom!...
Hey, Mom, guess what, I--
I know, I know! I'm sorry! But don't--
Huh? What?
Oh, really?
Oh, okay.
Okay, then I'll see you later, Mom.
Okay, bye.
...press 3. To check your current balance, press 4. To...
Hey, guess what, guys!
My mom just found out we can't go tonight! My uncle in Sacramento called and, uh, said he suddenly got called in for a business meeting...
Sweet!
Oh, cool!
Oh, wow!

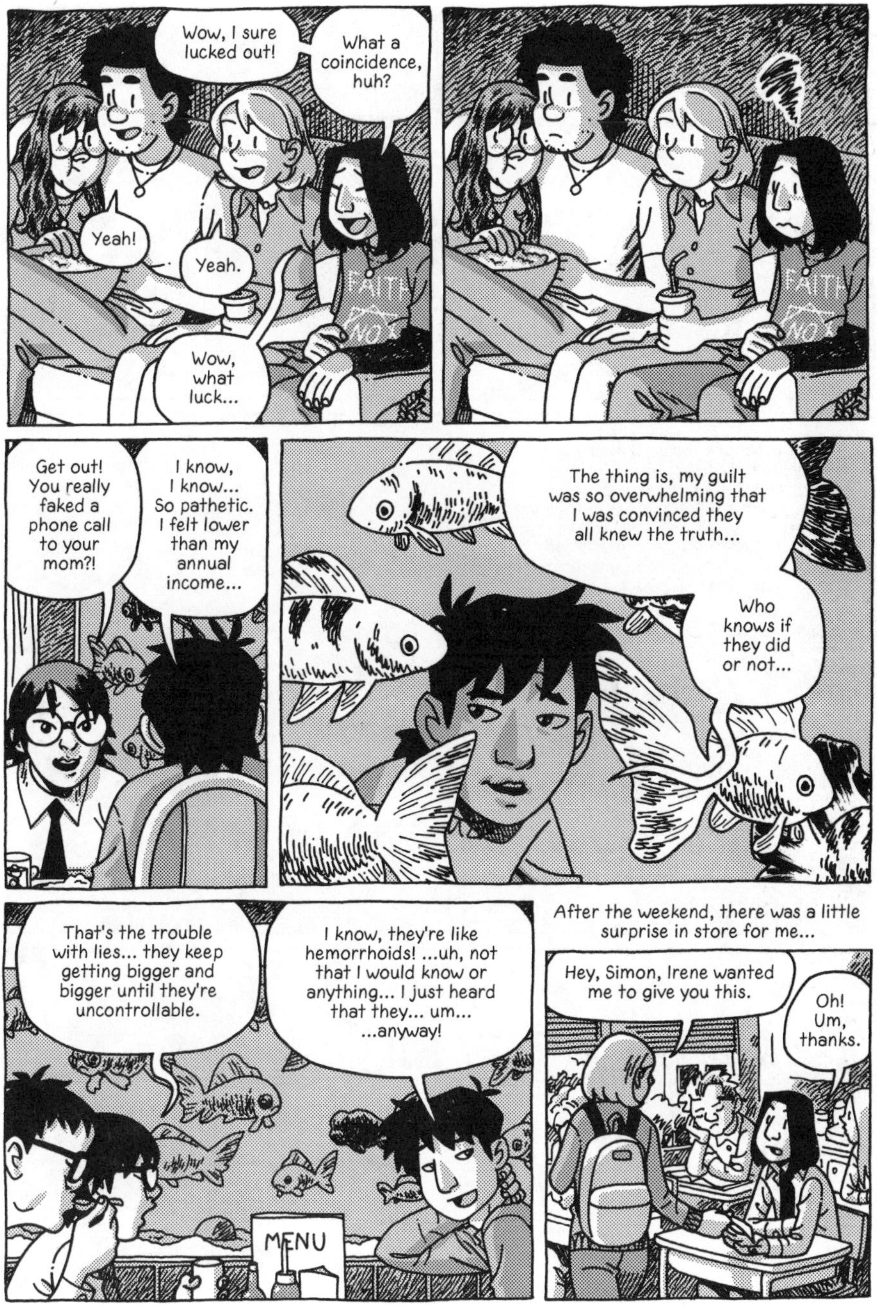

Wow, I sure lucked out!
What a coincidence, huh?
Yeah!
Yeah.
Wow, what luck...
Get out! You really faked a phone call to your mom?!
I know, I know... So pathetic. I felt lower than my annual income...
The thing is, my guilt was so overwhelming that I was convinced they all knew the truth...
Who knows if they did or not...
That's the trouble with lies... they keep getting bigger and bigger until they're uncontrollable.
I know, they're like hemorrhoids! ...uh, not that I would know or anything... I just heard that they... um... ...anyway!
MENU
After the weekend, there was a little surprise in store for me...
Hey, Simon, Irene wanted me to give you this.
Oh! Um, thanks.

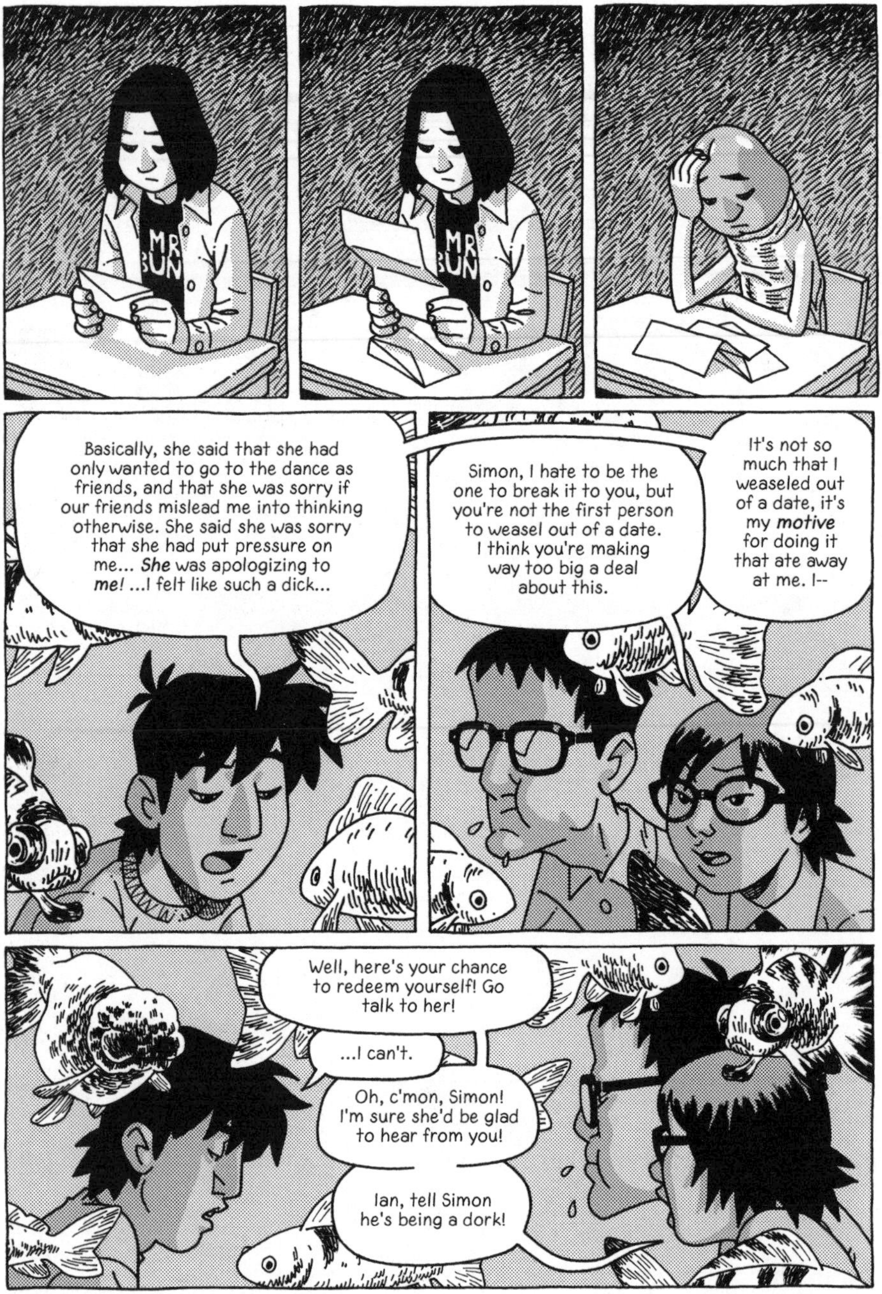
MR BUN
MR BUN
Basically, she said that she had only wanted to go to the dance as friends, and that she was sorry if our friends mislead me into thinking otherwise. She said she was sorry that she had put pressure on me... *She* was apologizing to *me!* ...I felt like such a dick...
Simon, I hate to be the one to break it to you, but you're not the first person to weasel out of a date. I think you're making way too big a deal about this.
It's not so much that I weaseled out of a date, it's my *motive* for doing it that ate away at me. I--
Well, here's your chance to redeem yourself! Go talk to her!
...I can't.
Oh, c'mon, Simon! I'm sure she'd be glad to hear from you!
Ian, tell Simon he's being a dork!

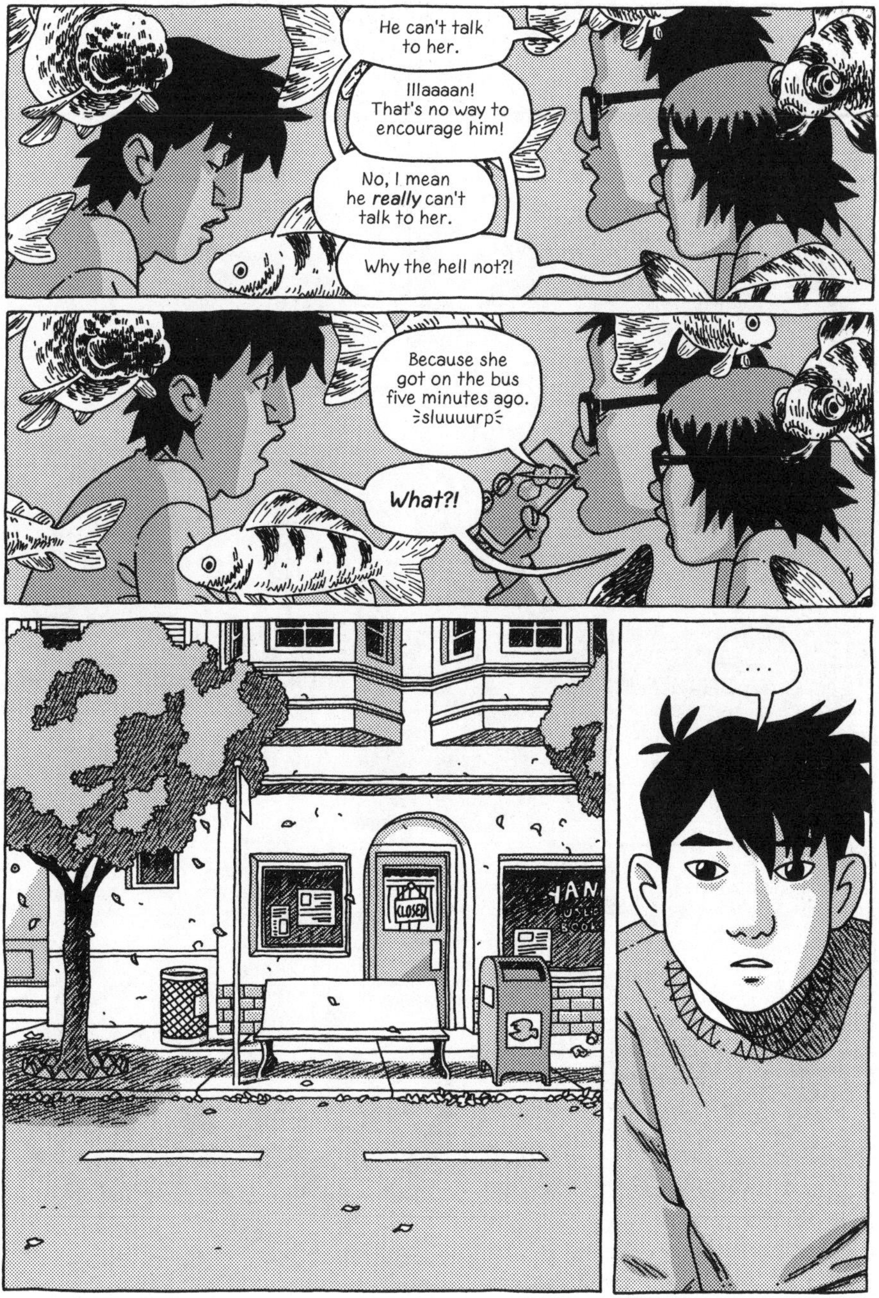
He can't talk to her.
Illaaaan! That's no way to encourage him!
No, I mean he *really* can't talk to her.
Why the hell not?!
Because she got on the bus five minutes ago. ⋨sluuuurp⋩
What?!
CLOSED
...

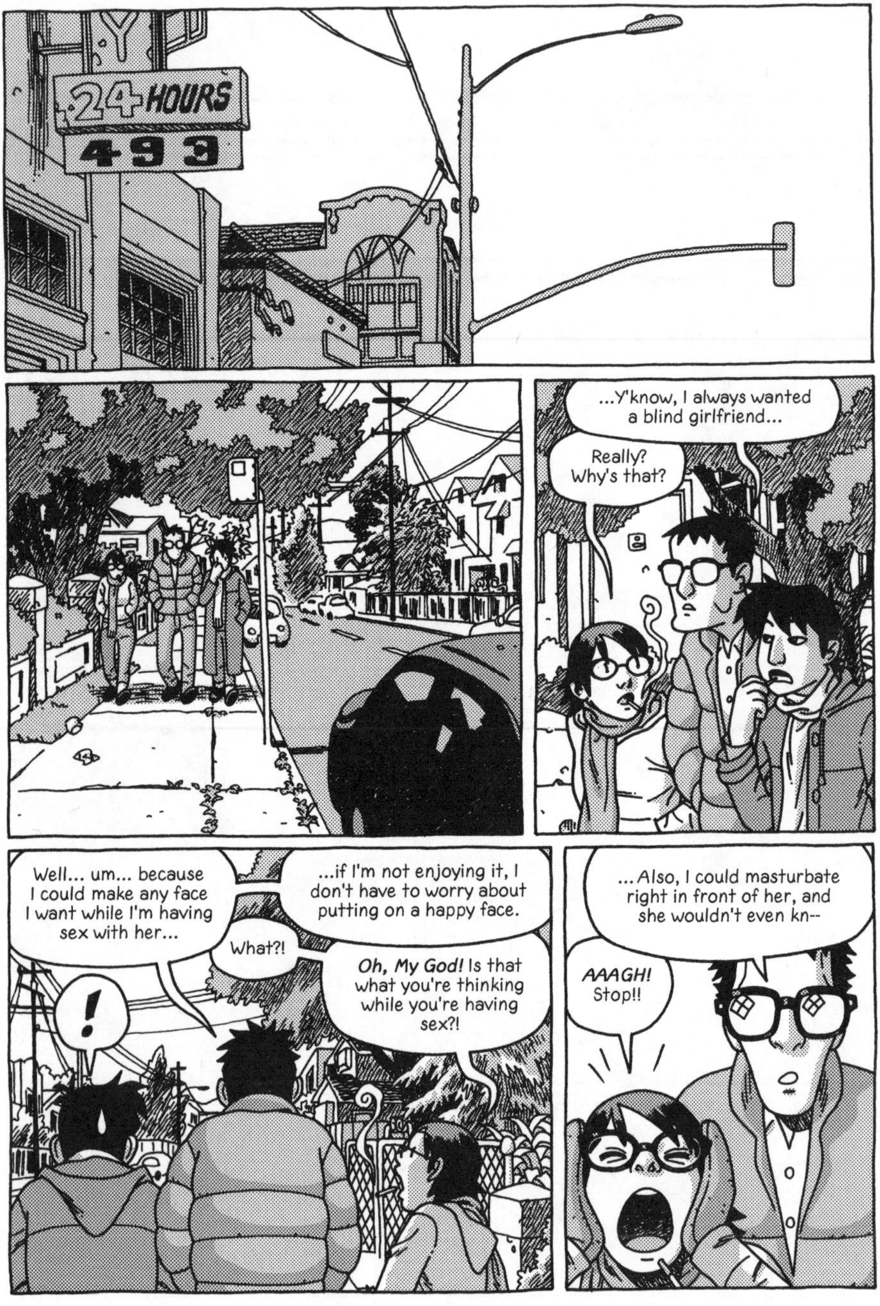

24 HOURS
493
...Y'know, I always wanted a blind girlfriend...
Really? Why's that?
Well... um... because I could make any face I want while I'm having sex with her...
...if I'm not enjoying it, I don't have to worry about putting on a happy face.
!
What?!
Oh, My God! Is that what you're thinking while you're having sex?!
...Also, I could masturbate right in front of her, and she wouldn't even kn--
AAAGH! Stop!!

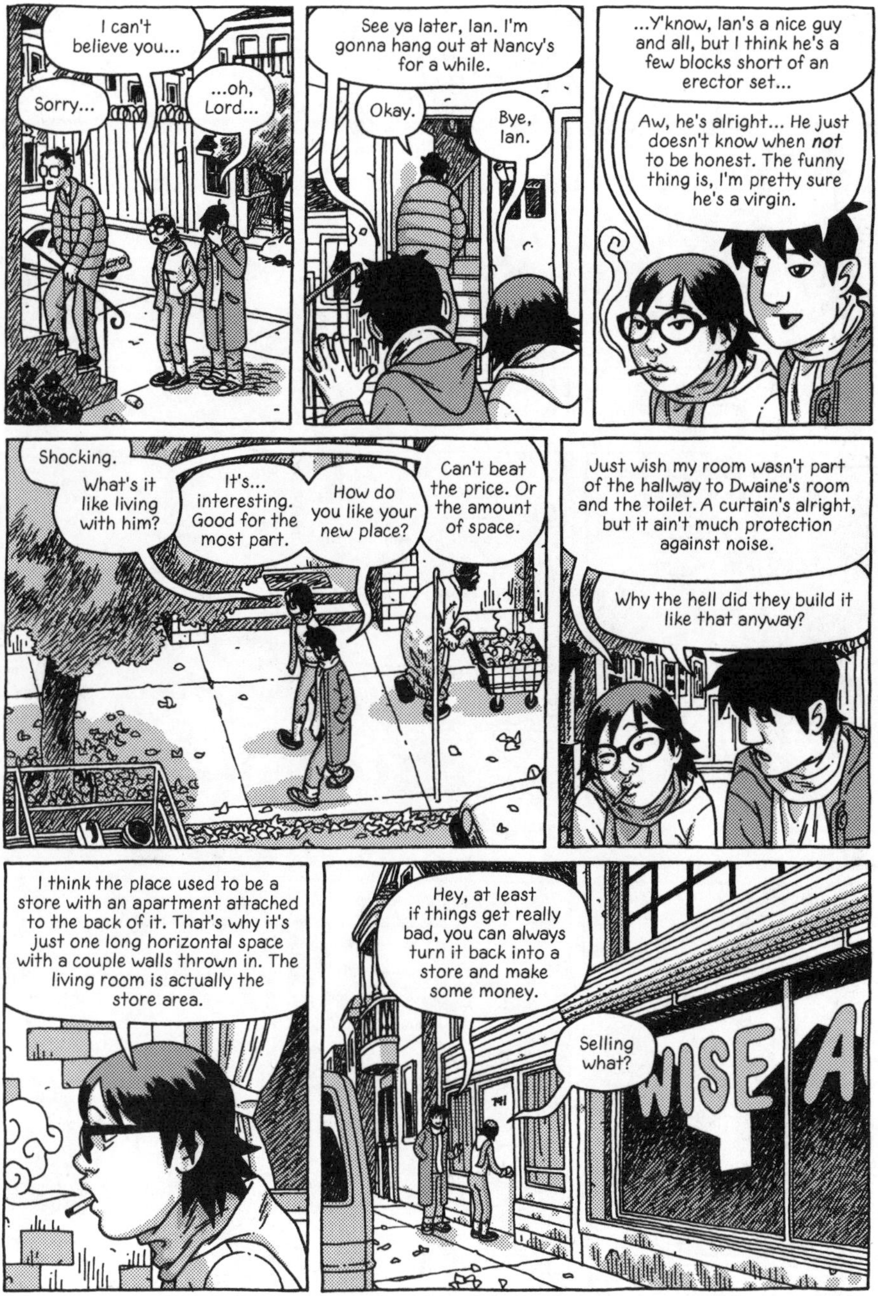
I can't believe you...
Sorry...
...oh, Lord...
See ya later, Ian. I'm gonna hang out at Nancy's for a while.
Okay.
Bye, Ian.
...Y'know, Ian's a nice guy and all, but I think he's a few blocks short of an erector set...
Aw, he's alright... He just doesn't know when **not** to be honest. The funny thing is, I'm pretty sure he's a virgin.
Shocking.
What's it like living with him?
It's... interesting. Good for the most part.
How do you like your new place?
Can't beat the price. Or the amount of space.
Just wish my room wasn't part of the hallway to Dwaine's room and the toilet. A curtain's alright, but it ain't much protection against noise.
Why the hell did they build it like that anyway?
I think the place used to be a store with an apartment attached to the back of it. That's why it's just one long horizontal space with a couple walls thrown in. The living room is actually the store area.
Hey, at least if things get really bad, you can always turn it back into a store and make some money.
Selling what?
WISE A

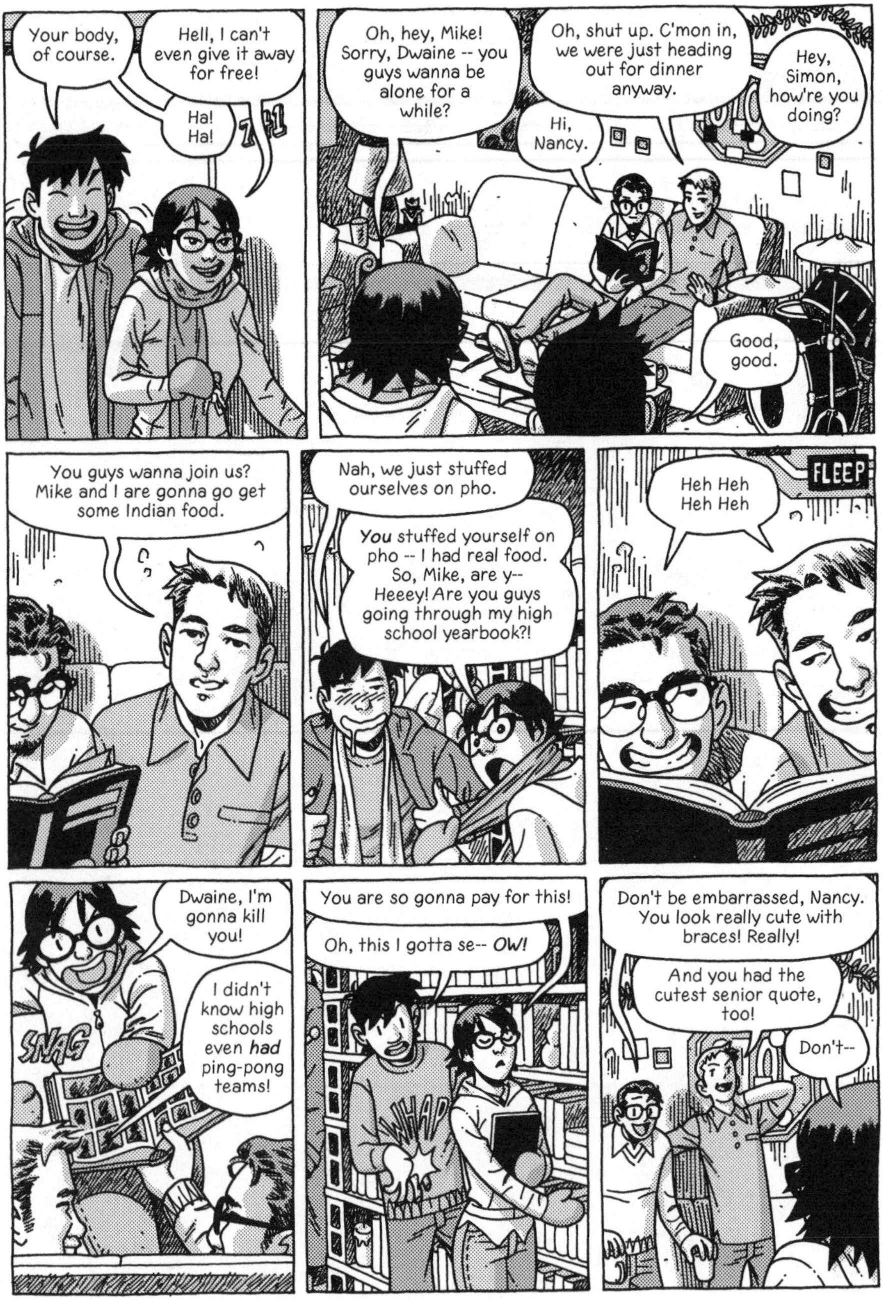

Your body, of course.
Hell, I can't even give it away for free!
Ha! Ha!
Oh, hey, Mike! Sorry, Dwaine -- you guys wanna be alone for a while?
Hi, Nancy.
Oh, shut up. C'mon in, we were just heading out for dinner anyway.
Hey, Simon, how're you doing?
Good, good.
You guys wanna join us? Mike and I are gonna go get some Indian food.
Nah, we just stuffed ourselves on pho.
You stuffed yourself on pho -- I had real food. So, Mike, are y-- Heeey! Are you guys going through my high school yearbook?!
FLEEP
Heh Heh Heh Heh
Dwaine, I'm gonna kill you!
SNAG
I didn't know high schools even *had* ping-pong teams!
You are so gonna pay for this!
Oh, this I gotta se-- *OW!*
WHAP
Don't be embarrassed, Nancy. You look really cute with braces! Really!
And you had the cutest senior quote, too!
Don't--

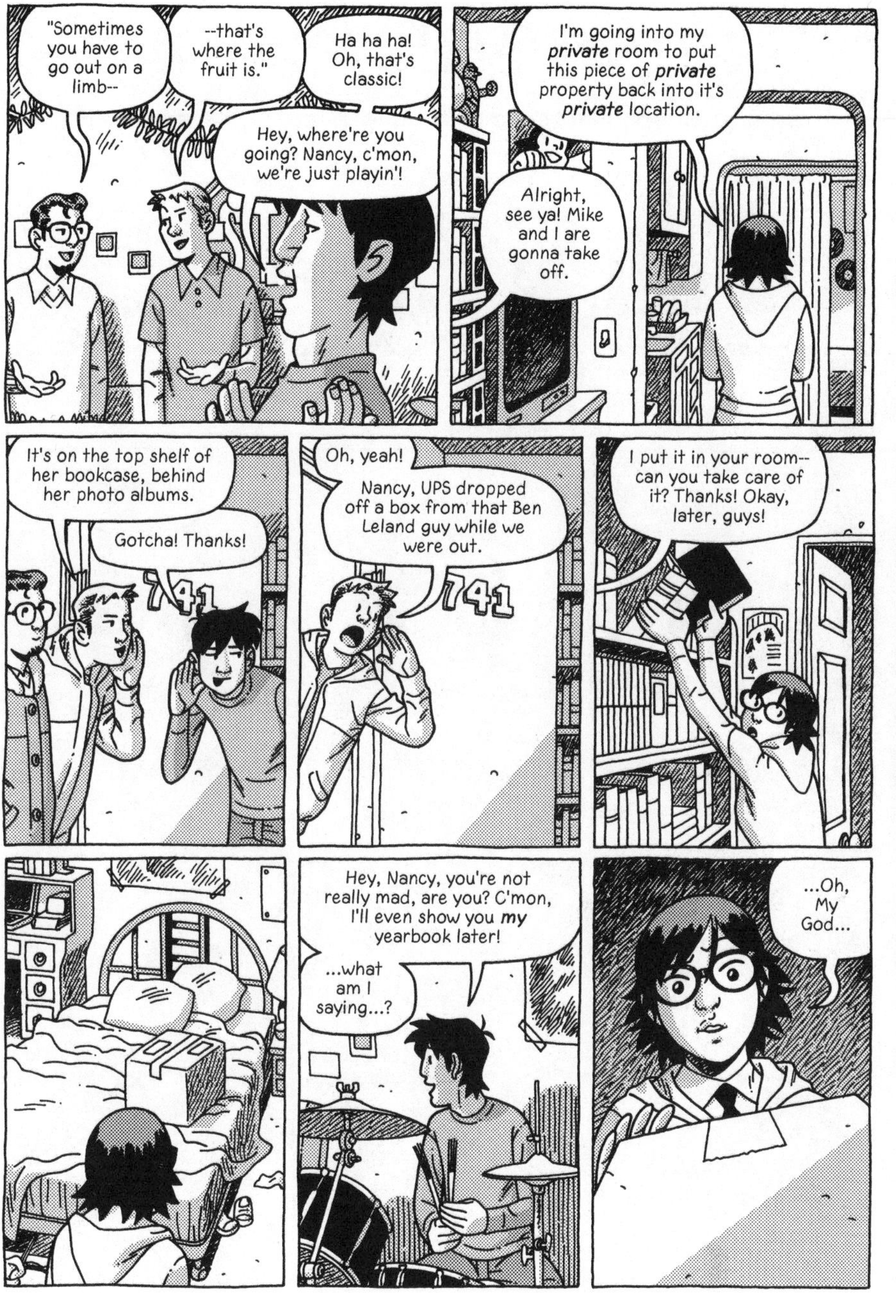
"Sometimes you have to go out on a limb--
--that's where the fruit is."
Ha ha ha! Oh, that's classic!
Hey, where're you going? Nancy, c'mon, we're just playin'!
I'm going into my *private* room to put this piece of *private* property back into it's *private* location.
Alright, see ya! Mike and I are gonna take off.
It's on the top shelf of her bookcase, behind her photo albums.
Gotcha! Thanks!
741
Oh, yeah!
Nancy, UPS dropped off a box from that Ben Leland guy while we were out.
741
I put it in your room--can you take care of it? Thanks! Okay, later, guys!
Hey, Nancy, you're not really mad, are you? C'mon, I'll even show you *my* yearbook later!
...what am I saying...?
...Oh, My God...

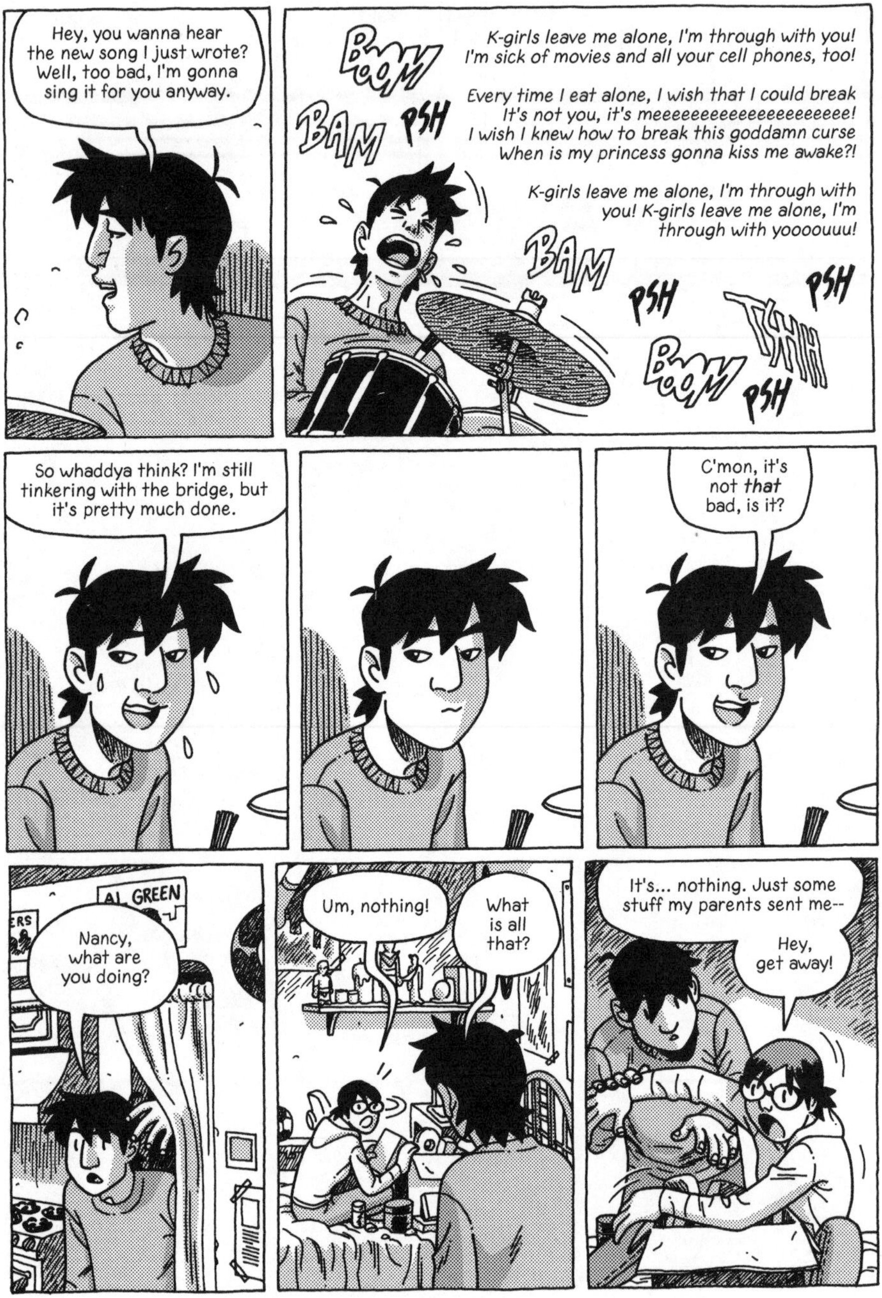

Hey, you wanna hear the new song I just wrote? Well, too bad, I'm gonna sing it for you anyway.
BOOM
BAM
PSH
K-girls leave me alone, I'm through with you! I'm sick of movies and all your cell phones, too!
Every time I eat alone, I wish that I could break It's not you, it's meeeeeeeeeeeeeeeeeeeee! I wish I knew how to break this goddamn curse When is my princess gonna kiss me awake?!
K-girls leave me alone, I'm through with you! K-girls leave me alone, I'm through with yoooouuu!
BAM
PSH
PSH
TSHH
BOOM
PSH
So whaddya think? I'm still tinkering with the bridge, but it's pretty much done.
C'mon, it's not *that* bad, is it?
AL GREEN
Nancy, what are you doing?
Um, nothing!
What is all that?
It's... nothing. Just some stuff my parents sent me--
Hey, get away!

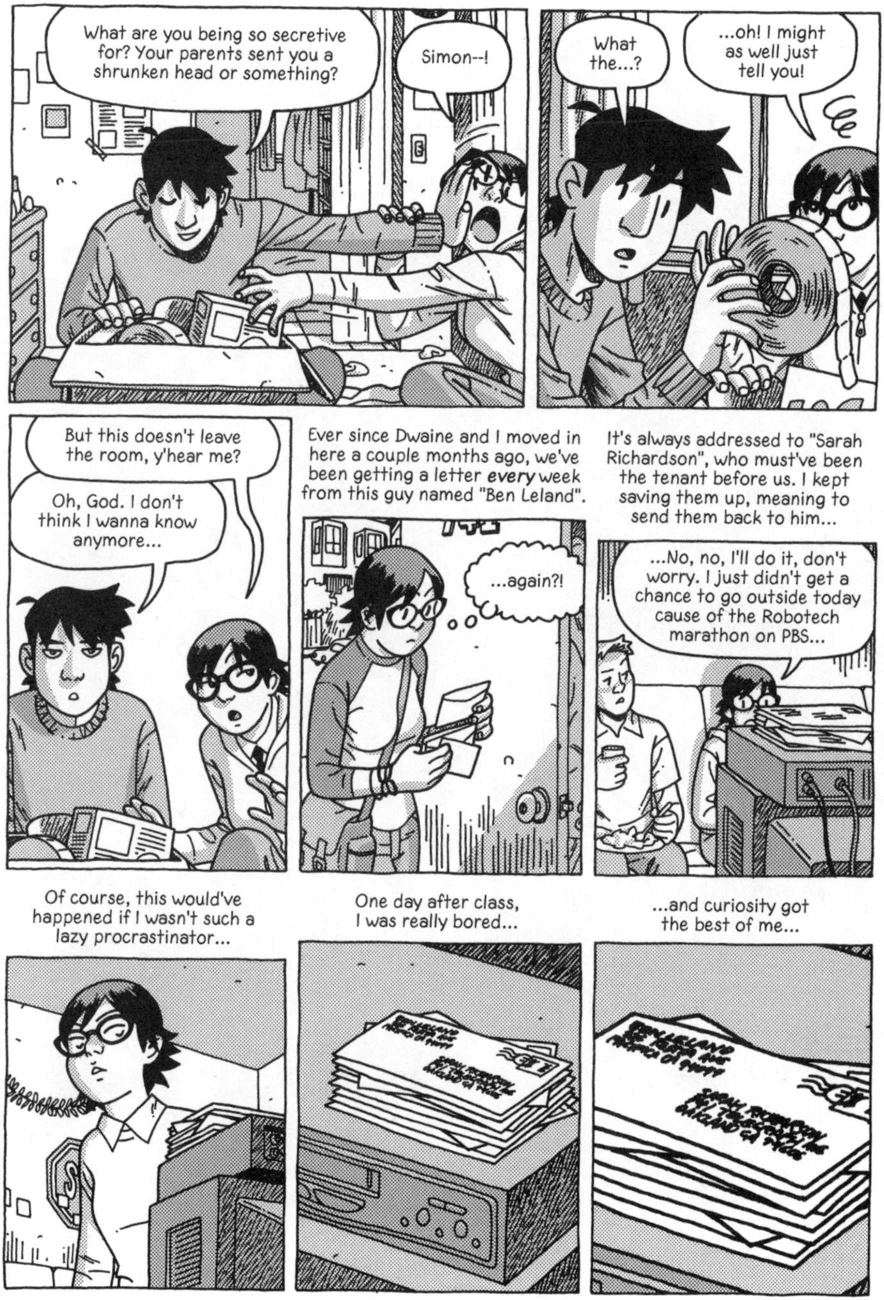
What are you being so secretive for? Your parents sent you a shrunken head or something?
Simon--!
What the...?
...oh! I might as well just tell you!
But this doesn't leave the room, y'hear me?
Oh, God. I don't think I wanna know anymore...
Ever since Dwaine and I moved in here a couple months ago, we've been getting a letter every week from this guy named "Ben Leland".
...again?!
It's always addressed to "Sarah Richardson", who must've been the tenant before us. I kept saving them up, meaning to send them back to him...
...No, no, I'll do it, don't worry. I just didn't get a chance to go outside today cause of the Robotech marathon on PBS...
Of course, this would've happened if I wasn't such a lazy procrastinator...
One day after class, I was really bored...
...and curiosity got the best of me...

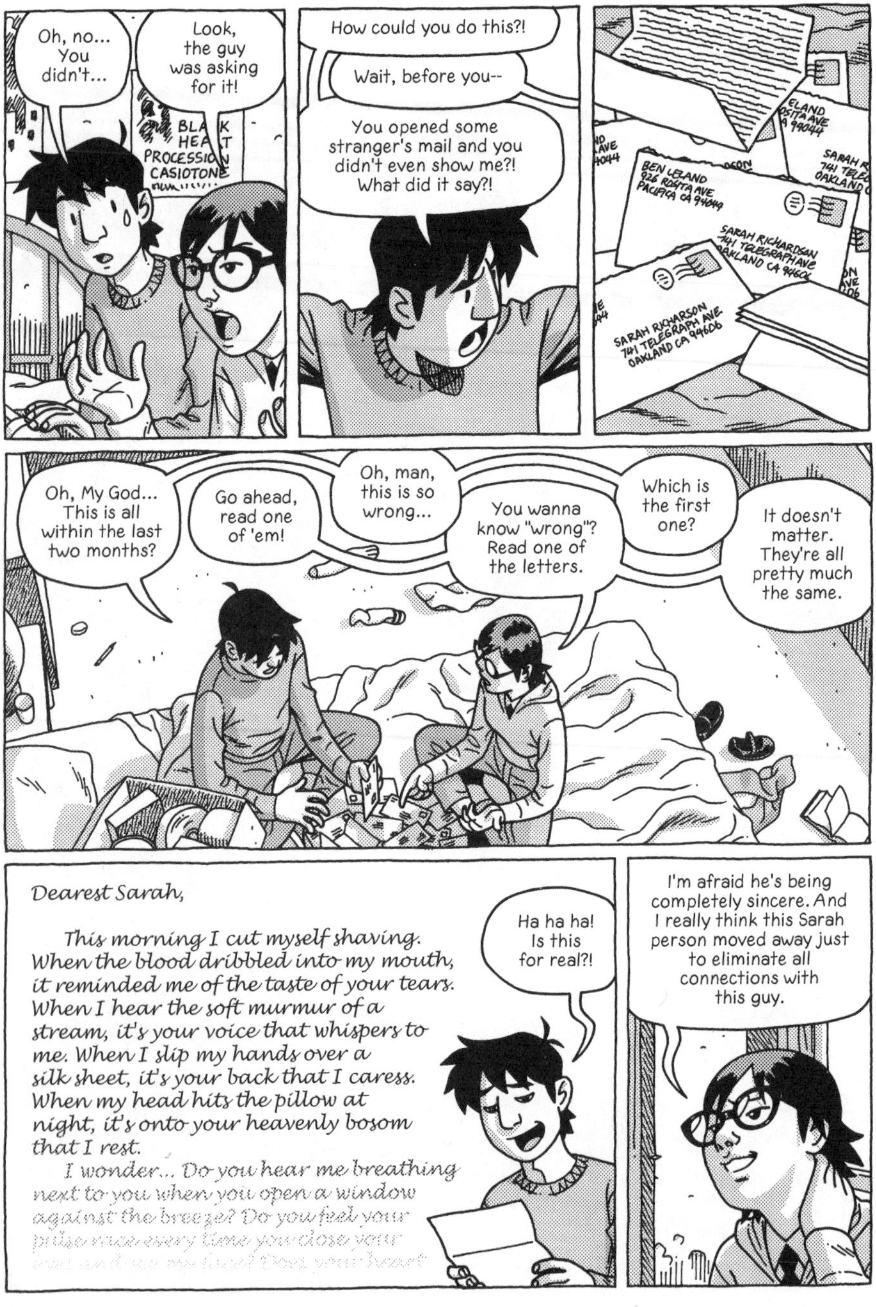
Oh, no... You didn't...
Look, the guy was asking for it!
How could you do this?!
Wait, before you--
You opened some stranger's mail and you didn't even show me?! What did it say?!
BEN LELAND 926 ROSITA AVE PACIFICA CA 94044
SARAH RICHARDSAN 741 TELEGRAPH AVE OAKLAND CA 94606
SARAH RICHARSON 741 TELEGRAPH AVE. OAKLAND CA 94606
Oh, My God... This is all within the last two months?
Go ahead, read one of 'em!
Oh, man, this is so wrong...
You wanna know "wrong"? Read one of the letters.
Which is the first one?
It doesn't matter. They're all pretty much the same.
Dearest Sarah,
This morning I cut myself shaving. When the blood dribbled into my mouth, it reminded me of the taste of your tears. When I hear the soft murmur of a stream, it's your voice that whispers to me. When I slip my hands over a silk sheet, it's your back that I caress. When my head hits the pillow at night, it's onto your heavenly bosom that I rest.
I wonder... Do you hear me breathing next to you when you open a window against the breeze? Do you feel your pulse race every time you close your
Ha ha ha! Is this for real?!
I'm afraid he's being completely sincere. And I really think this Sarah person moved away just to eliminate all connections with this guy.

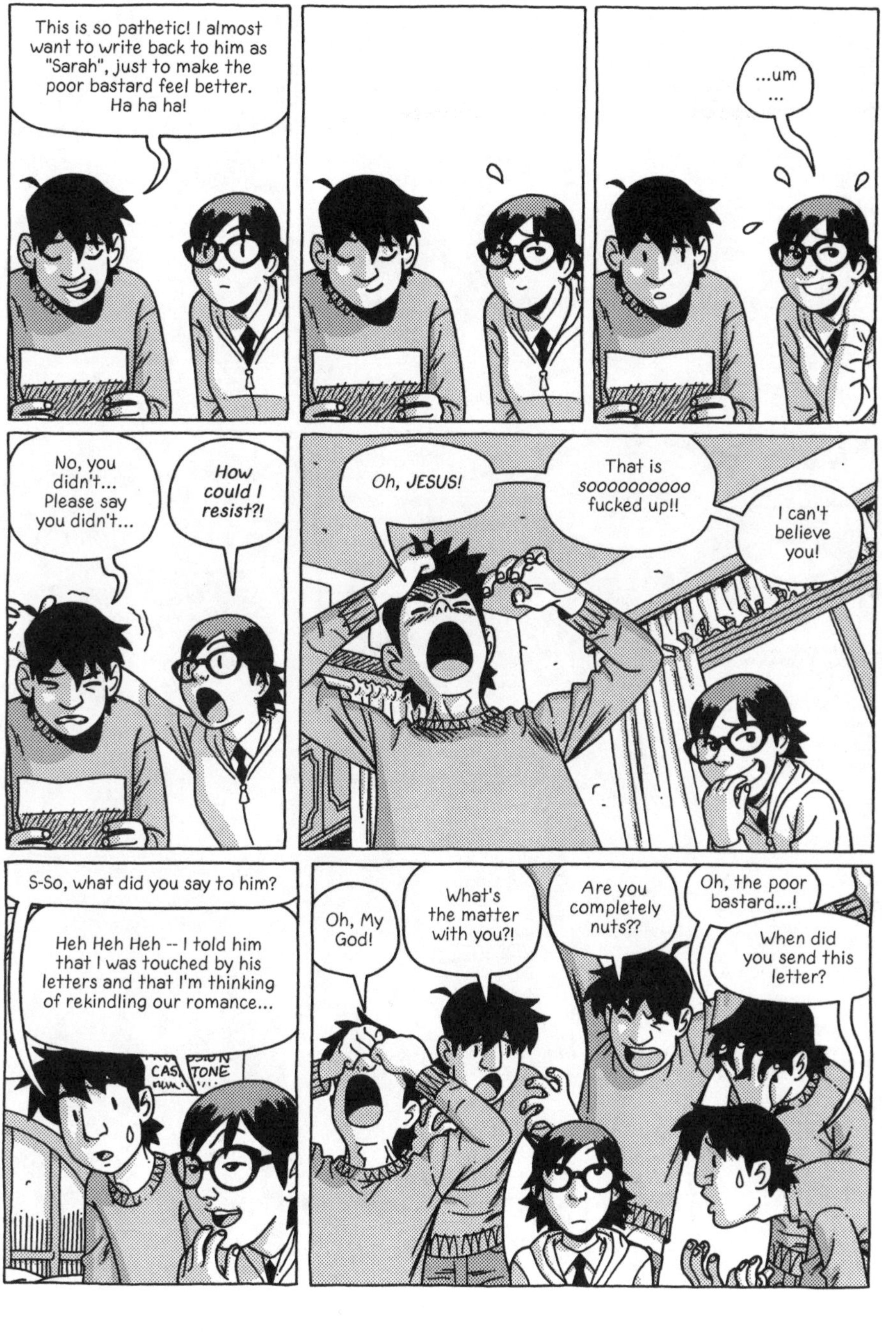
This is so pathetic! I almost want to write back to him as "Sarah", just to make the poor bastard feel better. Ha ha ha!
...um ...
No, you didn't... Please say you didn't...
How could I resist?!
Oh, JESUS!
That is sooooooooo fucked up!!
I can't believe you!
S-So, what did you say to him?
Heh Heh Heh -- I told him that I was touched by his letters and that I'm thinking of rekindling our romance...
Oh, My God!
What's the matter with you?!
Are you completely nuts??
Oh, the poor bastard...!
When did you send this letter?

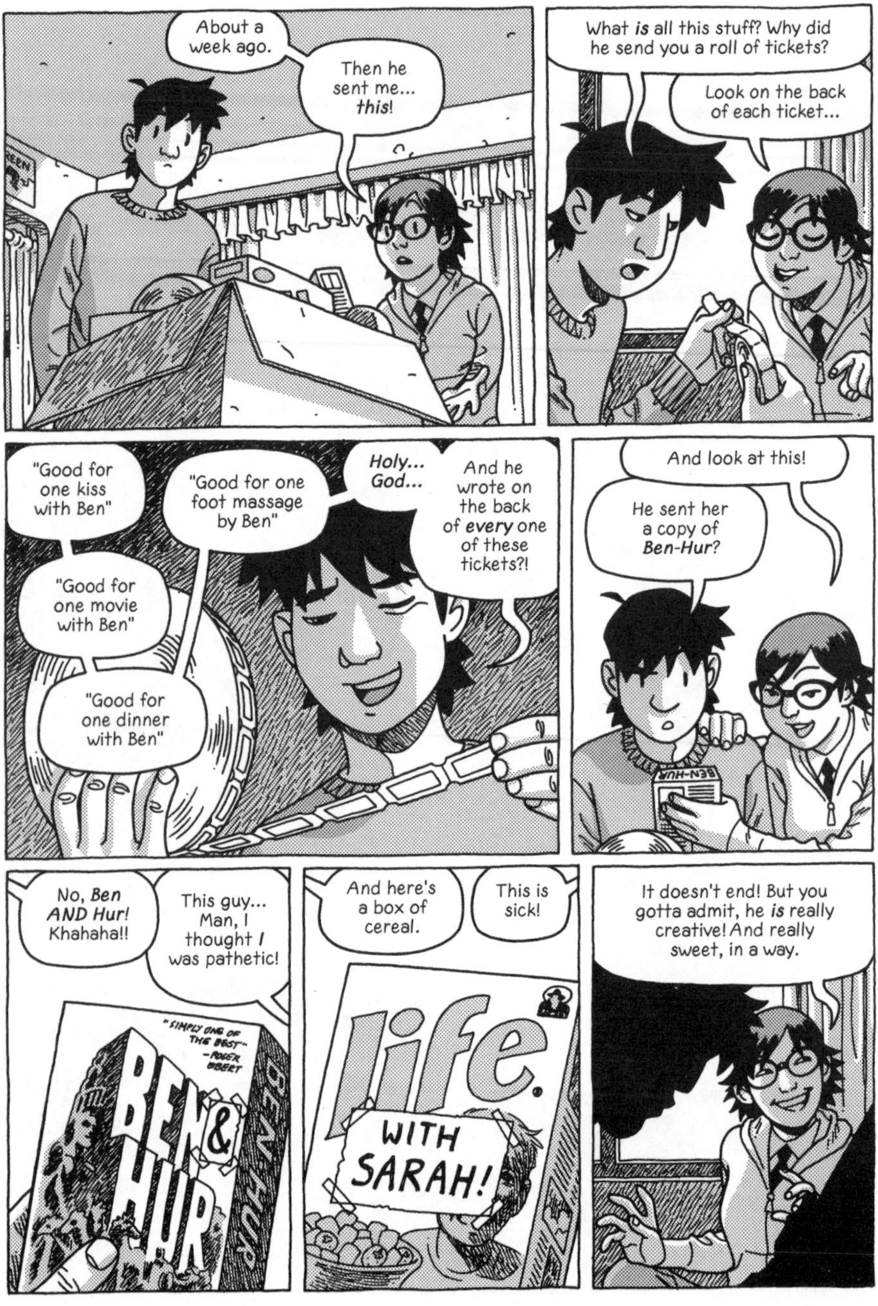

About a week ago.
Then he sent me... *this*!
What *is* all this stuff? Why did he send you a roll of tickets?
Look on the back of each ticket...
"Good for one kiss with Ben"
"Good for one movie with Ben"
"Good for one dinner with Ben"
"Good for one foot massage by Ben"
Holy... God...
And he wrote on the back of *every* one of these tickets?!
And look at this!
He sent her a copy of *Ben-Hur*?
BEN-HUR
No, *Ben AND Hur*! Khahaha!!
This guy... Man, I thought *I* was pathetic!
"SIMPLY ONE OF THE BEST" —ROGER EBERT
BEN & HUR
BEN & HUR
And here's a box of cereal.
This is sick!
life.
WITH SARAH!
It doesn't end! But you gotta admit, he *is* really creative! And really sweet, in a way.

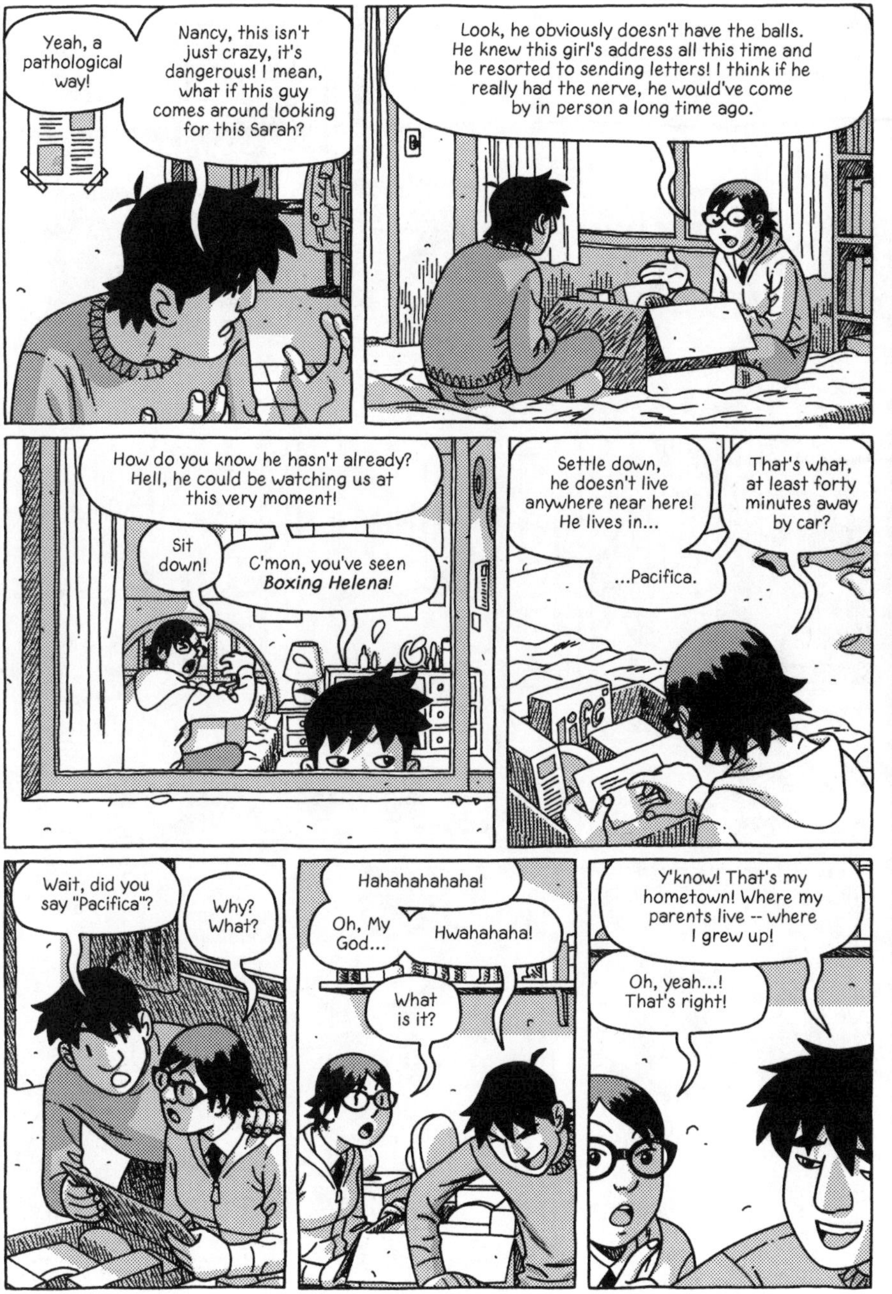
Yeah, a pathological way!
Nancy, this isn't just crazy, it's dangerous! I mean, what if this guy comes around looking for this Sarah?
Look, he obviously doesn't have the balls. He knew this girl's address all this time and he resorted to sending letters! I think if he really had the nerve, he would've come by in person a long time ago.
How do you know he hasn't already? Hell, he could be watching us at this very moment!
Sit down!
C'mon, you've seen *Boxing Helena*!
Settle down, he doesn't live anywhere near here! He lives in...
...Pacifica.
That's what, at least forty minutes away by car?
Wait, did you say "Pacifica"?
Why? What?
Hahahahahaha!
Oh, My God...
Hwahahaha!
What is it?
Y'know! That's my hometown! Where my parents live -- where I grew up!
Oh, yeah...! That's right!

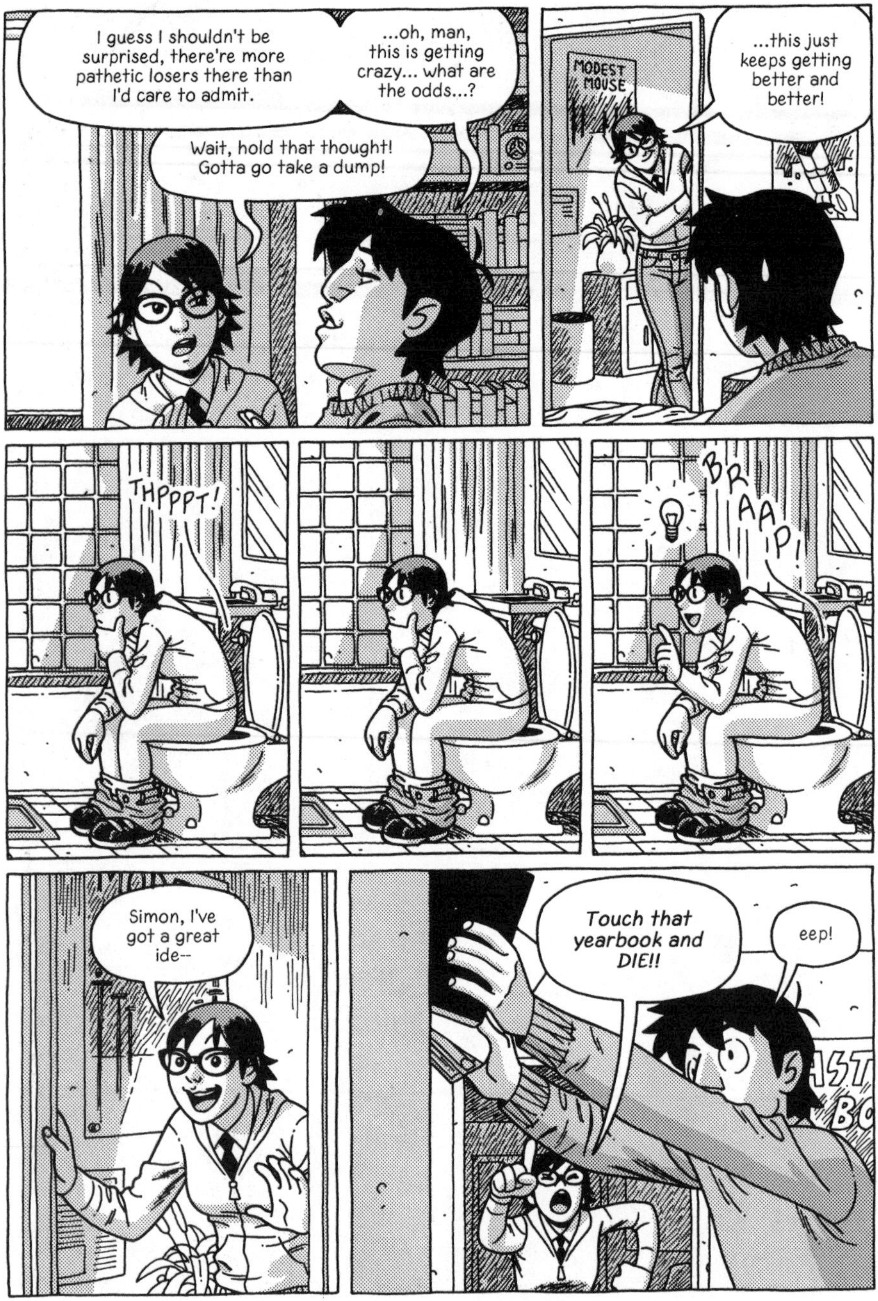
I guess I shouldn't be surprised, there're more pathetic losers there than I'd care to admit.
...oh, man, this is getting crazy... what are the odds...?
Wait, hold that thought! Gotta go take a dump!
MODEST MOUSE
...this just keeps getting better and better!
THPPPT!
BRAAAP!
Simon, I've got a great ide--
Touch that yearbook and DIE!!
eep!

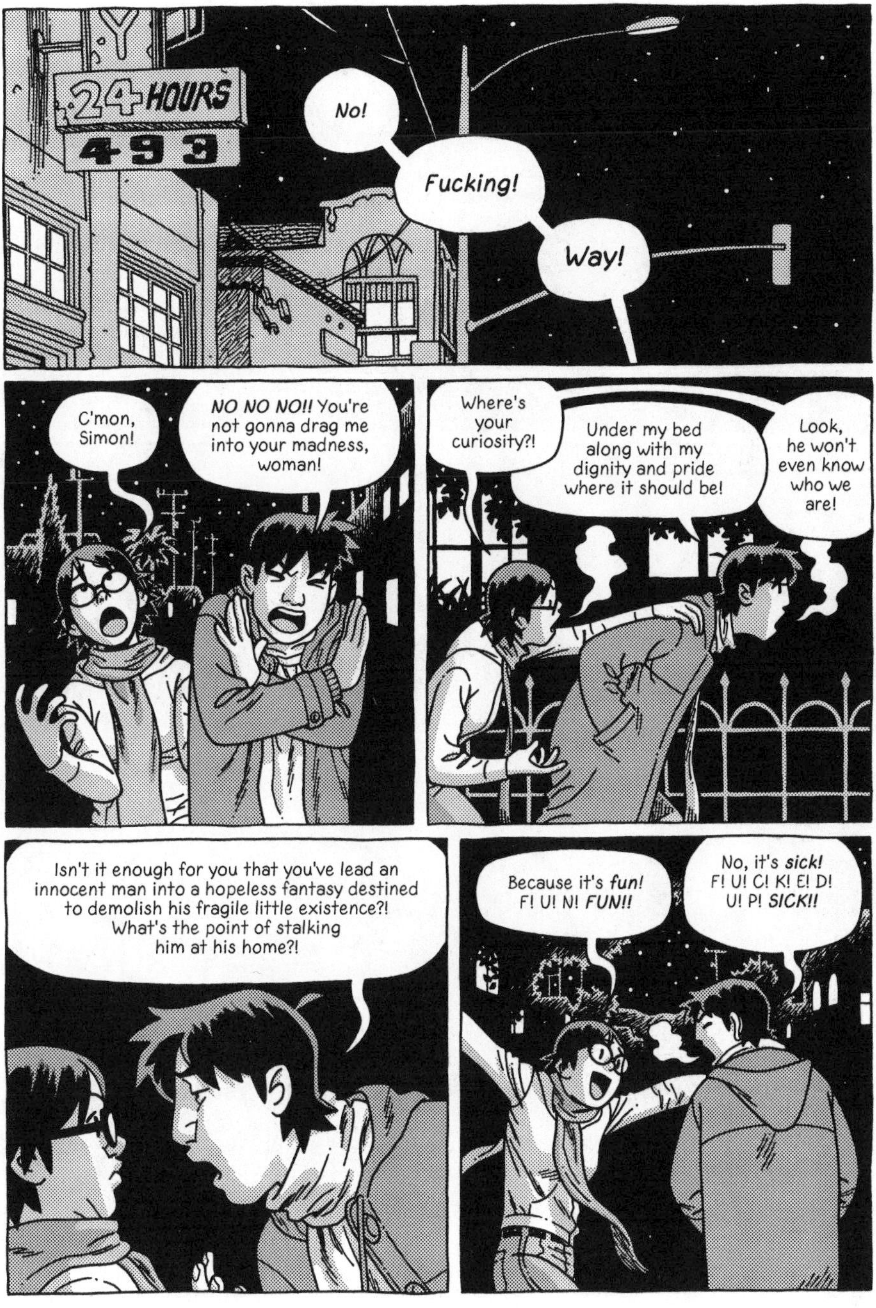
24 HOURS
493
No!
Fucking!
Way!
C'mon, Simon!
NO NO NO!! You're not gonna drag me into your madness, woman!
Where's your curiosity?!
Under my bed along with my dignity and pride where it should be!
Look, he won't even know who we are!
Isn't it enough for you that you've lead an innocent man into a hopeless fantasy destined to demolish his fragile little existence?! What's the point of stalking him at his home?!
Because it's fun! F! U! N! FUN!!
No, it's sick! F! U! C! K! E! D! U! P! SICK!!

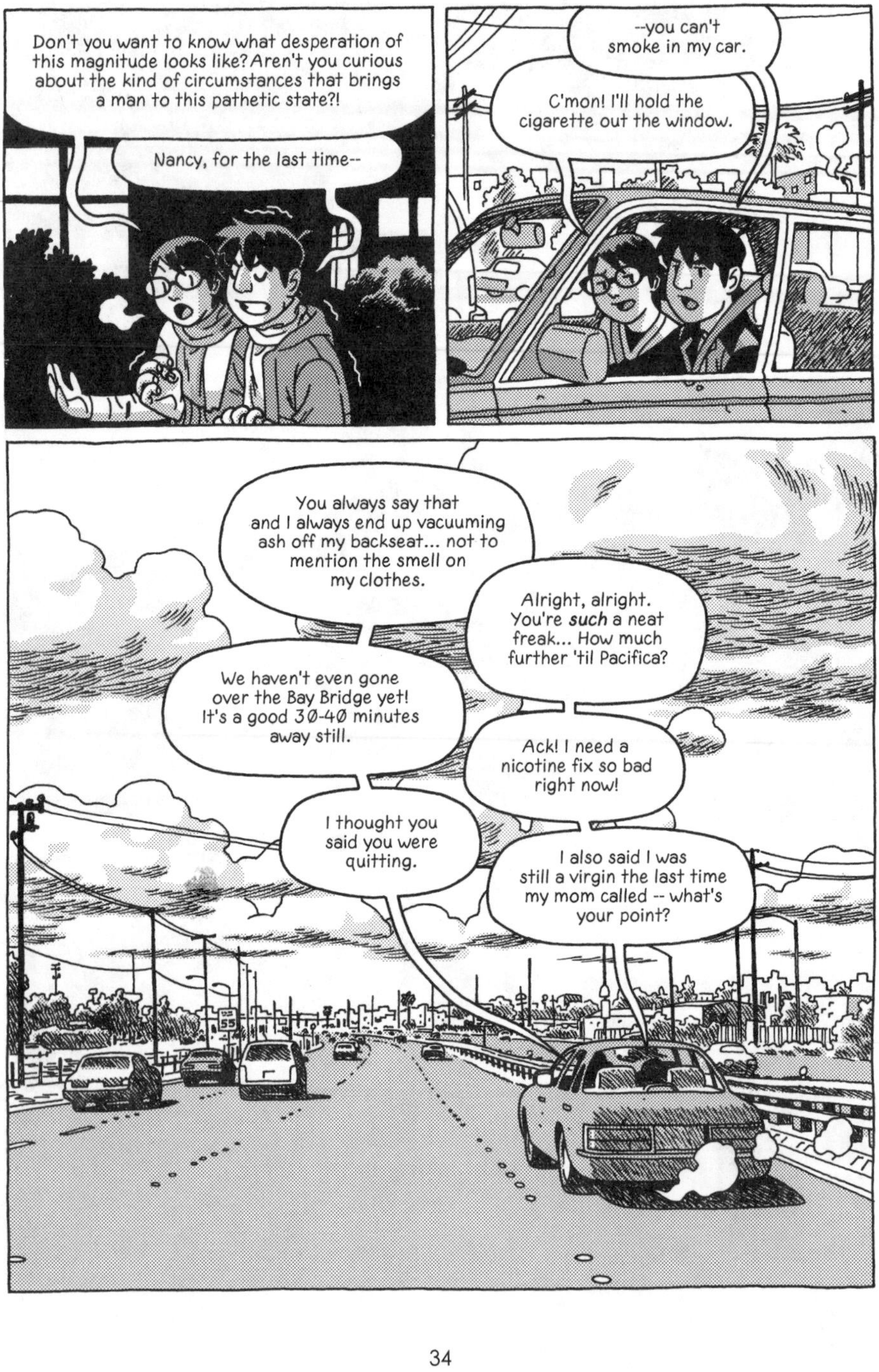
Don't you want to know what desperation of this magnitude looks like? Aren't you curious about the kind of circumstances that brings a man to this pathetic state?!
Nancy, for the last time--
--you can't smoke in my car.
C'mon! I'll hold the cigarette out the window.
You always say that and I always end up vacuuming ash off my backseat... not to mention the smell on my clothes.
Alright, alright. You're ***such*** a neat freak... How much further 'til Pacifica?
We haven't even gone over the Bay Bridge yet! It's a good 30-40 minutes away still.
Ack! I need a nicotine fix so bad right now!
I thought you said you were quitting.
I also said I was still a virgin the last time my mom called -- what's your point?

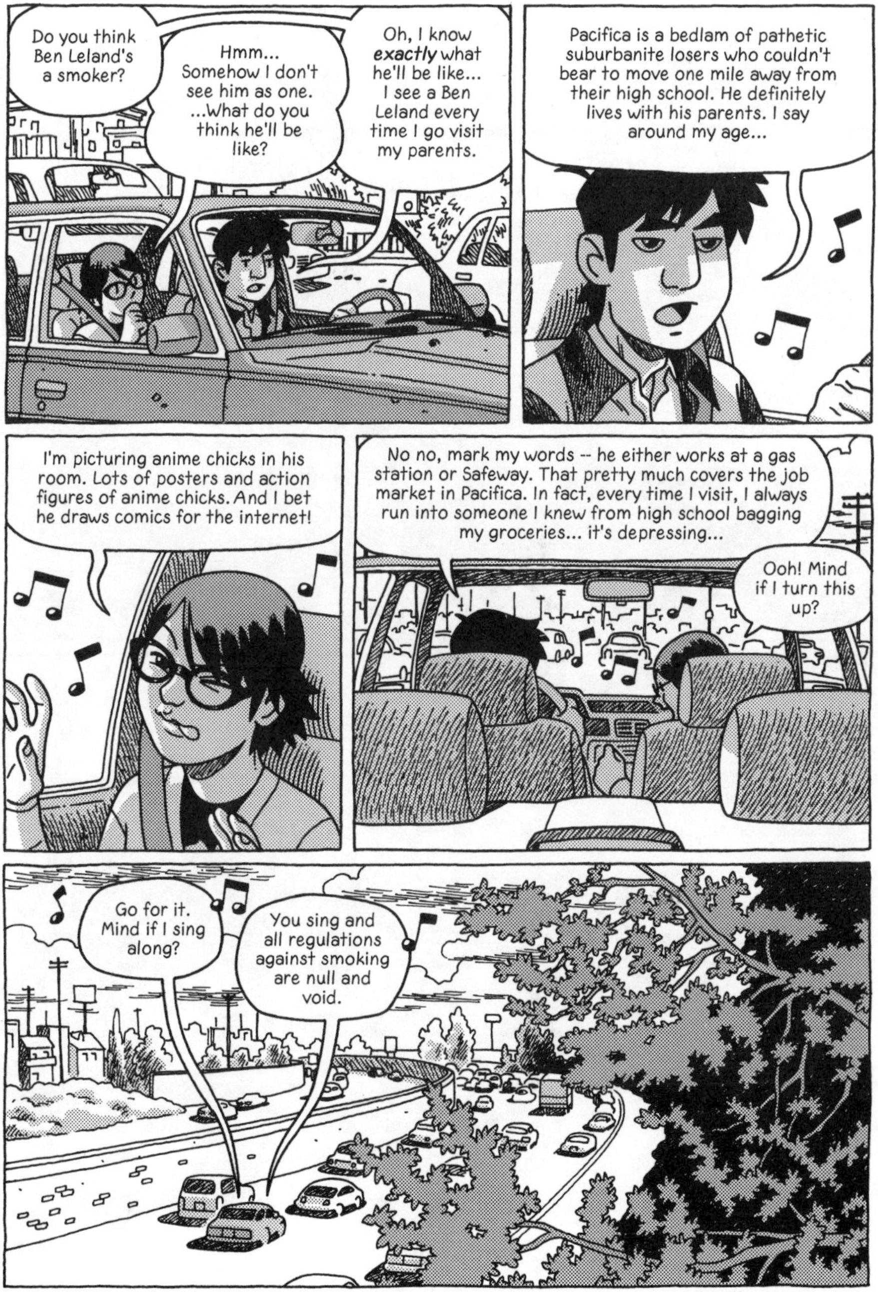
Do you think Ben Leland's a smoker?
Hmm... Somehow I don't see him as one. ...What do you think he'll be like?
Oh, I know *exactly* what he'll be like... I see a Ben Leland every time I go visit my parents.
Pacifica is a bedlam of pathetic suburbanite losers who couldn't bear to move one mile away from their high school. He definitely lives with his parents. I say around my age...
I'm picturing anime chicks in his room. Lots of posters and action figures of anime chicks. And I bet he draws comics for the internet!
No no, mark my words -- he either works at a gas station or Safeway. That pretty much covers the job market in Pacifica. In fact, every time I visit, I always run into someone I knew from high school bagging my groceries... it's depressing...
Ooh! Mind if I turn this up?
Go for it. Mind if I sing along?
You sing and all regulations against smoking are null and void.

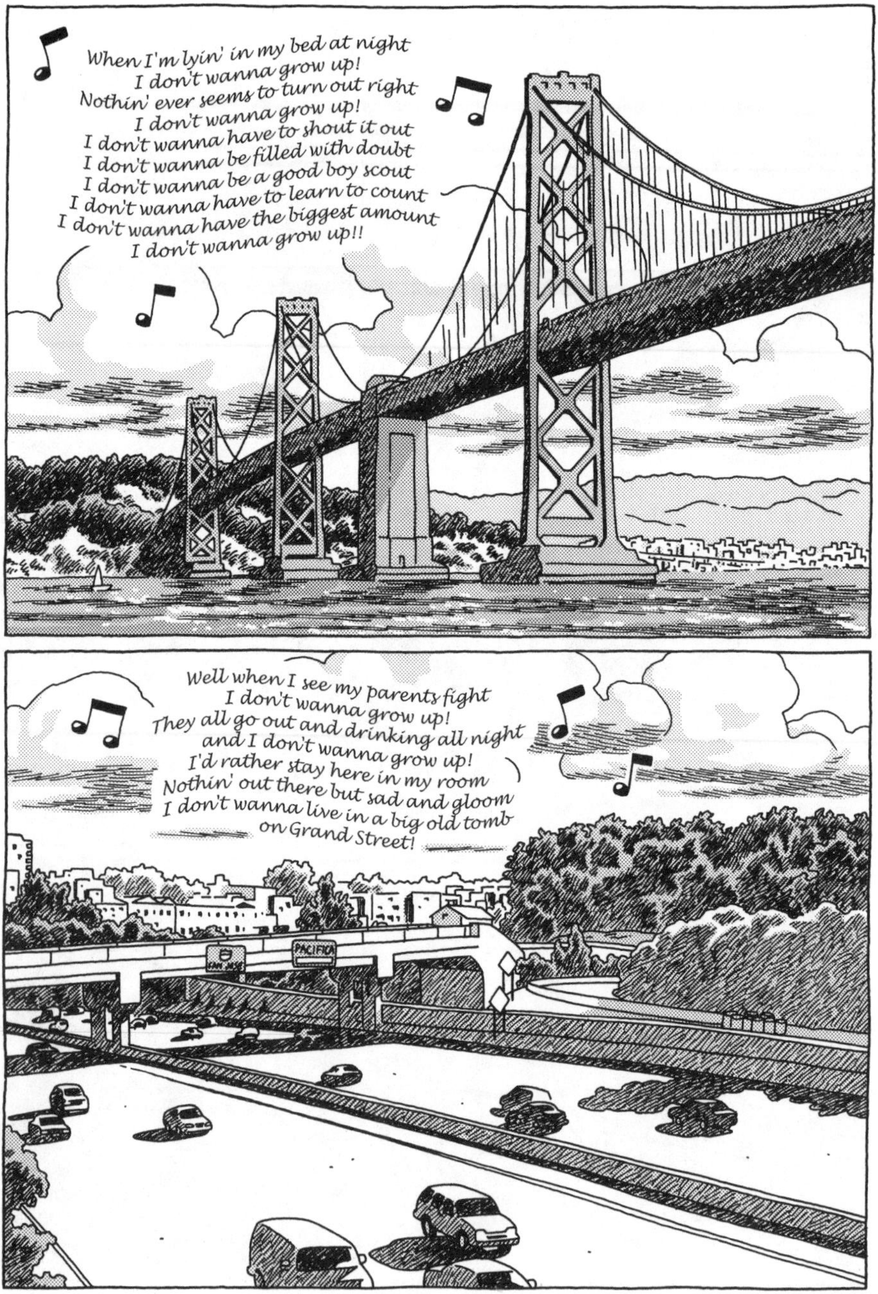
When I'm lyin' in my bed at night
I don't wanna grow up!
Nothin' ever seems to turn out right
I don't wanna grow up!
I don't wanna have to shout it out
I don't wanna be filled with doubt
I don't wanna be a good boy scout
I don't wanna have to learn to count
I don't wanna have the biggest amount
I don't wanna grow up!!
Well when I see my parents fight
I don't wanna grow up!
They all go out and drinking all night
and I don't wanna grow up!
I'd rather stay here in my room
Nothin' out there but sad and gloom
I don't wanna live in a big old tomb
on Grand Street!
PACIFICA

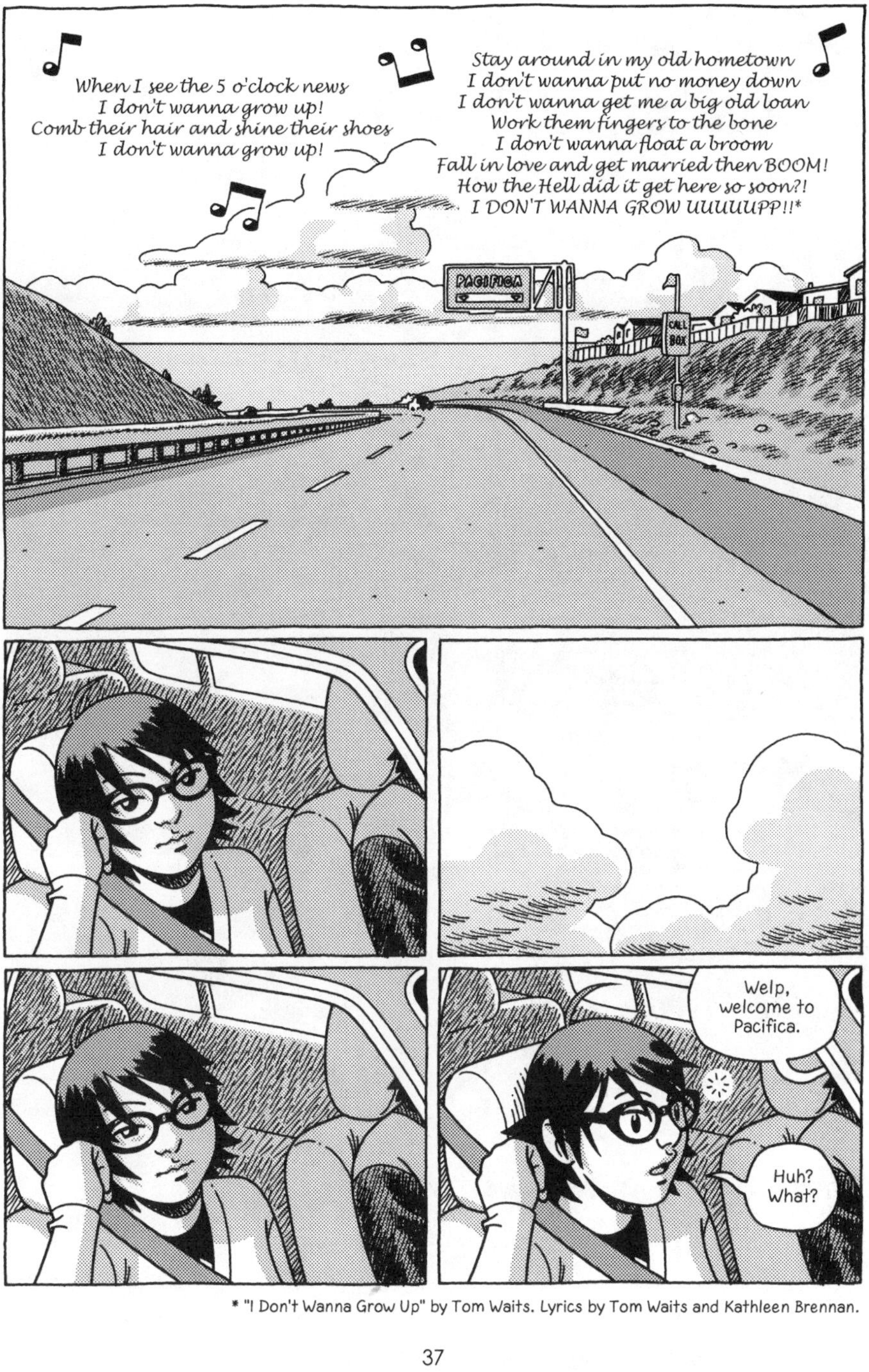
When I see the 5 o'clock news
I don't wanna grow up!
Comb their hair and shine their shoes
I don't wanna grow up!
Stay around in my old hometown
I don't wanna put no money down
I don't wanna get me a big old loan
Work them fingers to the bone
I don't wanna float a broom
Fall in love and get married then BOOM!
How the Hell did it get here so soon?!
I DON'T WANNA GROW UUUUUPP!!*
PACIFICA
CALL BOX
Welp, welcome to Pacifica.
Huh? What?

* "I Don't Wanna Grow Up" by Tom Waits. Lyrics by Tom Waits and Kathleen Brennan.

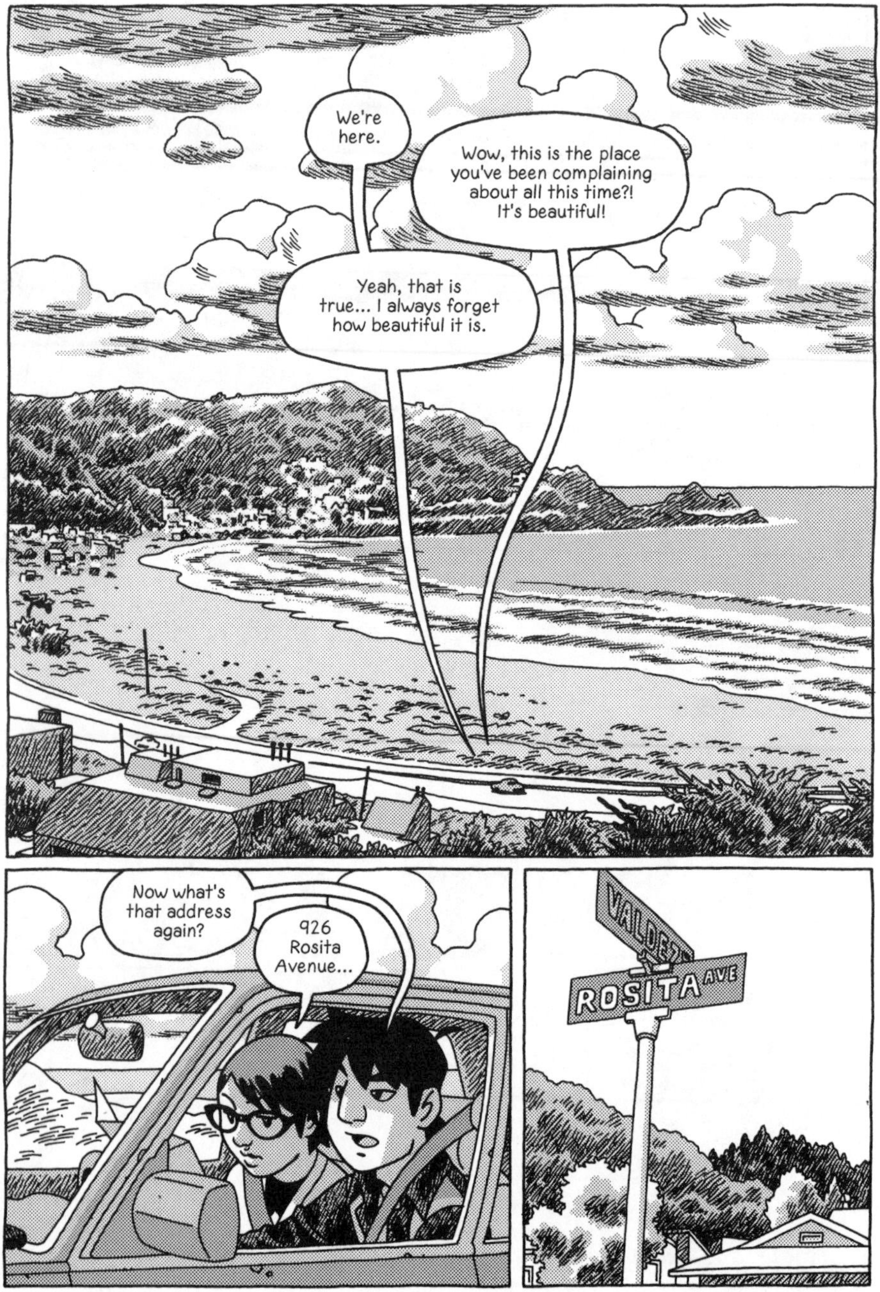
We're here.
Wow, this is the place you've been complaining about all this time?! It's beautiful!
Yeah, that is true... I always forget how beautiful it is.
Now what's that address again?
926 Rosita Avenue...
ROSITA AVE

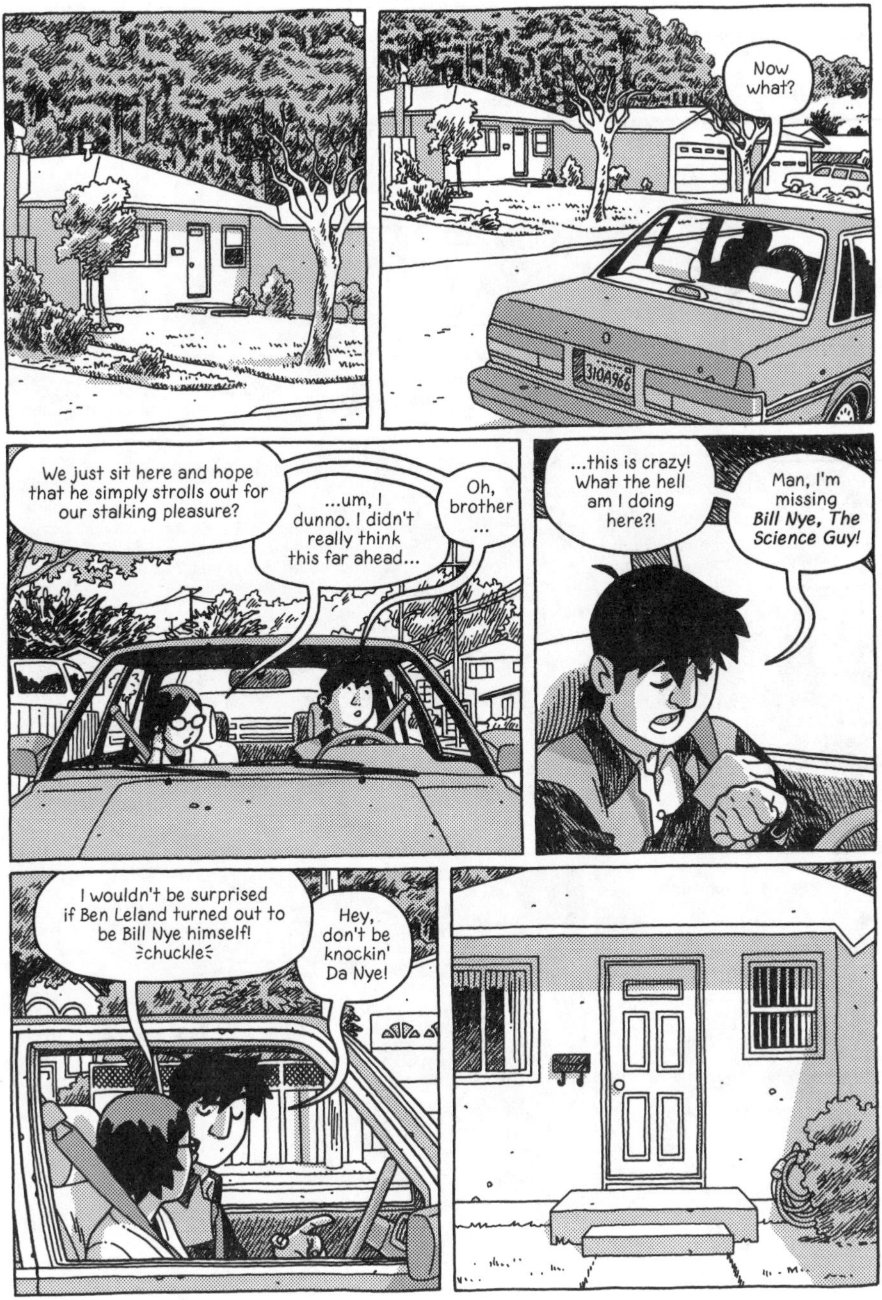
Now what?
We just sit here and hope that he simply strolls out for our stalking pleasure?
...um, I dunno. I didn't really think this far ahead...
Oh, brother ...
...this is crazy! What the hell am I doing here?!
Man, I'm missing *Bill Nye, The Science Guy!*
I wouldn't be surprised if Ben Leland turned out to be Bill Nye himself! ≷chuckle≶
Hey, don't be knockin' Da Nye!

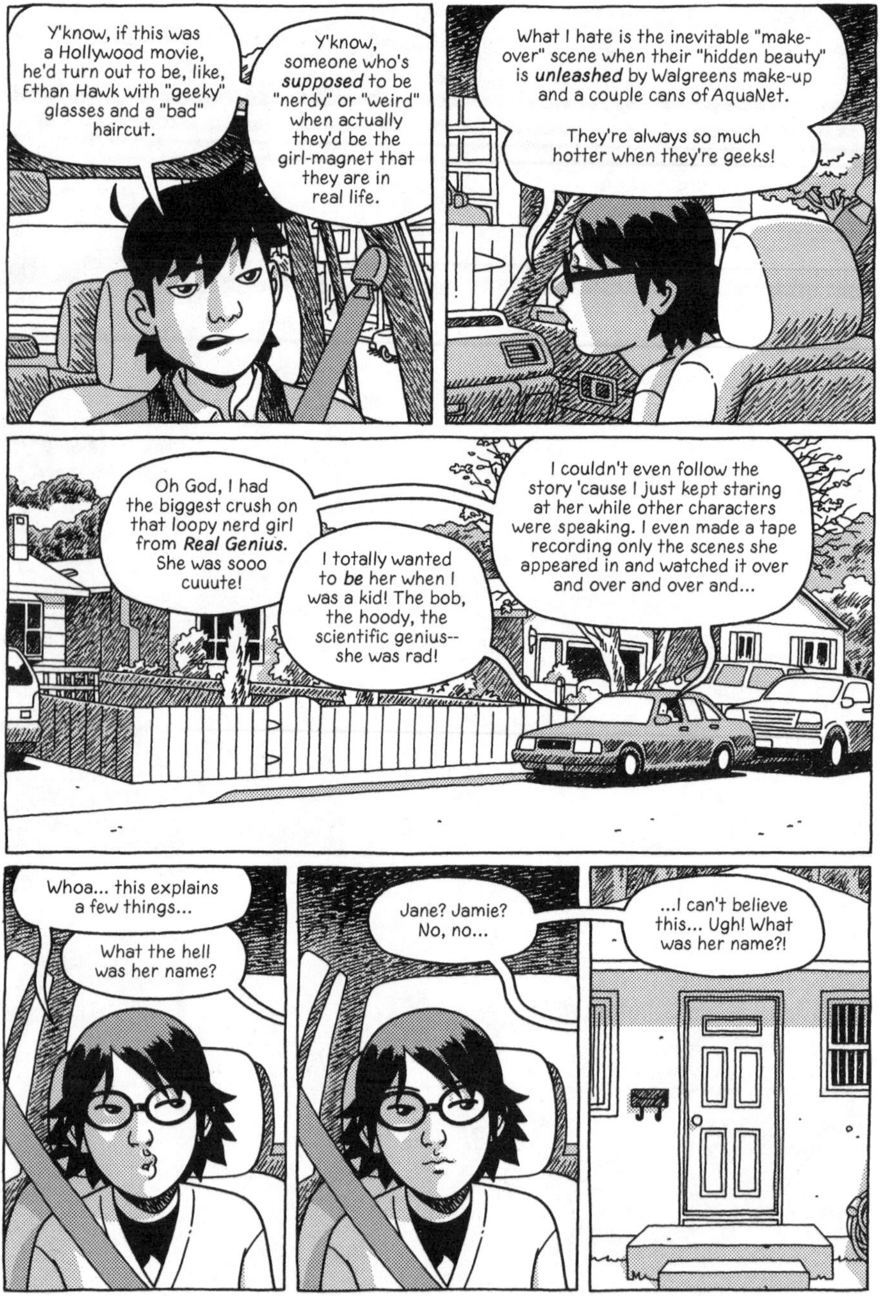
Y'know, if this was a Hollywood movie, he'd turn out to be, like, Ethan Hawk with "geeky" glasses and a "bad" haircut.
Y'know, someone who's ***supposed*** to be "nerdy" or "weird" when actually they'd be the girl-magnet that they are in real life.
What I hate is the inevitable "make-over" scene when their "hidden beauty" is ***unleashed*** by Walgreens make-up and a couple cans of AquaNet.
They're always so much hotter when they're geeks!
Oh God, I had the biggest crush on that loopy nerd girl from ***Real Genius.*** She was sooo cuuute!
I totally wanted to ***be*** her when I was a kid! The bob, the hoody, the scientific genius-- she was rad!
I couldn't even follow the story 'cause I just kept staring at her while other characters were speaking. I even made a tape recording only the scenes she appeared in and watched it over and over and over and...
Whoa... this explains a few things...
What the hell was her name?
Jane? Jamie? No, no...
...I can't believe this... Ugh! What was her name?!

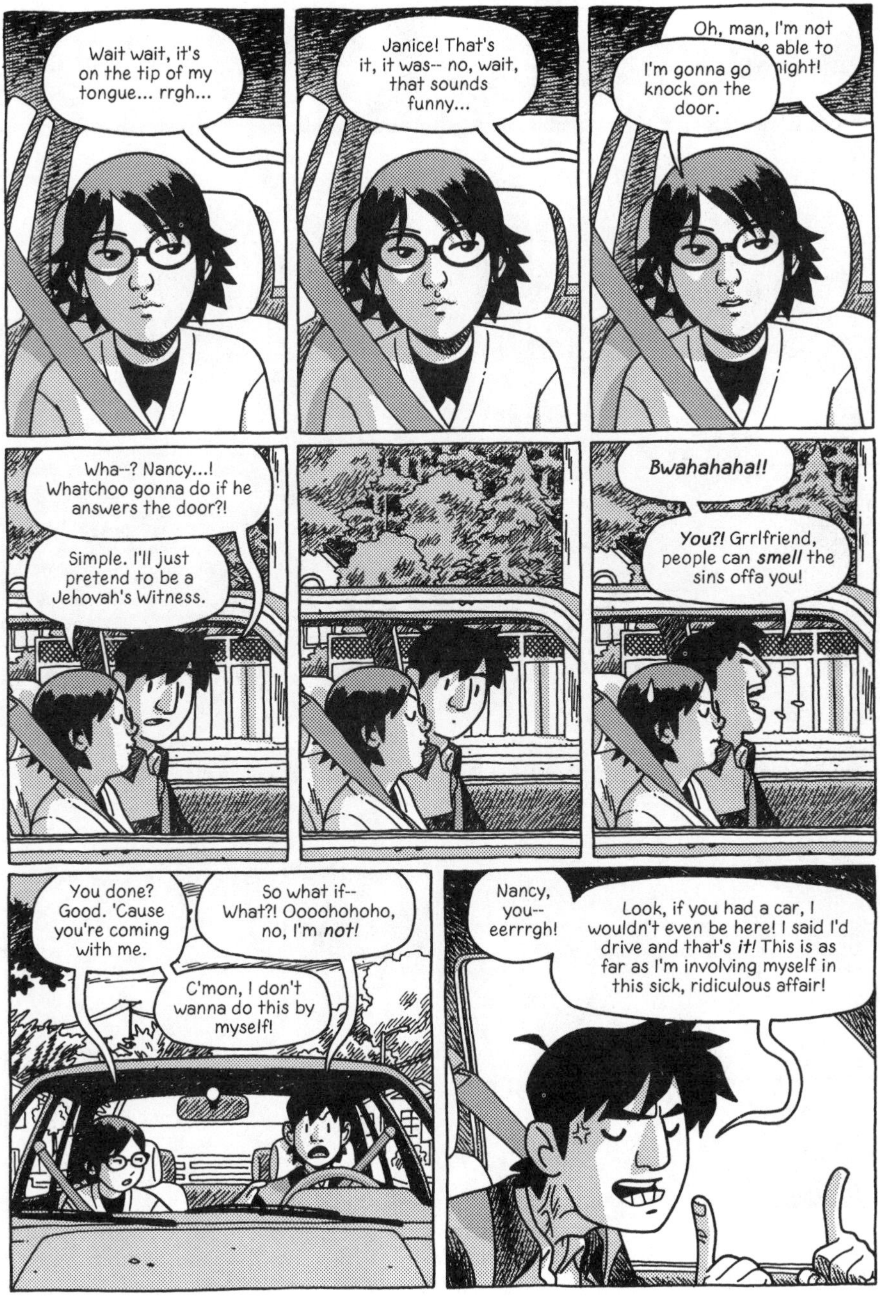

Wait wait, it's on the tip of my tongue... rrgh...
Janice! That's it, it was-- no, wait, that sounds funny...
Oh, man, I'm not
I'm gonna go knock on the door.
Wha--? Nancy...! Whatchoo gonna do if he answers the door?!
Simple. I'll just pretend to be a Jehovah's Witness.
Bwahahaha!!
You?! Grrlfriend, people can smell the sins offa you!
You done? Good. 'Cause you're coming with me.
So what if-- What?! Ooookohoho, no, I'm not!
C'mon, I don't wanna do this by myself!
Nancy, you-- eerrrgh!
Look, if you had a car, I wouldn't even be here! I said I'd drive and that's it! This is as far as I'm involving myself in this sick, ridiculous affair!

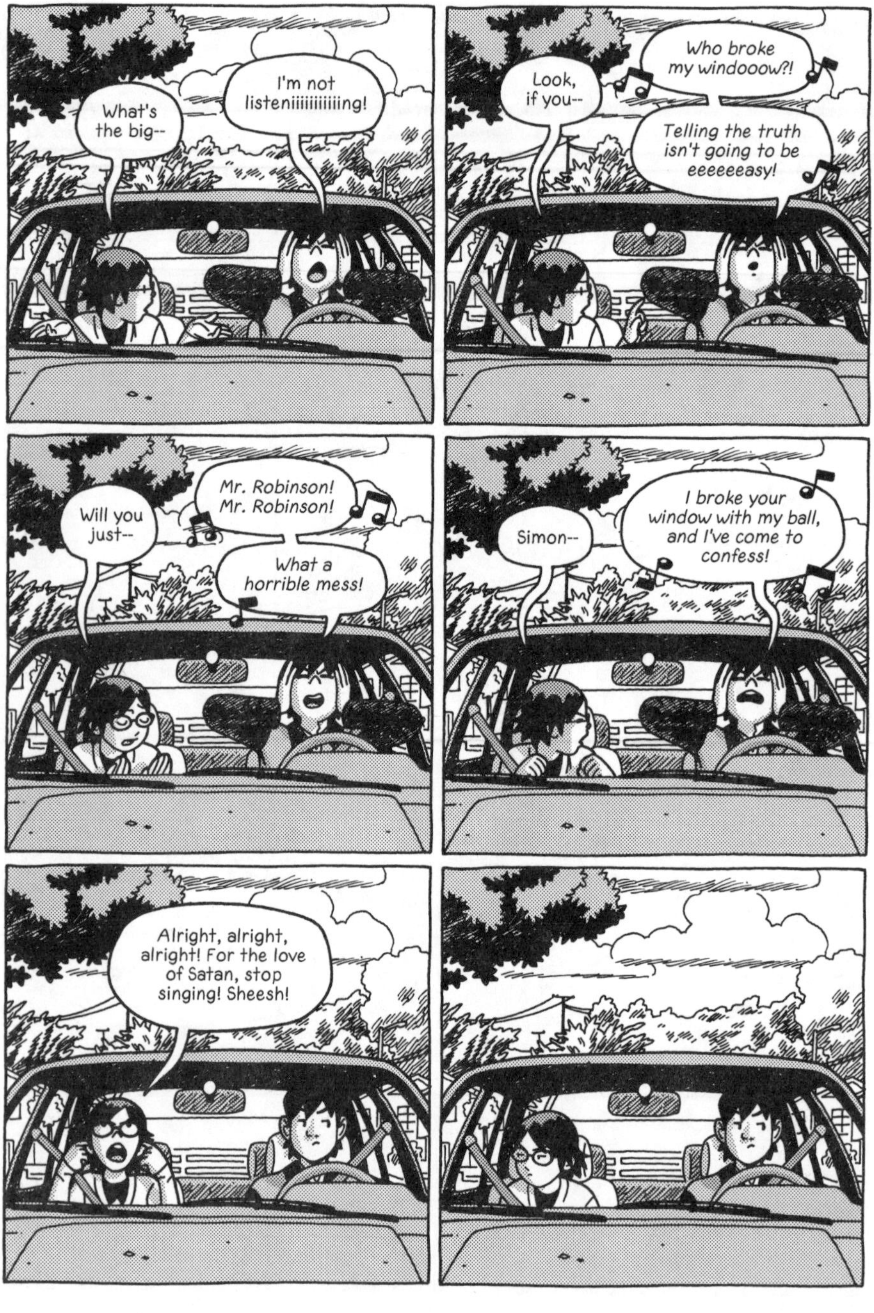
What's the big--
I'm not listeniiiiiiiiiiing!
Look, if you--
Who broke my windooow?!
Telling the truth isn't going to be eeeeeeasy!
Will you just--
Mr. Robinson! Mr. Robinson!
What a horrible mess!
Simon--
I broke your window with my ball, and I've come to confess!
Alright, alright, alright! For the love of Satan, stop singing! Sheesh!

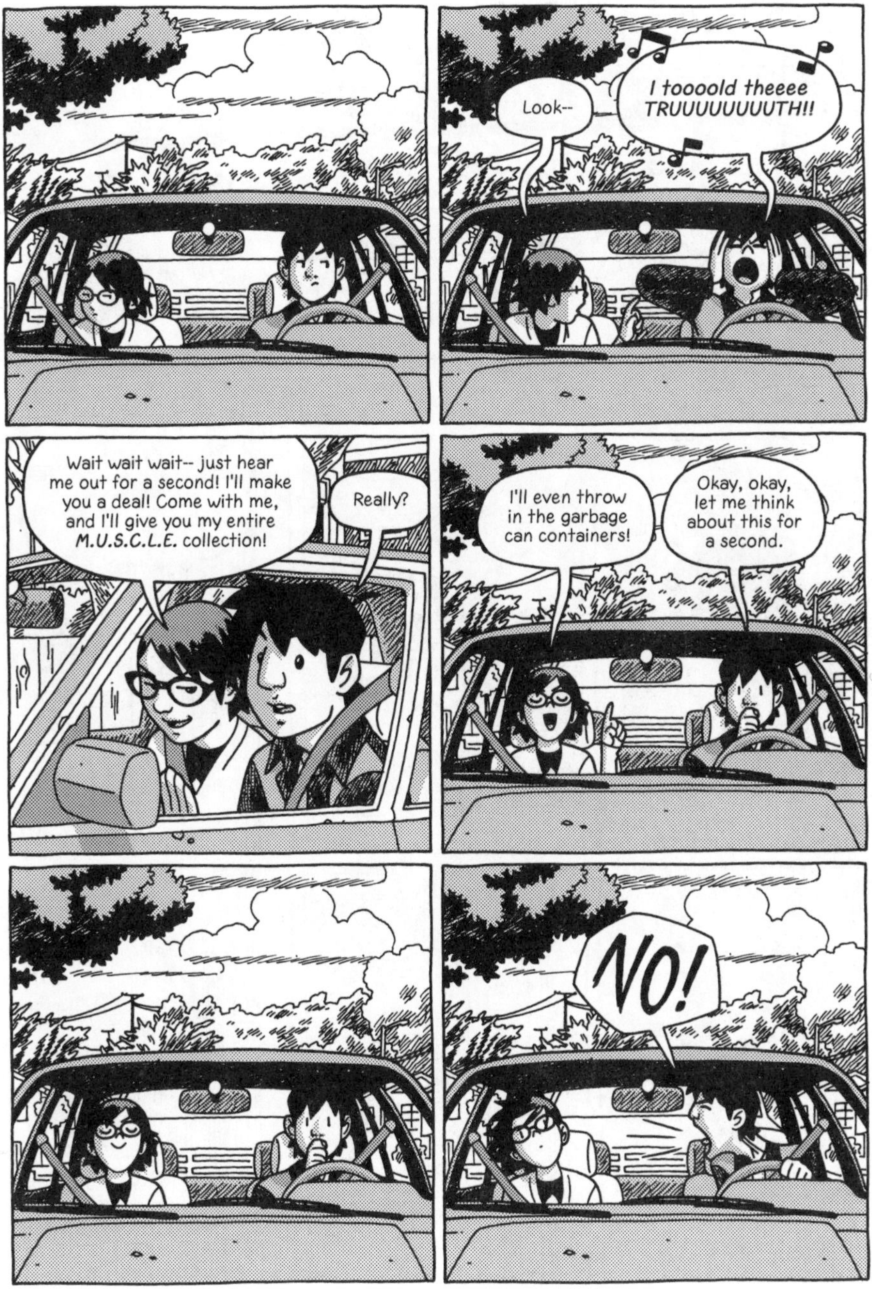
Look--
I tooold theeee TRUUUUUUUUTH!!
Wait wait wait-- just hear me out for a second! I'll make you a deal! Come with me, and I'll give you my entire *M.U.S.C.L.E.* collection!
Really?
I'll even throw in the garbage can containers!
Okay, okay, let me think about this for a second.
NO!

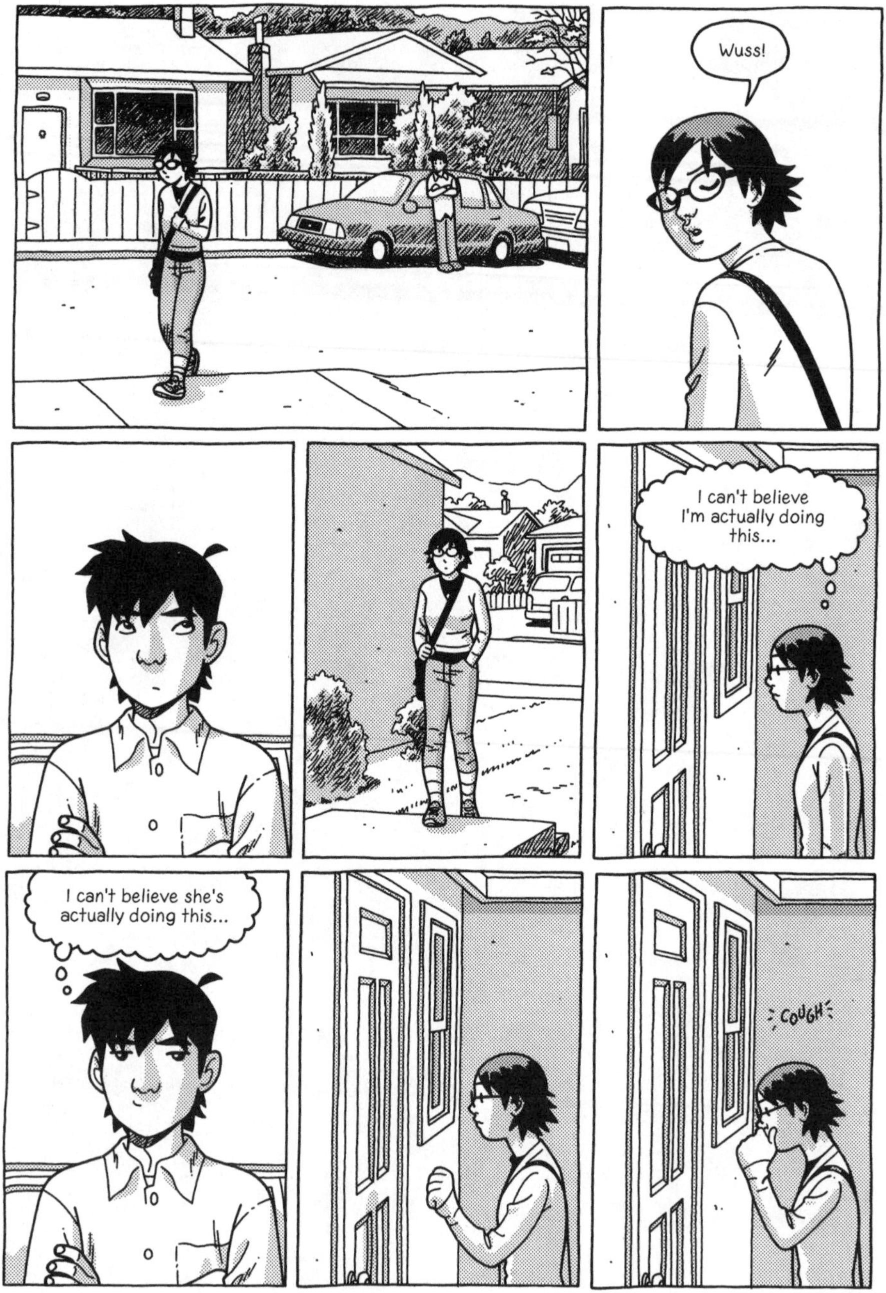
Wuss!
I can't believe I'm actually doing this...
I can't believe she's actually doing this...
COUGH

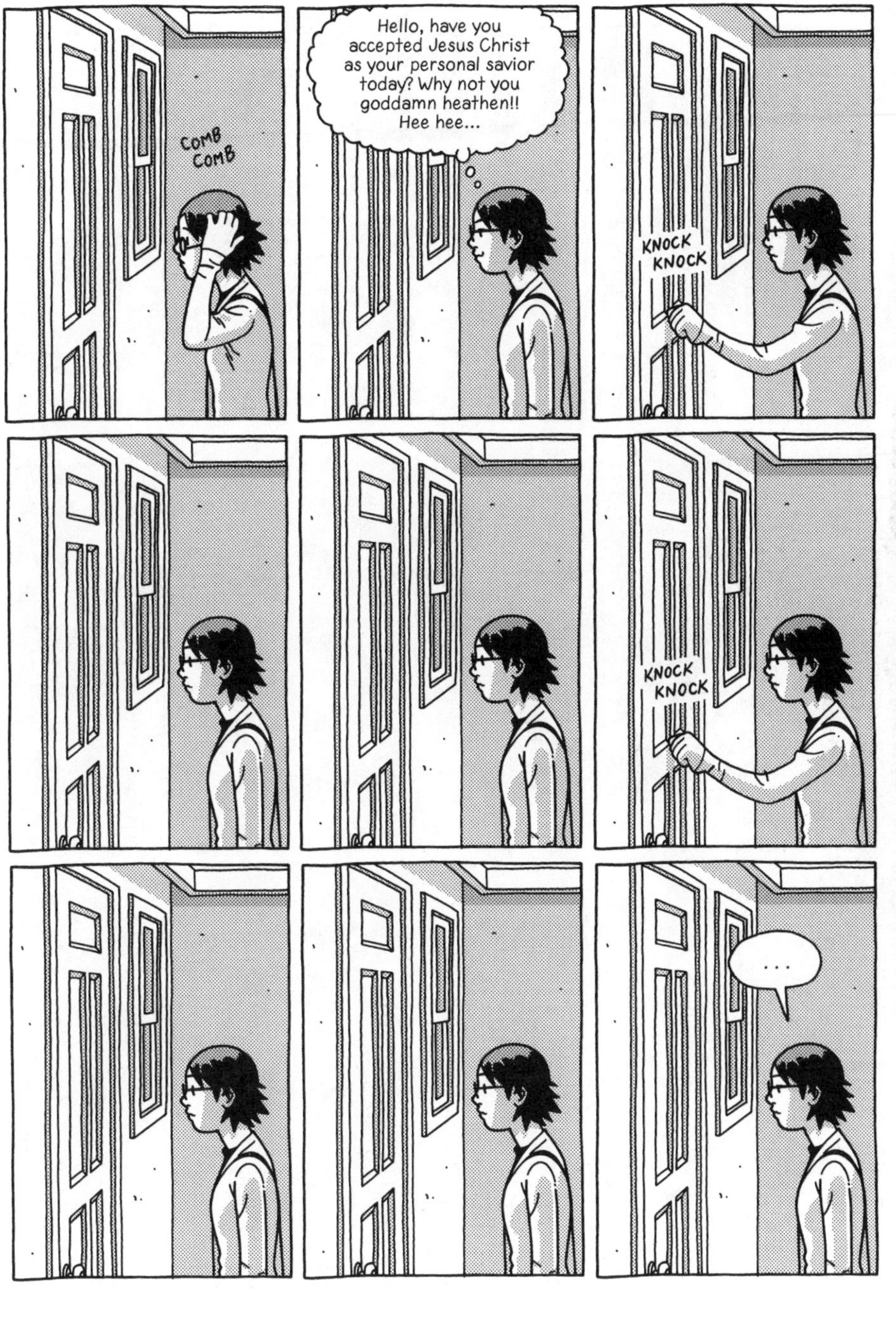
COMB
COMB
Hello, have you accepted Jesus Christ as your personal savior today? Why not you goddamn heathen!! Hee hee...
KNOCK
KNOCK
KNOCK
KNOCK
. . .

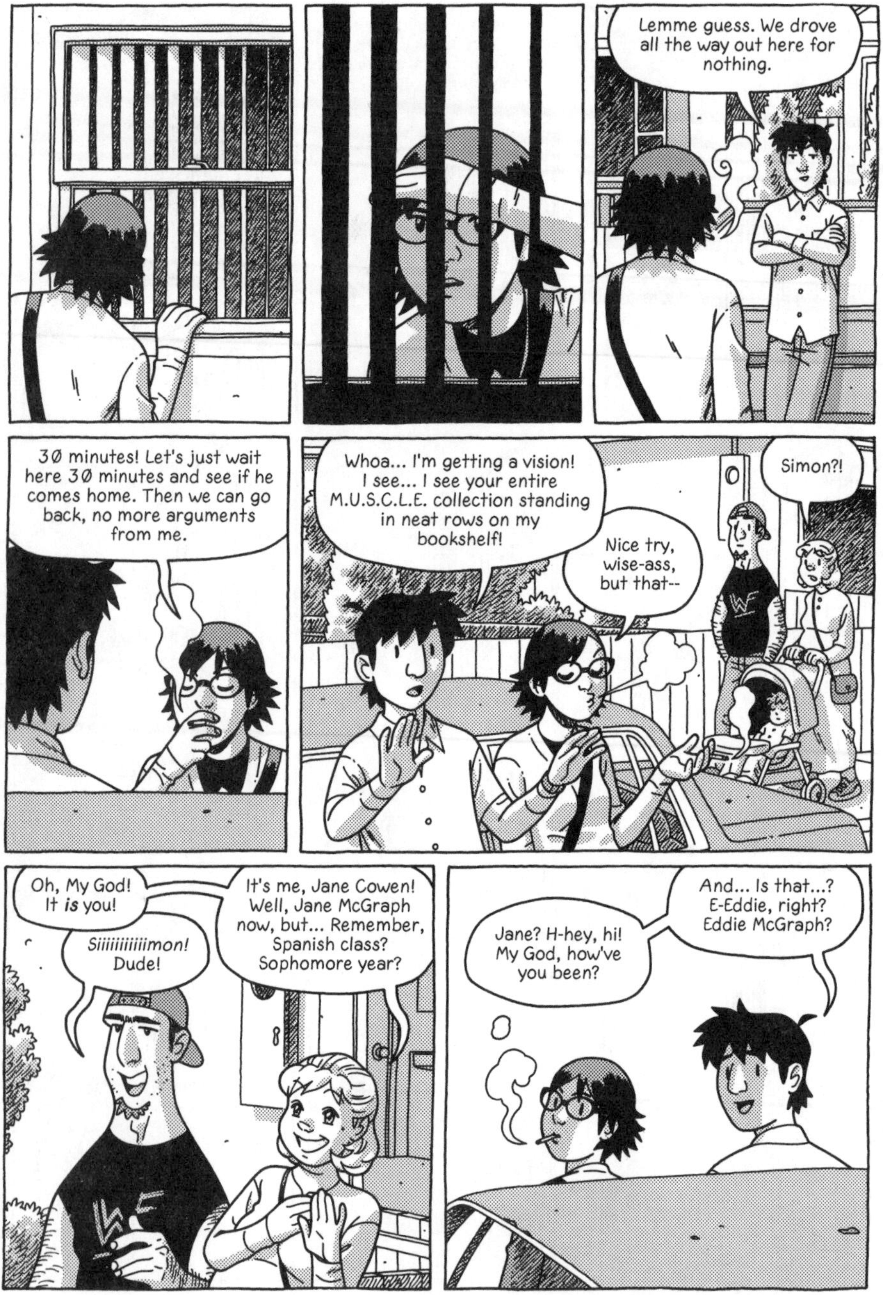
Lemme guess. We drove all the way out here for nothing.
3Ø minutes! Let's just wait here 3Ø minutes and see if he comes home. Then we can go back, no more arguments from me.
Whoa... I'm getting a vision! I see... I see your entire M.U.S.C.L.E. collection standing in neat rows on my bookshelf!
Nice try, wise-ass, but that--
Simon?!
Oh, My God! It *is* you!
Siiiiiiiiiimon! Dude!
It's me, Jane Cowen! Well, Jane McGraph now, but... Remember, Spanish class? Sophomore year?
Jane? H-hey, hi! My God, how've you been?
And... Is that...? E-Eddie, right? Eddie McGraph?

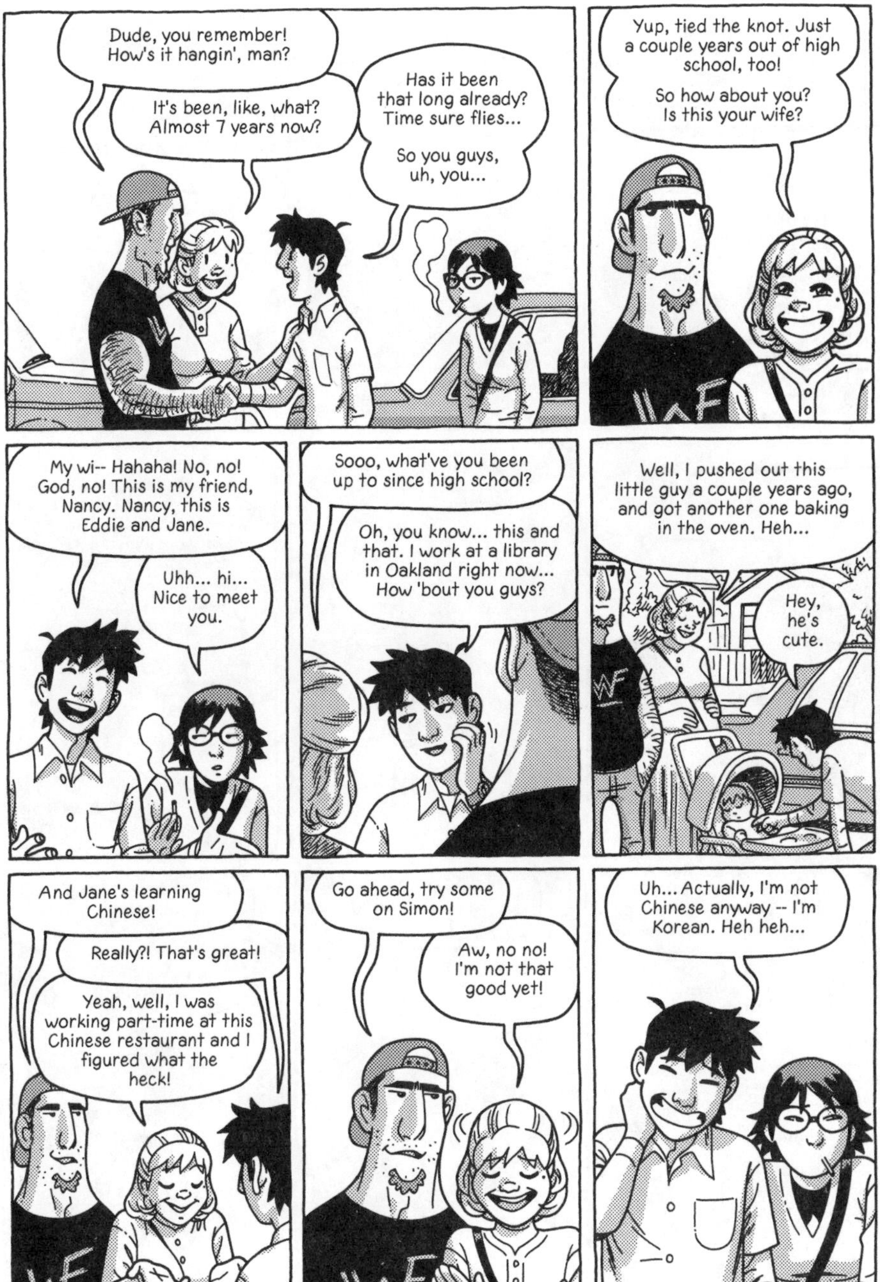
Dude, you remember! How's it hangin', man?
It's been, like, what? Almost 7 years now?
Has it been that long already? Time sure flies...
So you guys, uh, you...
Yup, tied the knot. Just a couple years out of high school, too!
So how about you? Is this your wife?
My wi-- Hahaha! No, no! God, no! This is my friend, Nancy. Nancy, this is Eddie and Jane.
Uhh... hi... Nice to meet you.
Sooo, what've you been up to since high school?
Oh, you know... this and that. I work at a library in Oakland right now... How 'bout you guys?
Well, I pushed out this little guy a couple years ago, and got another one baking in the oven. Heh...
Hey, he's cute.
And Jane's learning Chinese!
Really?! That's great!
Yeah, well, I was working part-time at this Chinese restaurant and I figured what the heck!
Go ahead, try some on Simon!
Aw, no no! I'm not that good yet!
Uh... Actually, I'm not Chinese anyway -- I'm Korean. Heh heh...

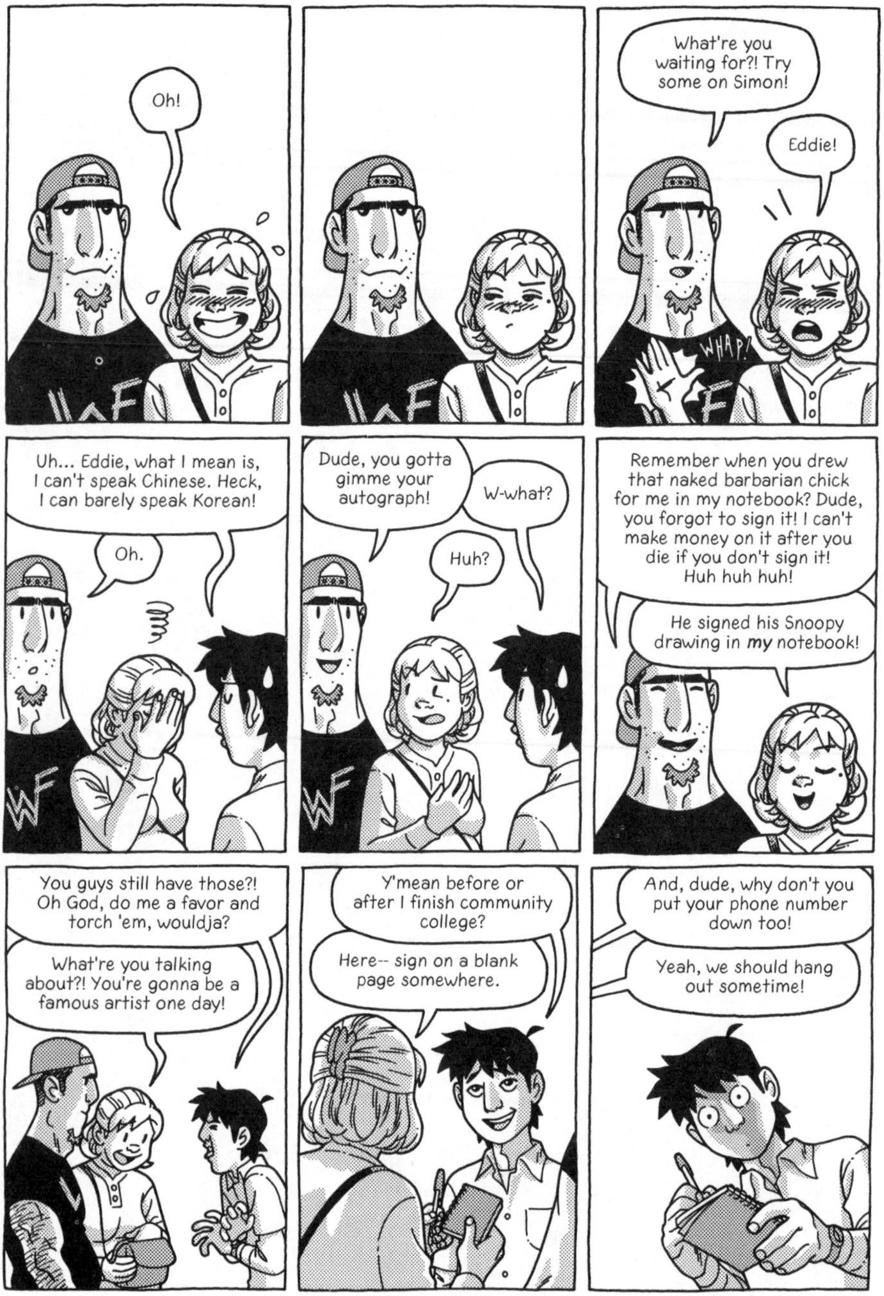
Oh!
What're you waiting for?! Try some on Simon!
Eddie!
WHAP!
Uh... Eddie, what I mean is, I can't speak Chinese. Heck, I can barely speak Korean!
Oh.
Dude, you gotta gimme your autograph!
W-what?
Huh?
Remember when you drew that naked barbarian chick for me in my notebook? Dude, you forgot to sign it! I can't make money on it after you die if you don't sign it! Huh huh huh!
He signed his Snoopy drawing in **my** notebook!
You guys still have those?! Oh God, do me a favor and torch 'em, wouldja?
What're you talking about?! You're gonna be a famous artist one day!
Y'mean before or after I finish community college?
Here-- sign on a blank page somewhere.
And, dude, why don't you put your phone number down too!
Yeah, we should hang out sometime!

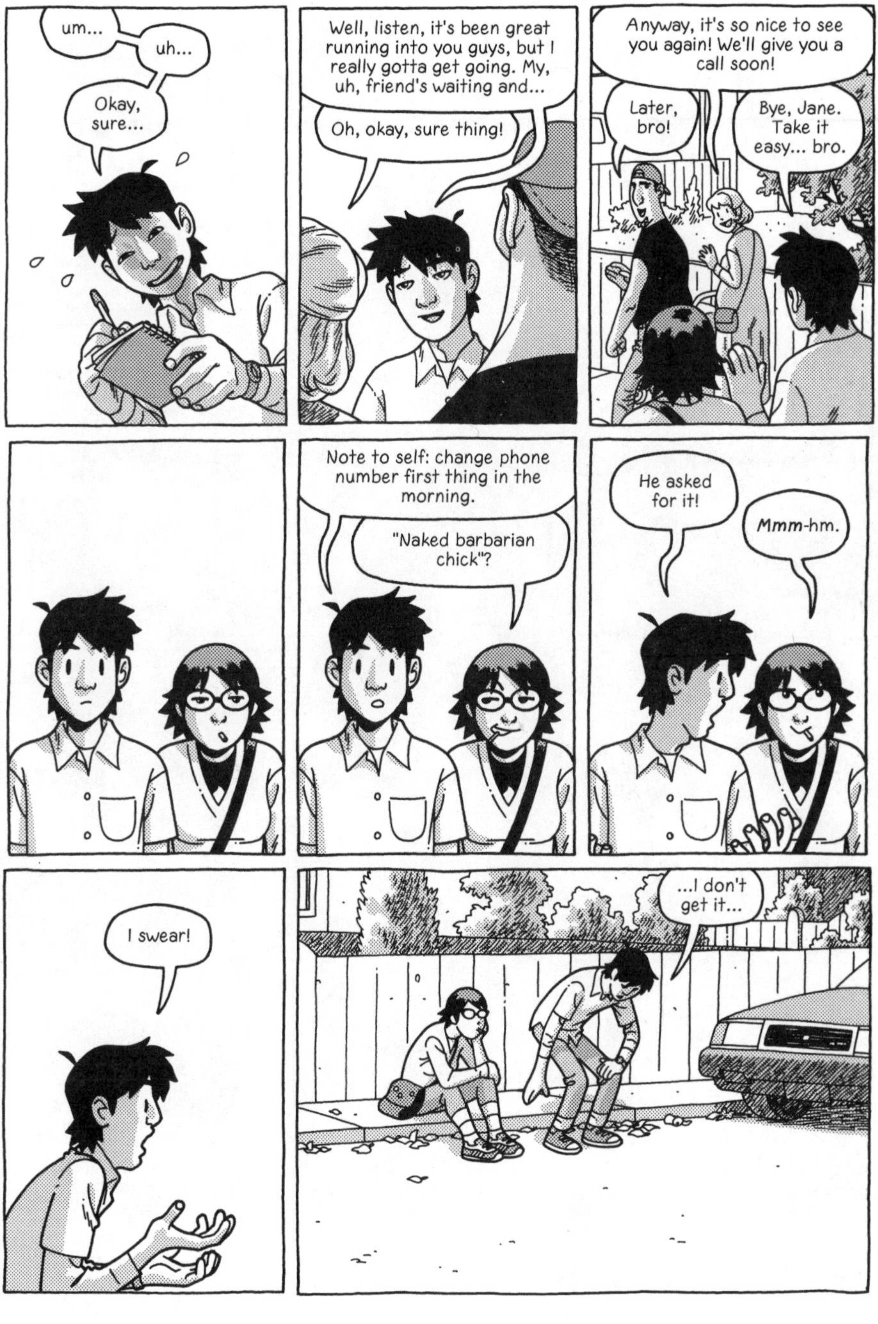

um...
uh...
Okay, sure...
Well, listen, it's been great running into you guys, but I really gotta get going. My, uh, friend's waiting and...
Oh, okay, sure thing!
Anyway, it's so nice to see you again! We'll give you a call soon!
Later, bro!
Bye, Jane. Take it easy... bro.
Note to self: change phone number first thing in the morning.
"Naked barbarian chick"?
He asked for it!
Mmm-hm.
I swear!
...I don't get it...

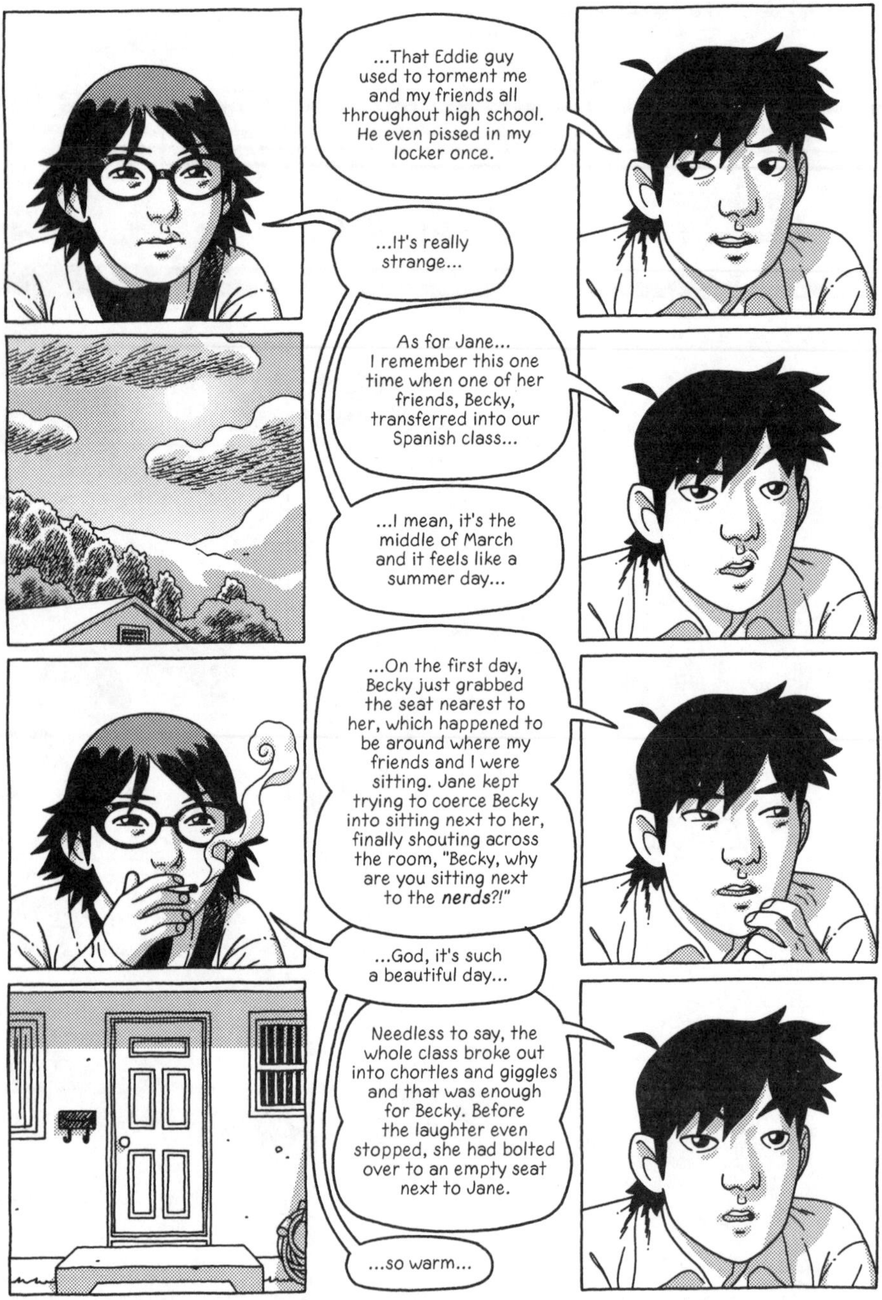
...That Eddie guy used to torment me and my friends all throughout high school. He even pissed in my locker once.
...It's really strange...
As for Jane... I remember this one time when one of her friends, Becky, transferred into our Spanish class...
...I mean, it's the middle of March and it feels like a summer day...
...On the first day, Becky just grabbed the seat nearest to her, which happened to be around where my friends and I were sitting. Jane kept trying to coerce Becky into sitting next to her, finally shouting across the room, "Becky, why are you sitting next to the *nerds*?!"
...God, it's such a beautiful day...
Needless to say, the whole class broke out into chortles and giggles and that was enough for Becky. Before the laughter even stopped, she had bolted over to an empty seat next to Jane.
...so warm...

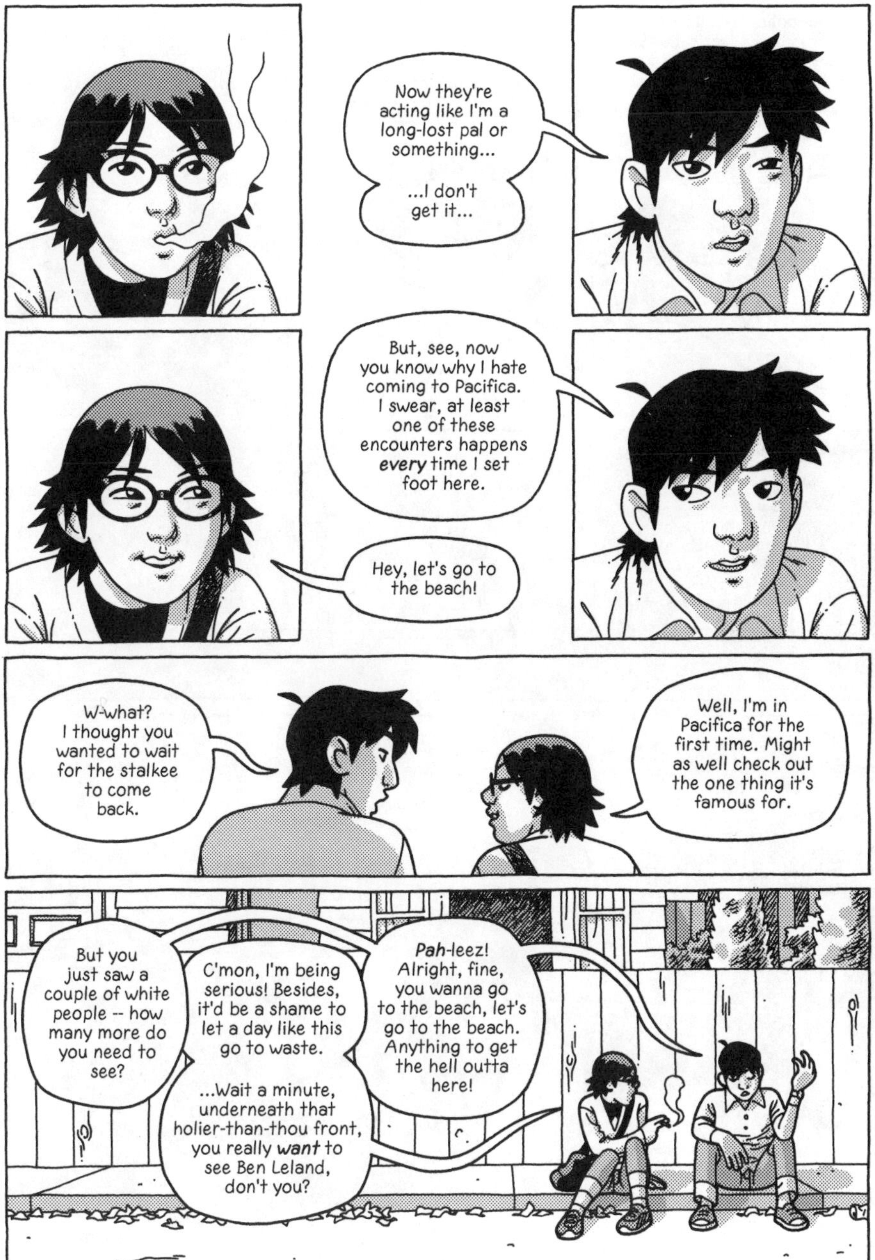
Now they're acting like I'm a long-lost pal or something...
...I don't get it...
But, see, now you know why I hate coming to Pacifica. I swear, at least one of these encounters happens *every* time I set foot here.
Hey, let's go to the beach!
W-what? I thought you wanted to wait for the stalkee to come back.
Well, I'm in Pacifica for the first time. Might as well check out the one thing it's famous for.
But you just saw a couple of white people -- how many more do you need to see?
C'mon, I'm being serious! Besides, it'd be a shame to let a day like this go to waste.
...Wait a minute, underneath that holier-than-thou front, you really *want* to see Ben Leland, don't you?
Pah-leez! Alright, fine, you wanna go to the beach, let's go to the beach. Anything to get the hell outta here!

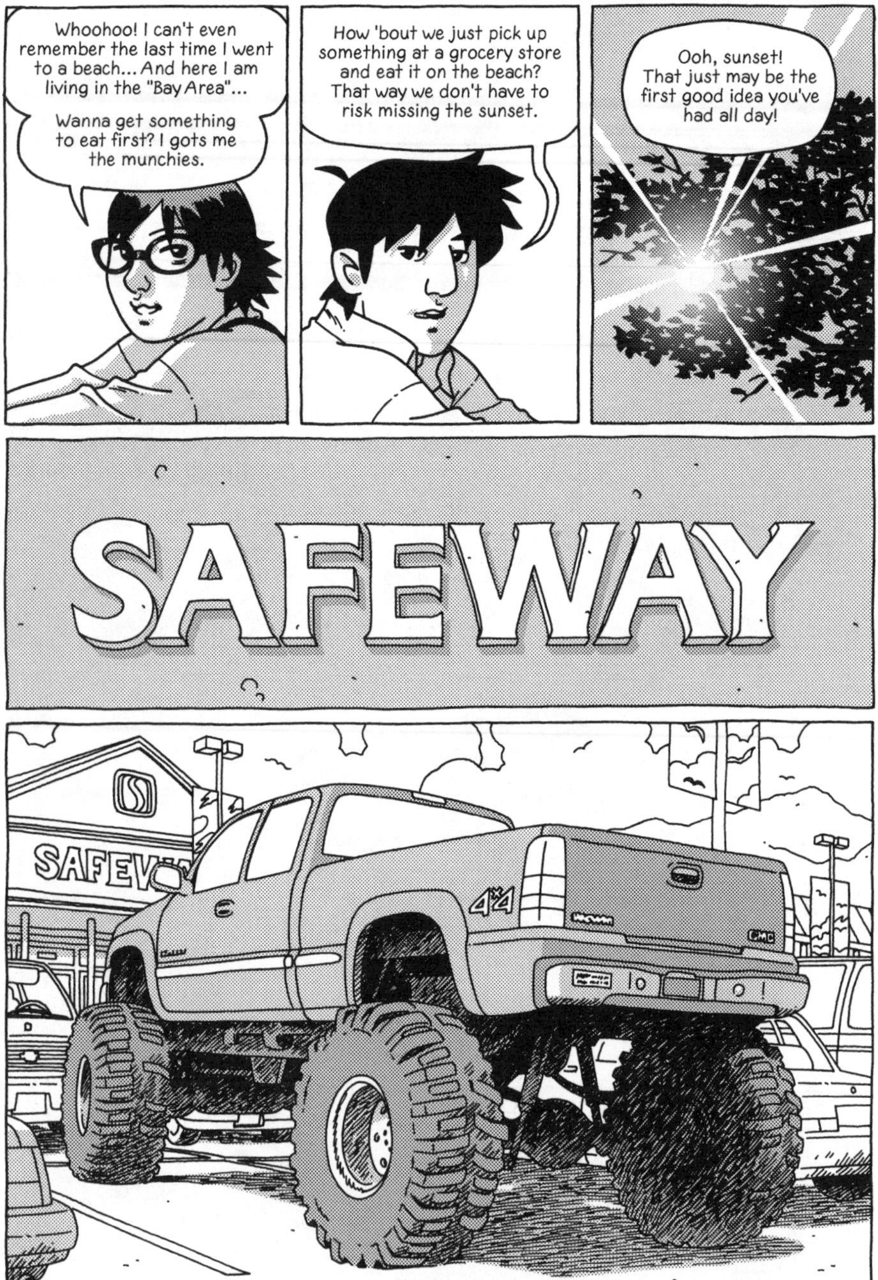
Whoohoo! I can't even remember the last time I went to a beach... And here I am living in the "Bay Area"...
Wanna get something to eat first? I gots me the munchies.
How 'bout we just pick up something at a grocery store and eat it on the beach? That way we don't have to risk missing the sunset.
Ooh, sunset! That just may be the first good idea you've had all day!
SAFEWAY
4x4
GMC

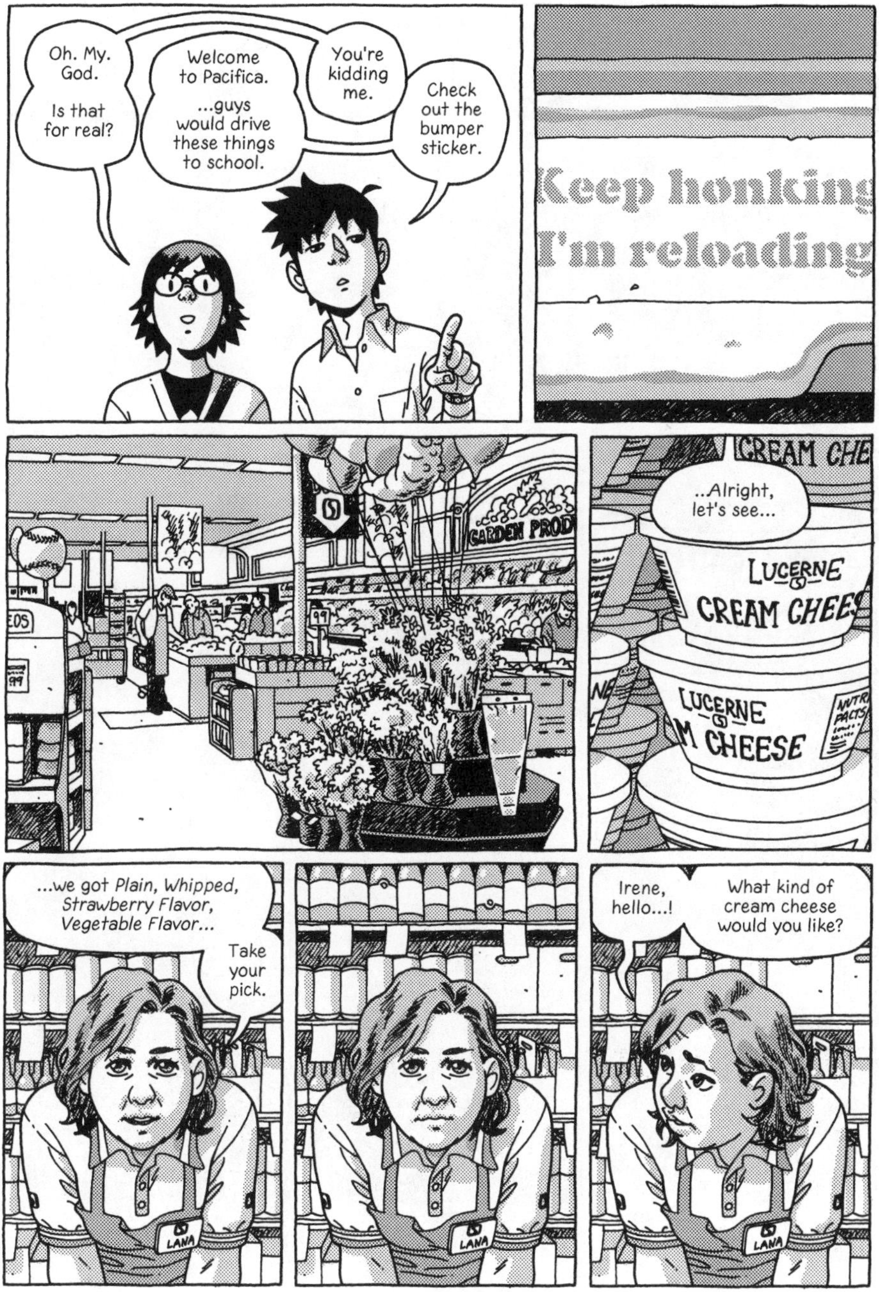

Oh. My. God.
Is that for real?
Welcome to Pacifica.
...guys would drive these things to school.
You're kidding me.
Check out the bumper sticker.
Keep honking
I'm reloading
GARDEN PROD
CREAM CHE
..Alright, let's see...
LUCERNE
CREAM CHEES
LUCERNE
M CHEESE
...we got Plain, Whipped, Strawberry Flavor, Vegetable Flavor...
Take your pick.
LANA
LANA
Irene, hello...!
What kind of cream cheese would you like?
LANA

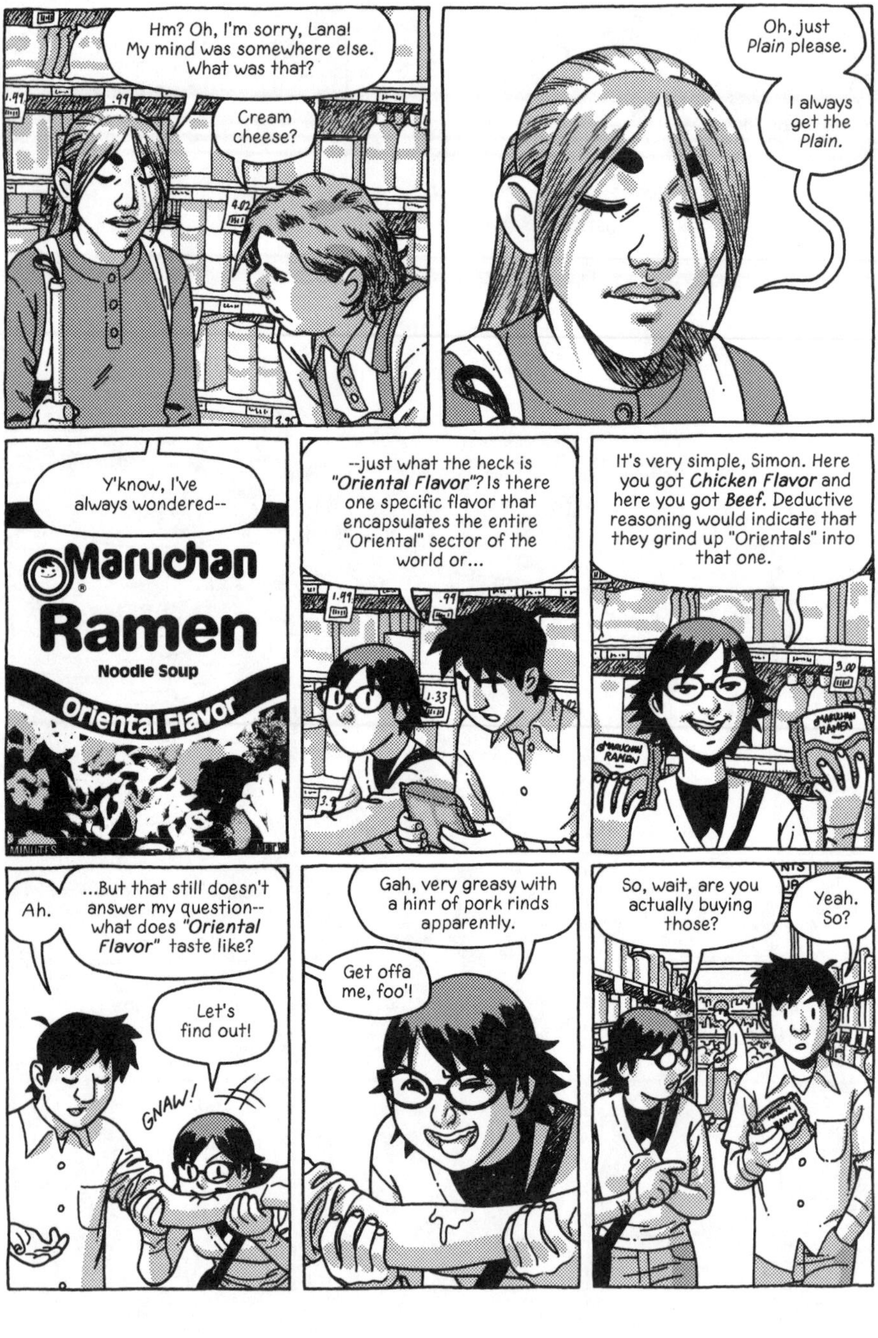

Hm? Oh, I'm sorry, Lana! My mind was somewhere else. What was that?
Cream cheese?
Oh, just *Plain* please.
I always get the *Plain.*
Y'know, I've always wondered--
Maruchan
Ramen
Noodle Soup
Oriental Flavor
--just what the heck is *"Oriental Flavor"*? Is there one specific flavor that encapsulates the entire "Oriental" sector of the world or...
It's very simple, Simon. Here you got ***Chicken Flavor*** and here you got ***Beef.*** Deductive reasoning would indicate that they grind up "Orientals" into that one.
Ah.
...But that still doesn't answer my question-- what does *"Oriental Flavor"* taste like?
Let's find out!
GNAW!
Gah, very greasy with a hint of pork rinds apparently.
Get offa me, foo'!
So, wait, are you actually buying those?
Yeah. So?

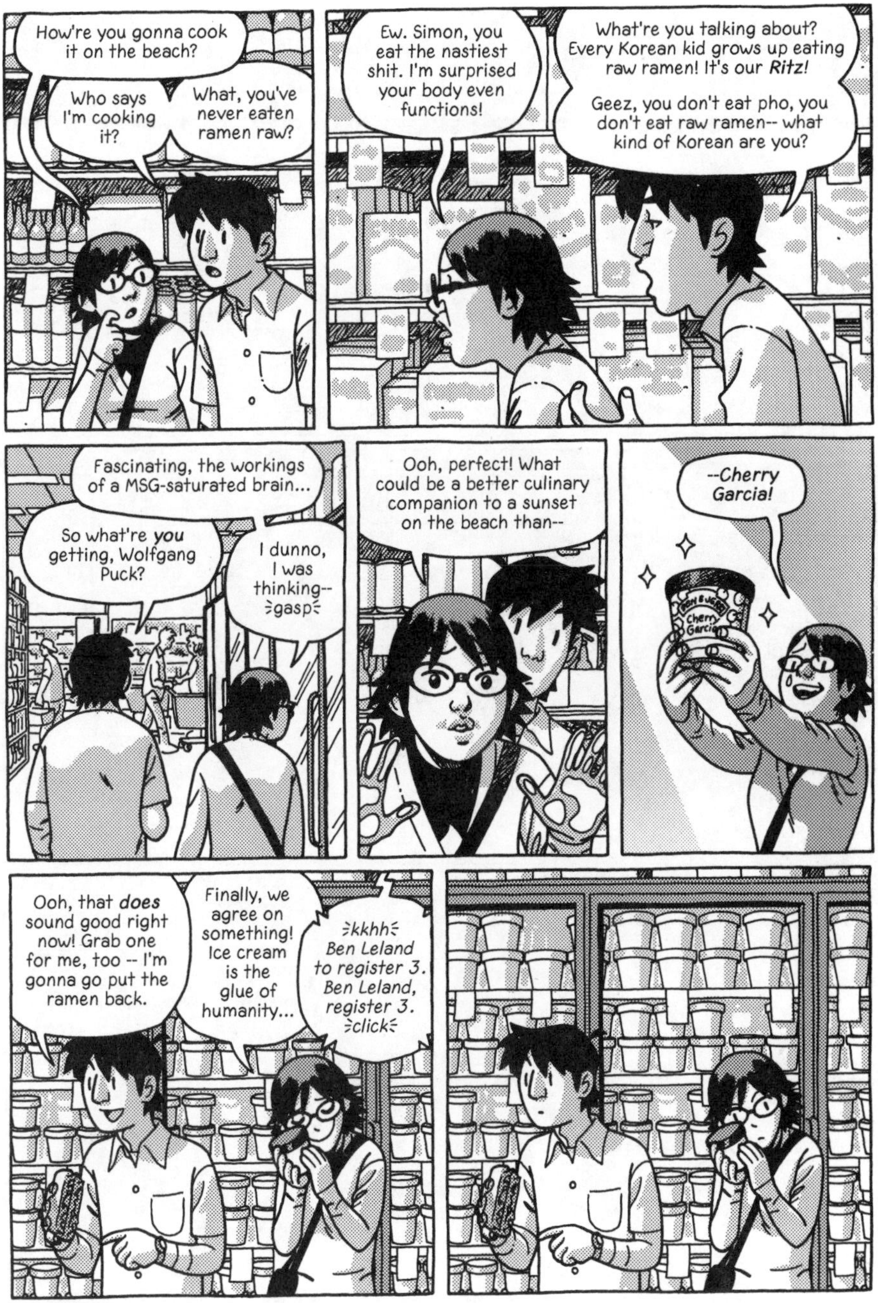
How're you gonna cook it on the beach?
Who says I'm cooking it?
What, you've never eaten ramen raw?
Ew. Simon, you eat the nastiest shit. I'm surprised your body even functions!
What're you talking about? Every Korean kid grows up eating raw ramen! It's our Ritz!
Geez, you don't eat pho, you don't eat raw ramen-- what kind of Korean are you?
Fascinating, the workings of a MSG-saturated brain...
So what're you getting, Wolfgang Puck?
I dunno, I was thinking-- gasp
Ooh, perfect! What could be a better culinary companion to a sunset on the beach than--
--Cherry Garcia!
Ben & Jerry's Cherry Garcia
Ooh, that does sound good right now! Grab one for me, too -- I'm gonna go put the ramen back.
Finally, we agree on something! Ice cream is the glue of humanity...
kkhh Ben Leland to register 3. Ben Leland, register 3. click

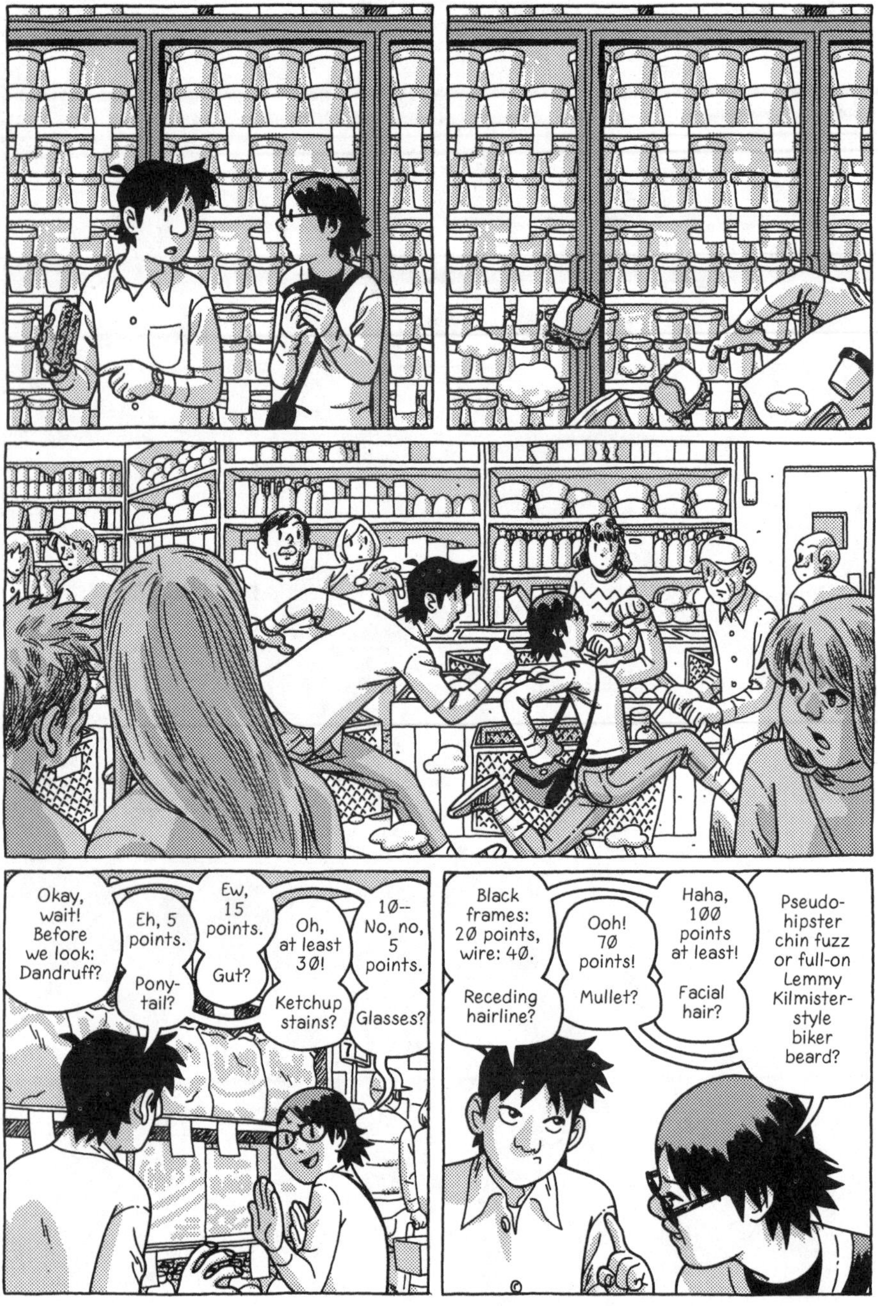
Okay, wait! Before we look: Dandruff?
Eh, 5 points.
Pony-tail?
Ew, 15 points.
Gut?
Oh, at least 3Ø!
Ketchup stains?
1Ø-- No, no, 5 points.
Glasses?
Black frames: 2Ø points, wire: 4Ø.
Receding hairline?
Ooh! 7Ø points!
Mullet?
Haha, 1ØØ points at least!
Facial hair?
Pseudo-hipster chin fuzz or full-on Lemmy Kilmister-style biker beard?

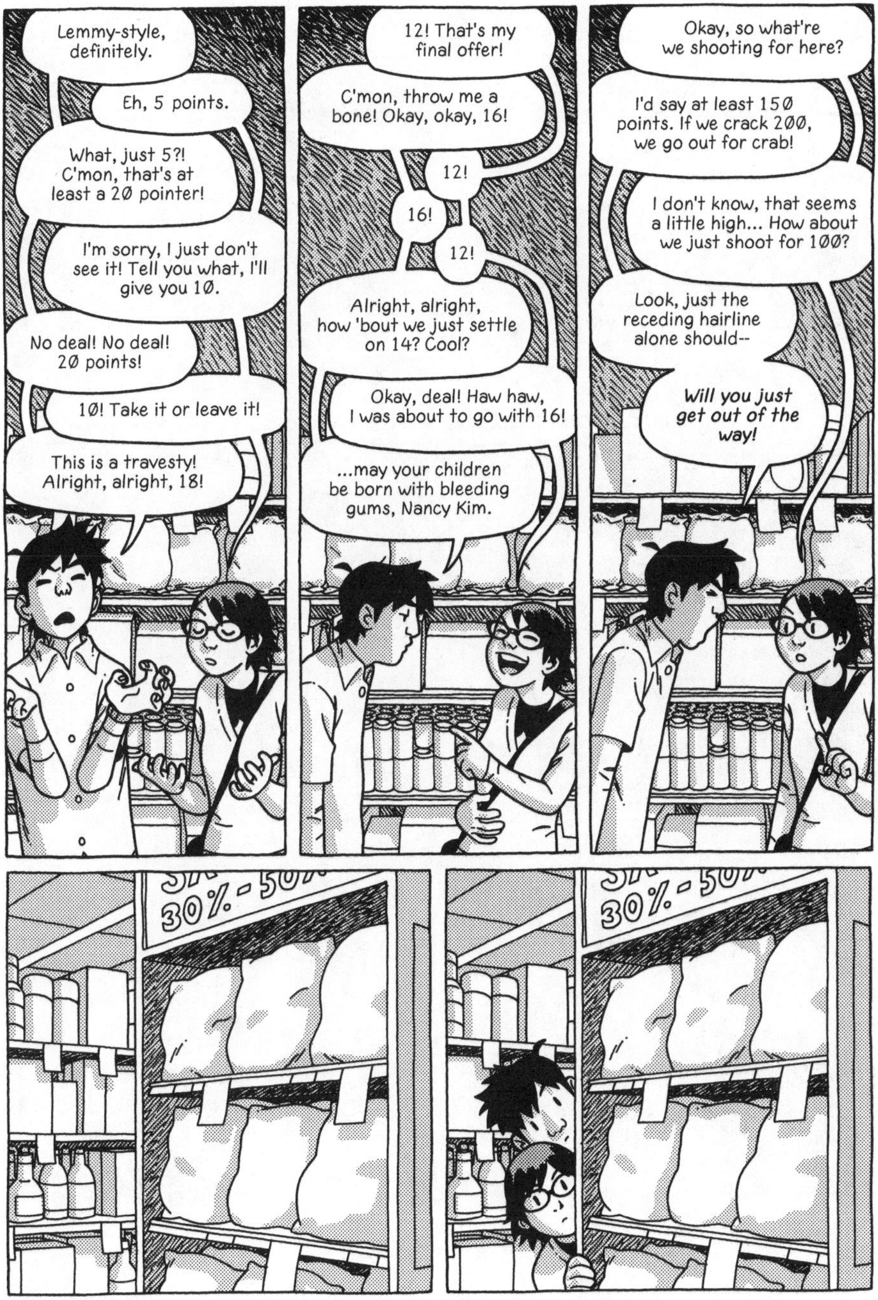
Lemmy-style, definitely.
Eh, 5 points.
What, just 5?! C'mon, that's at least a 2Ø pointer!
I'm sorry, I just don't see it! Tell you what, I'll give you 1Ø.
No deal! No deal! 2Ø points!
1Ø! Take it or leave it!
This is a travesty! Alright, alright, 18!
12! That's my final offer!
C'mon, throw me a bone! Okay, okay, 16!
12!
16!
12!
Alright, alright, how 'bout we just settle on 14? Cool?
Okay, deal! Haw haw, I was about to go with 16!
...may your children be born with bleeding gums, Nancy Kim.
Okay, so what're we shooting for here?
I'd say at least 15Ø points. If we crack 2ØØ, we go out for crab!
I don't know, that seems a little high... How about we just shoot for 1ØØ?
Look, just the receding hairline alone should--
Will you just get out of the way!

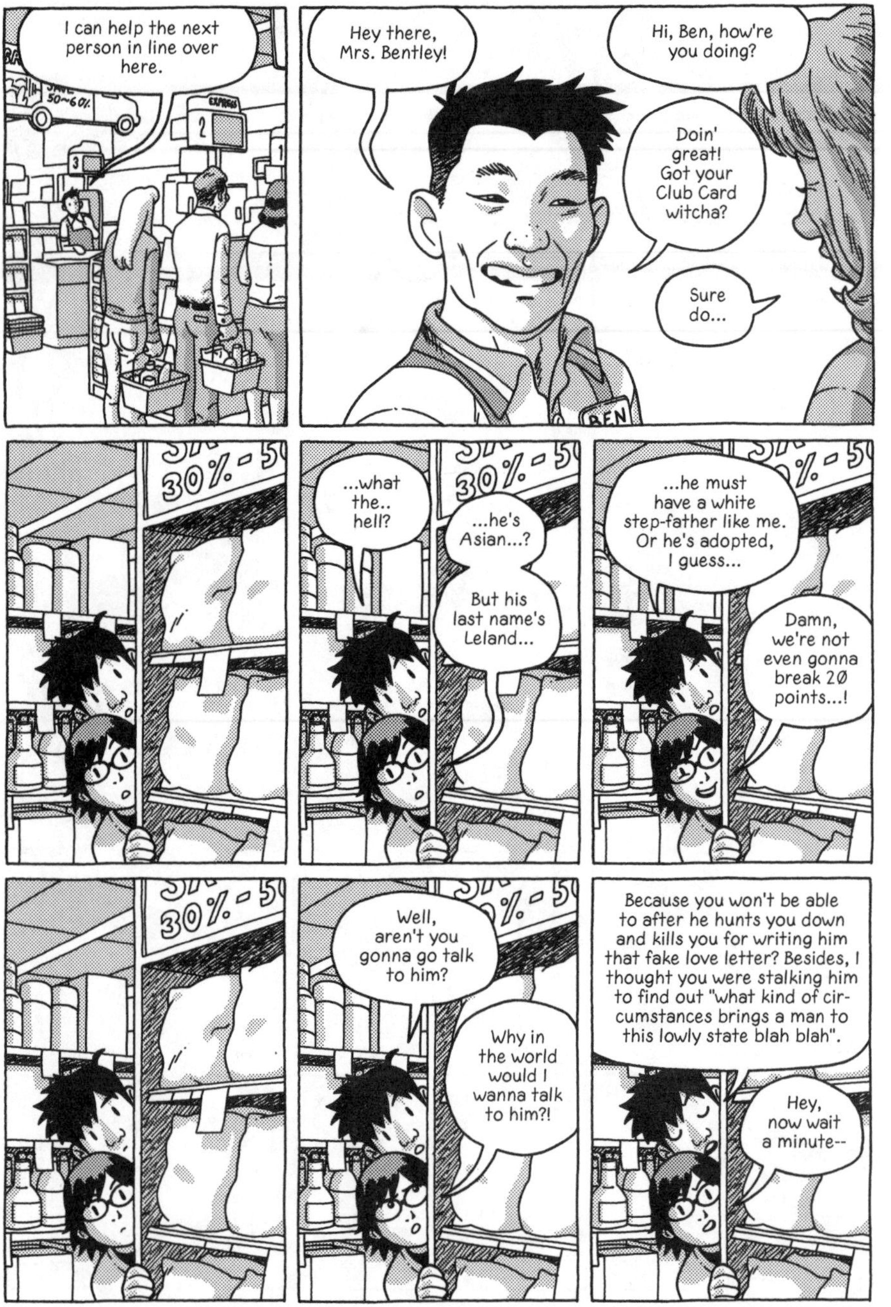
I can help the next person in line over here.
SAVE 50~60%
EXPRESS
Hey there, Mrs. Bentley!
Hi, Ben, how're you doing?
Doin' great! Got your Club Card witcha?
Sure do...
BEN
30% - 5
...what the.. hell?
...he's Asian...?
But his last name's Leland...
...he must have a white step-father like me. Or he's adopted, I guess...
Damn, we're not even gonna break 20 points...!
Well, aren't you gonna go talk to him?
Why in the world would I wanna talk to him?!
Because you won't be able to after he hunts you down and kills you for writing him that fake love letter? Besides, I thought you were stalking him to find out "what kind of circumstances brings a man to this lowly state blah blah".
Hey, now wait a minute--

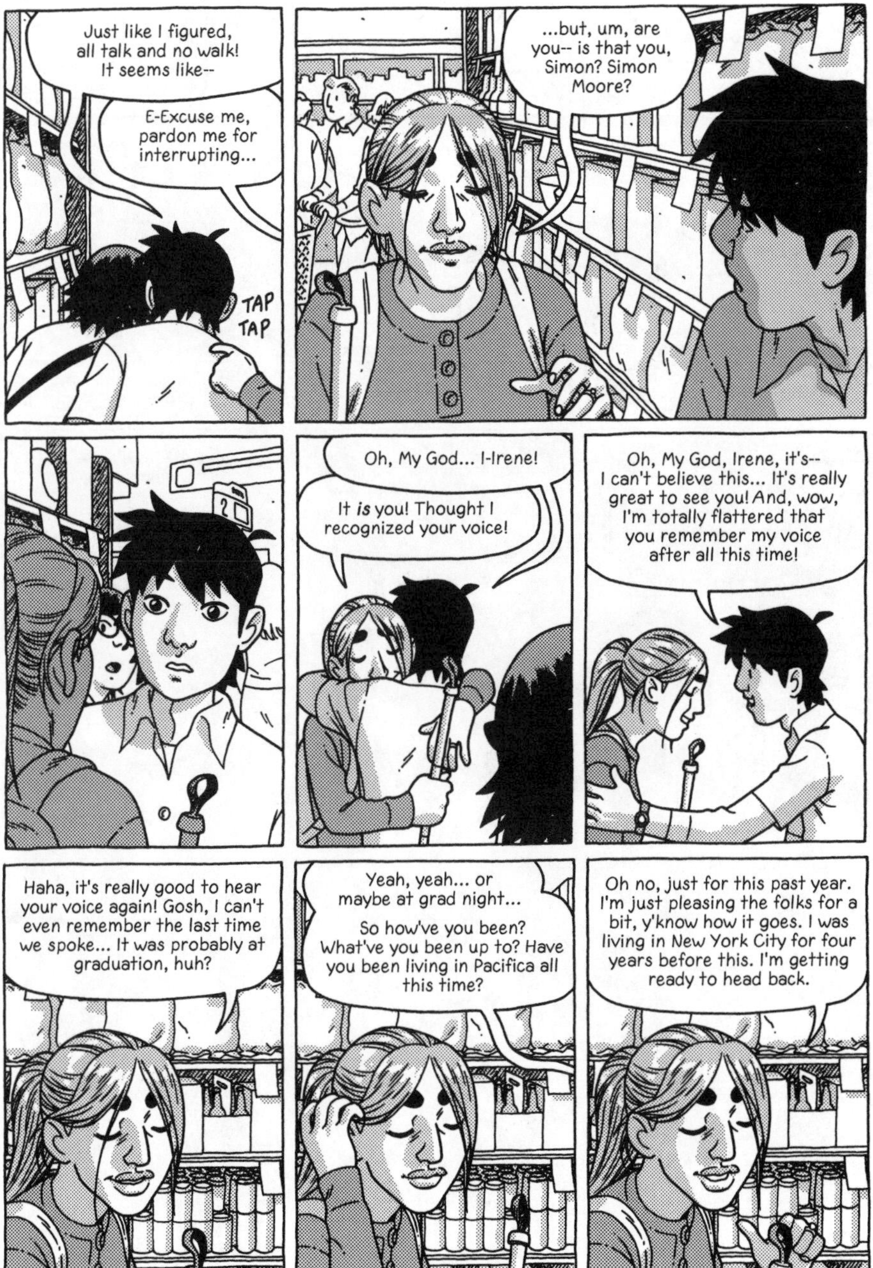
Just like I figured, all talk and no walk! It seems like--
E-Excuse me, pardon me for interrupting...
TAP TAP
...but, um, are you-- is that you, Simon? Simon Moore?
Oh, My God... I-Irene!
It *is* you! Thought I recognized your voice!
Oh, My God, Irene, it's-- I can't believe this... It's really great to see you! And, wow, I'm totally flattered that you remember my voice after all this time!
Haha, it's really good to hear your voice again! Gosh, I can't even remember the last time we spoke... It was probably at graduation, huh?
Yeah, yeah... or maybe at grad night...
So how've you been? What've you been up to? Have you been living in Pacifica all this time?
Oh no, just for this past year. I'm just pleasing the folks for a bit, y'know how it goes. I was living in New York City for four years before this. I'm getting ready to head back.

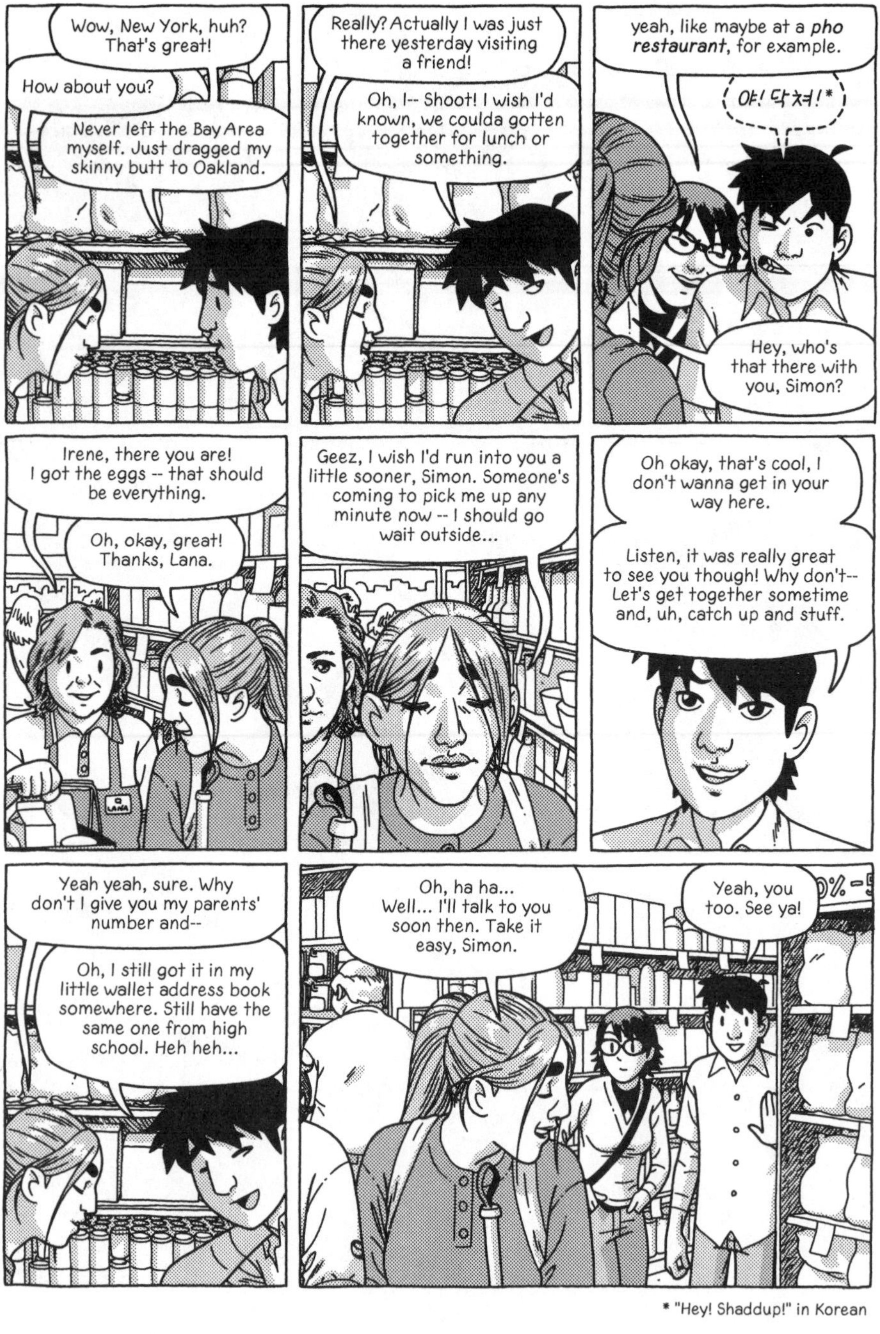
Wow, New York, huh? That's great!
How about you?
Never left the Bay Area myself. Just dragged my skinny butt to Oakland.
Really? Actually I was just there yesterday visiting a friend!
Oh, I-- Shoot! I wish I'd known, we coulda gotten together for lunch or something.
yeah, like maybe at a *pho restaurant*, for example.
야! 닥쳐!*
Hey, who's that there with you, Simon?
Irene, there you are! I got the eggs -- that should be everything.
Oh, okay, great! Thanks, Lana.
Geez, I wish I'd run into you a little sooner, Simon. Someone's coming to pick me up any minute now -- I should go wait outside...
Oh okay, that's cool, I don't wanna get in your way here.
Listen, it was really great to see you though! Why don't-- Let's get together sometime and, uh, catch up and stuff.
Yeah yeah, sure. Why don't I give you my parents' number and--
Oh, I still got it in my little wallet address book somewhere. Still have the same one from high school. Heh heh...
Oh, ha ha... Well... I'll talk to you soon then. Take it easy, Simon.
Yeah, you too. See ya!

* "Hey! Shaddup!" in Korean

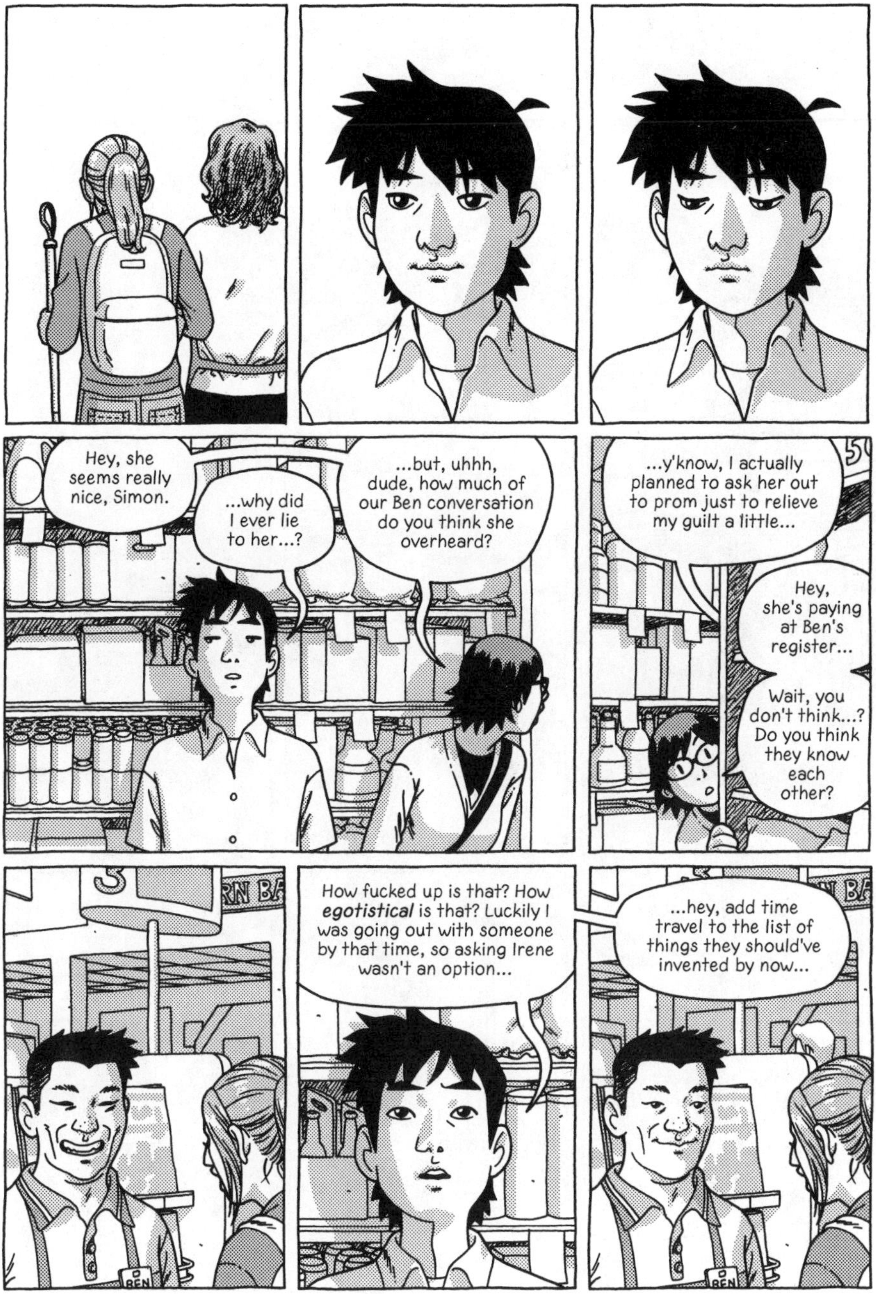
Hey, she seems really nice, Simon.
...why did I ever lie to her...?
...but, uhhh, dude, how much of our Ben conversation do you think she overheard?
...y'know, I actually planned to ask her out to prom just to relieve my guilt a little...
Hey, she's paying at Ben's register...
Wait, you don't think...? Do you think they know each other?
RN BA
BEN
How fucked up is that? How *egotistical* is that? Luckily I was going out with someone by that time, so asking Irene wasn't an option...
...hey, add time travel to the list of things they should've invented by now...
BEN

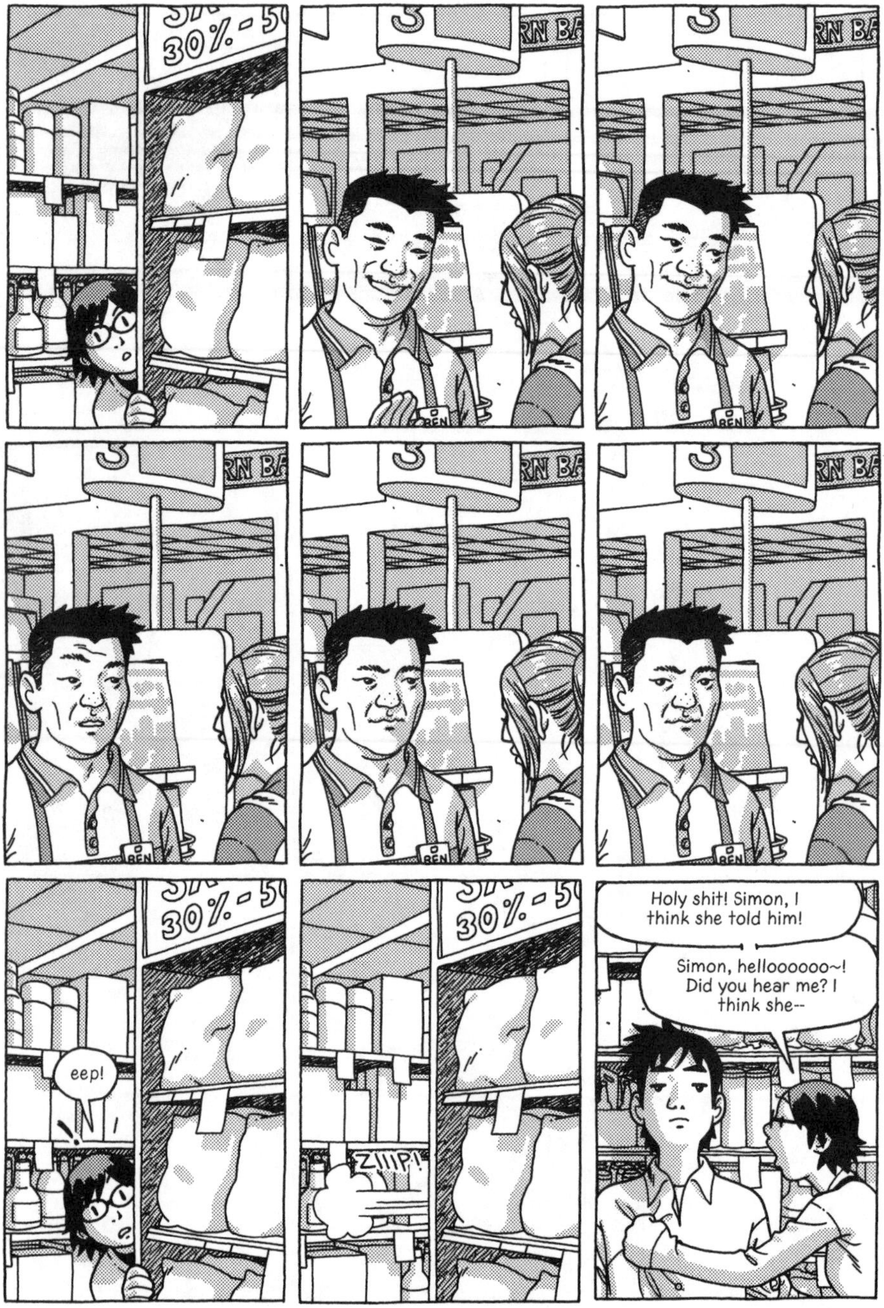
eep!
ZIIIP!
Holy shit! Simon, I think she told him!
Simon, hellooooo~! Did you hear me? I think she--

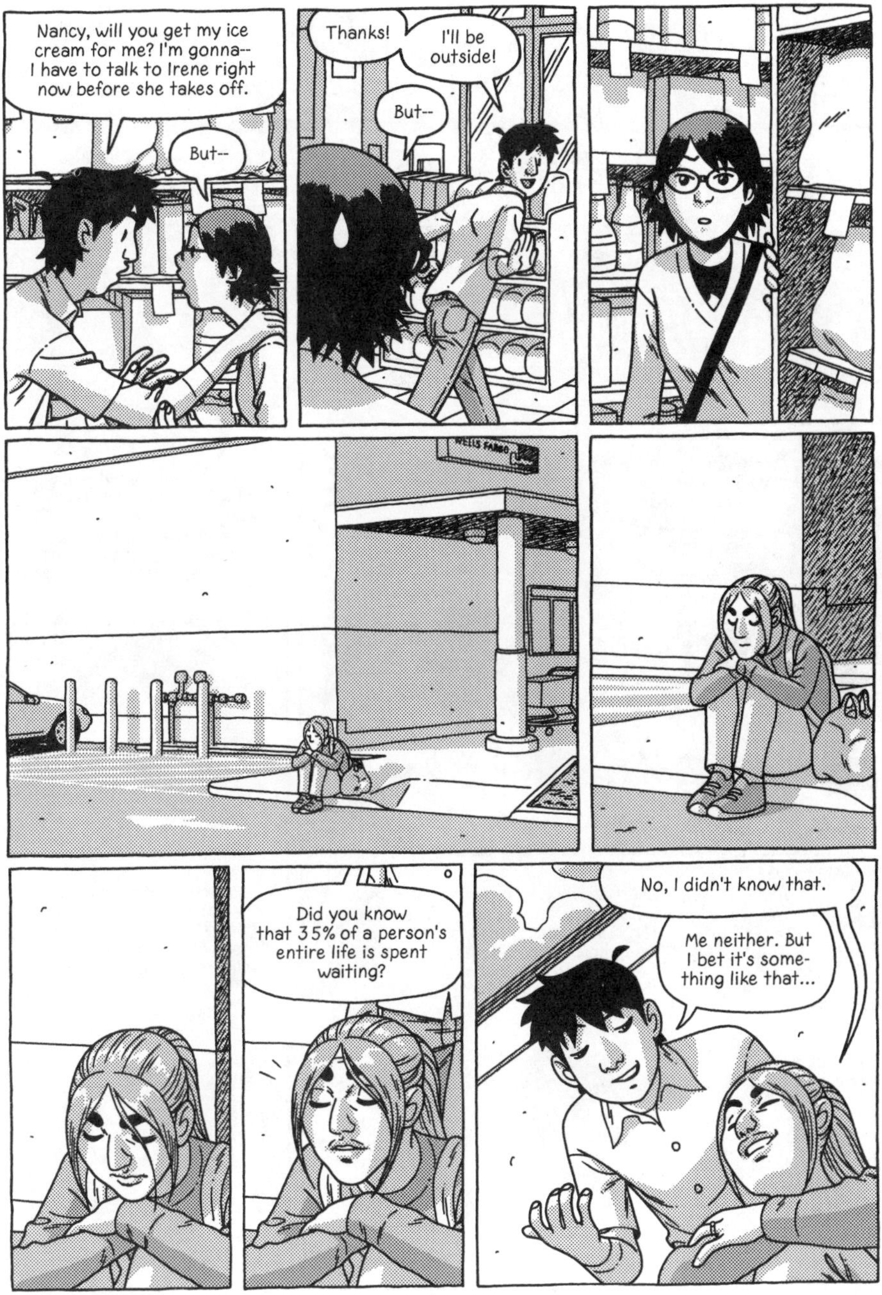
Nancy, will you get my ice cream for me? I'm gonna-- I have to talk to Irene right now before she takes off.
But--
Thanks!
I'll be outside!
But--
WELLS FARGO
Did you know that 35% of a person's entire life is spent waiting?
No, I didn't know that.
Me neither. But I bet it's something like that...

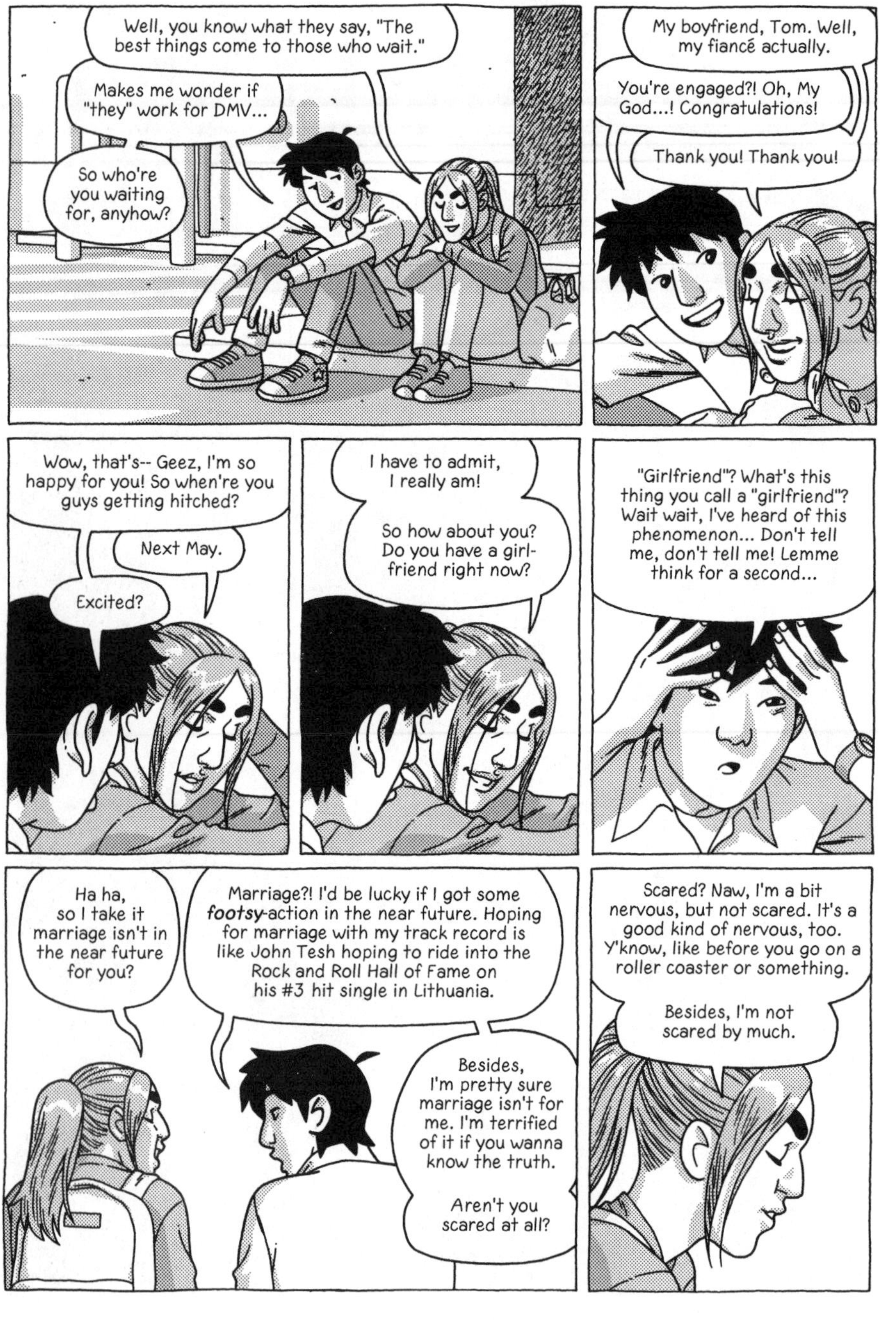
Well, you know what they say, "The best things come to those who wait."
Makes me wonder if "they" work for DMV...
So who're you waiting for, anyhow?
My boyfriend, Tom. Well, my fiancé actually.
You're engaged?! Oh, My God...! Congratulations!
Thank you! Thank you!
Wow, that's-- Geez, I'm so happy for you! So when're you guys getting hitched?
Next May.
Excited?
I have to admit, I really am!
So how about you? Do you have a girl-friend right now?
"Girlfriend"? What's this thing you call a "girlfriend"? Wait wait, I've heard of this phenomenon... Don't tell me, don't tell me! Lemme think for a second...
Ha ha, so I take it marriage isn't in the near future for you?
Marriage?! I'd be lucky if I got some *footsy*-action in the near future. Hoping for marriage with my track record is like John Tesh hoping to ride into the Rock and Roll Hall of Fame on his #3 hit single in Lithuania.
Besides, I'm pretty sure marriage isn't for me. I'm terrified of it if you wanna know the truth.
Aren't you scared at all?
Scared? Naw, I'm a bit nervous, but not scared. It's a good kind of nervous, too. Y'know, like before you go on a roller coaster or something.
Besides, I'm not scared by much.

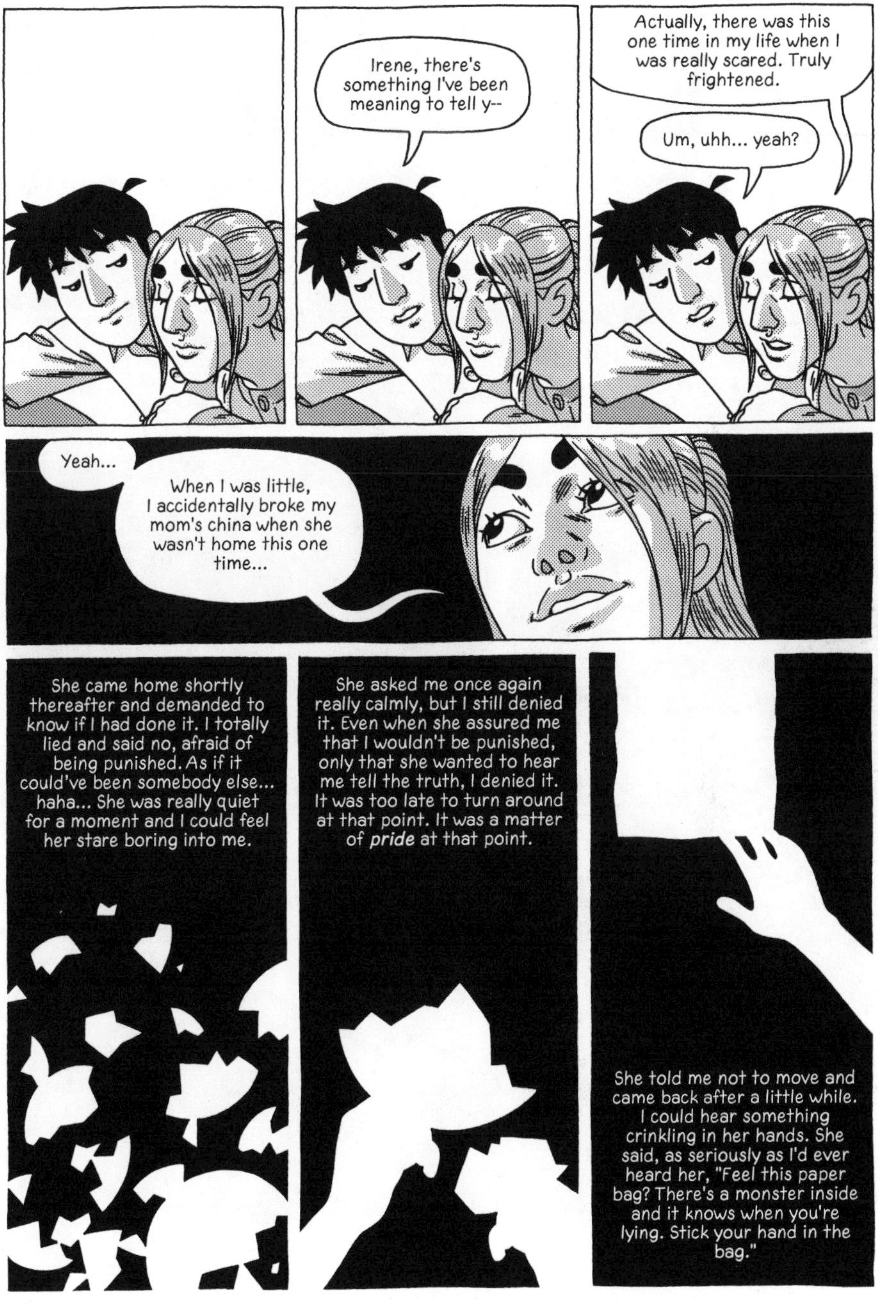
Irene, there's something I've been meaning to tell y--
Actually, there was this one time in my life when I was really scared. Truly frightened.
Um, uhh... yeah?
Yeah...
When I was little, I accidentally broke my mom's china when she wasn't home this one time...
She came home shortly thereafter and demanded to know if I had done it. I totally lied and said no, afraid of being punished. As if it could've been somebody else... haha... She was really quiet for a moment and I could feel her stare boring into me.
She asked me once again really calmly, but I still denied it. Even when she assured me that I wouldn't be punished, only that she wanted to hear me tell the truth, I denied it. It was too late to turn around at that point. It was a matter of *pride* at that point.
She told me not to move and came back after a little while. I could hear something crinkling in her hands. She said, as seriously as I'd ever heard her, "Feel this paper bag? There's a monster inside and it knows when you're lying. Stick your hand in the bag."

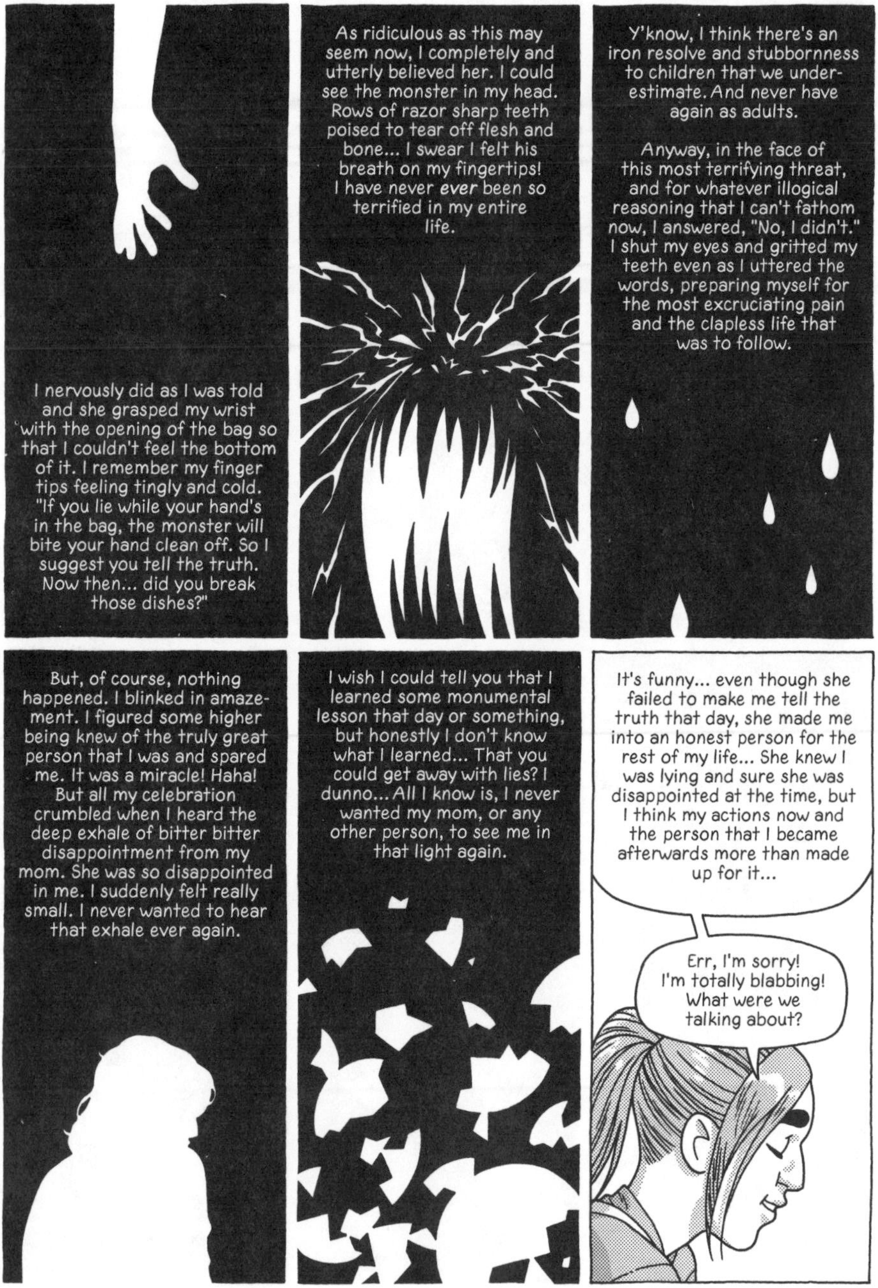

I nervously did as I was told and she grasped my wrist with the opening of the bag so that I couldn't feel the bottom of it. I remember my finger tips feeling tingly and cold. "If you lie while your hand's in the bag, the monster will bite your hand clean off. So I suggest you tell the truth. Now then... did you break those dishes?"
As ridiculous as this may seem now, I completely and utterly believed her. I could see the monster in my head. Rows of razor sharp teeth poised to tear off flesh and bone... I swear I felt his breath on my fingertips! I have never *ever* been so terrified in my entire life.
Y'know, I think there's an iron resolve and stubbornness to children that we underestimate. And never have again as adults.
Anyway, in the face of this most terrifying threat, and for whatever illogical reasoning that I can't fathom now, I answered, "No, I didn't." I shut my eyes and gritted my teeth even as I uttered the words, preparing myself for the most excruciating pain and the clapless life that was to follow.
But, of course, nothing happened. I blinked in amazement. I figured some higher being knew of the truly great person that I was and spared me. It was a miracle! Haha! But all my celebration crumbled when I heard the deep exhale of bitter bitter disappointment from my mom. She was so disappointed in me. I suddenly felt really small. I never wanted to hear that exhale ever again.
I wish I could tell you that I learned some monumental lesson that day or something, but honestly I don't know what I learned... That you could get away with lies? I dunno... All I know is, I never wanted my mom, or any other person, to see me in that light again.
It's funny... even though she failed to make me tell the truth that day, she made me into an honest person for the rest of my life... She knew I was lying and sure she was disappointed at the time, but I think my actions now and the person that I became afterwards more than made up for it...
Err, I'm sorry! I'm totally blabbing! What were we talking about?

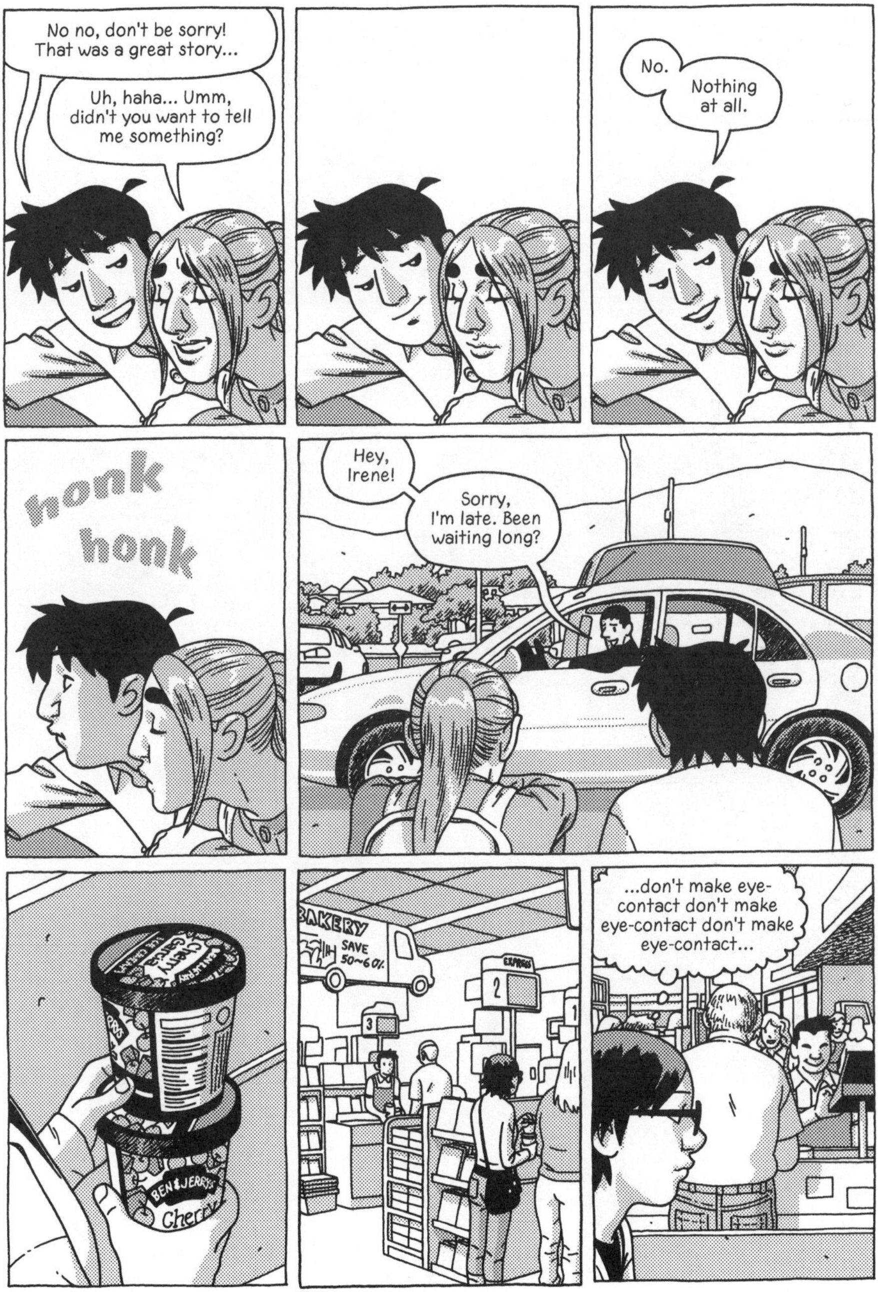
No no, don't be sorry! That was a great story...
Uh, haha... Umm, didn't you want to tell me something?
No.
Nothing at all.
honk
honk
Hey, Irene!
Sorry, I'm late. Been waiting long?
Cherry Garcia
BEN&JERRY'S
Cherry
BAKERY
SAVE
EXPRESS
...don't make eye-contact don't make eye-contact don't make eye-contact...

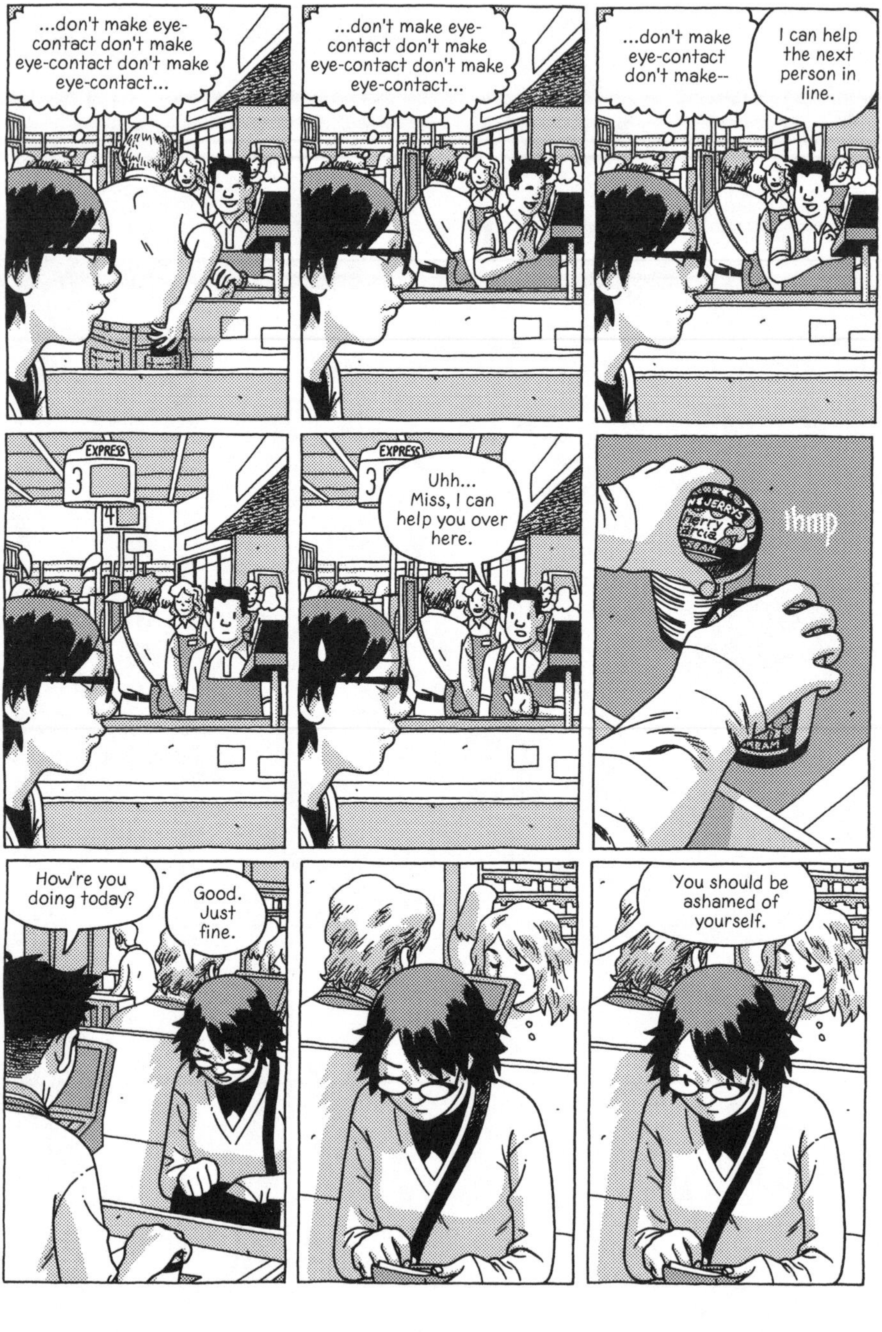
...don't make eye-contact don't make eye-contact don't make eye-contact...
...don't make eye-contact don't make eye-contact don't make eye-contact...
...don't make eye-contact don't make--
I can help the next person in line.
EXPRESS
3
4
EXPRESS
3
Uhh... Miss, I can help you over here.
thmp
How're you doing today?
Good. Just fine.
You should be ashamed of yourself.

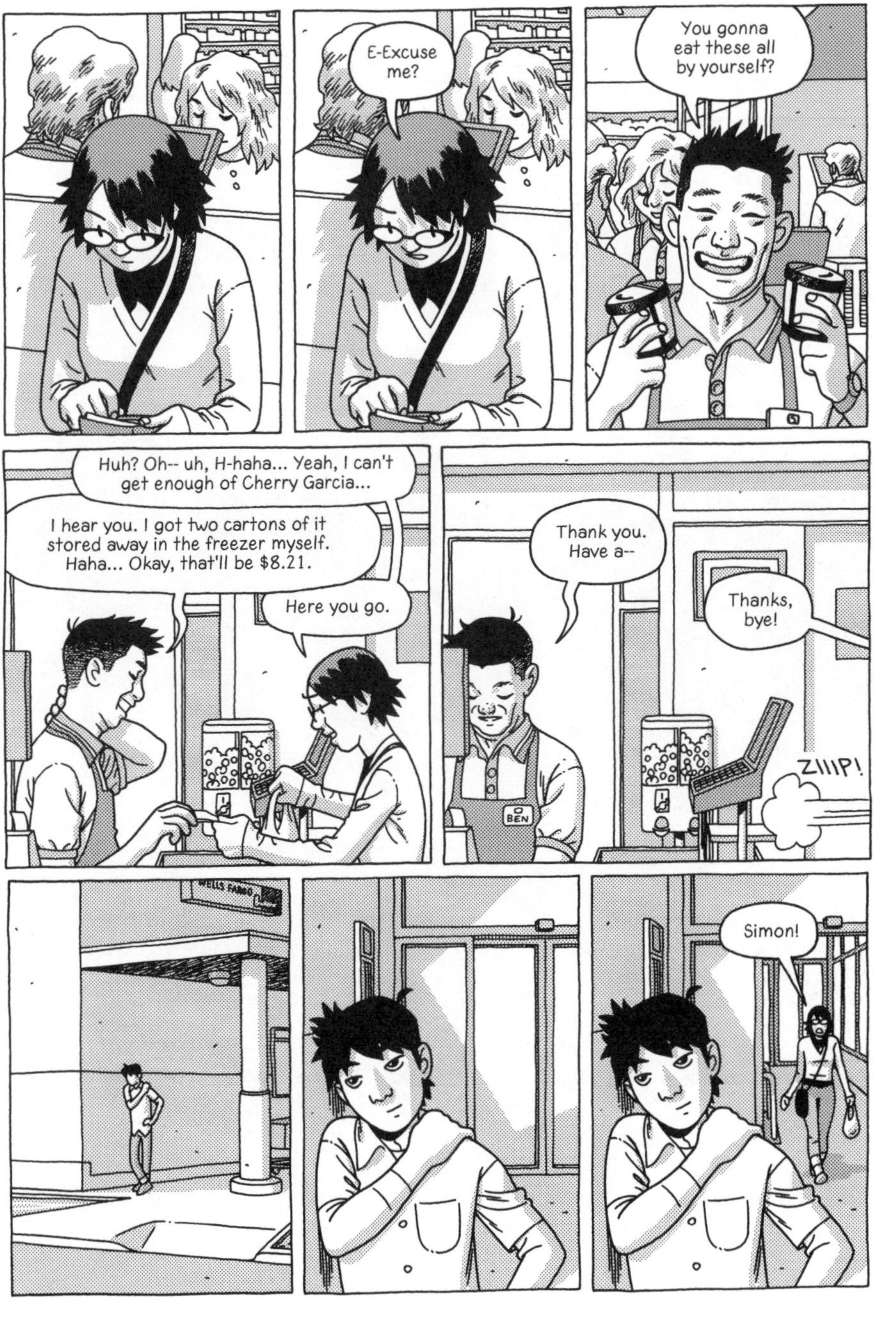
E-Excuse me?
You gonna eat these all by yourself?
Huh? Oh-- uh, H-haha... Yeah, I can't get enough of Cherry Garcia...
I hear you. I got two cartons of it stored away in the freezer myself. Haha... Okay, that'll be $8.21.
Here you go.
BEN
Thank you. Have a--
Thanks, bye!
ZIIIP!
WELLS FARGO
Simon!

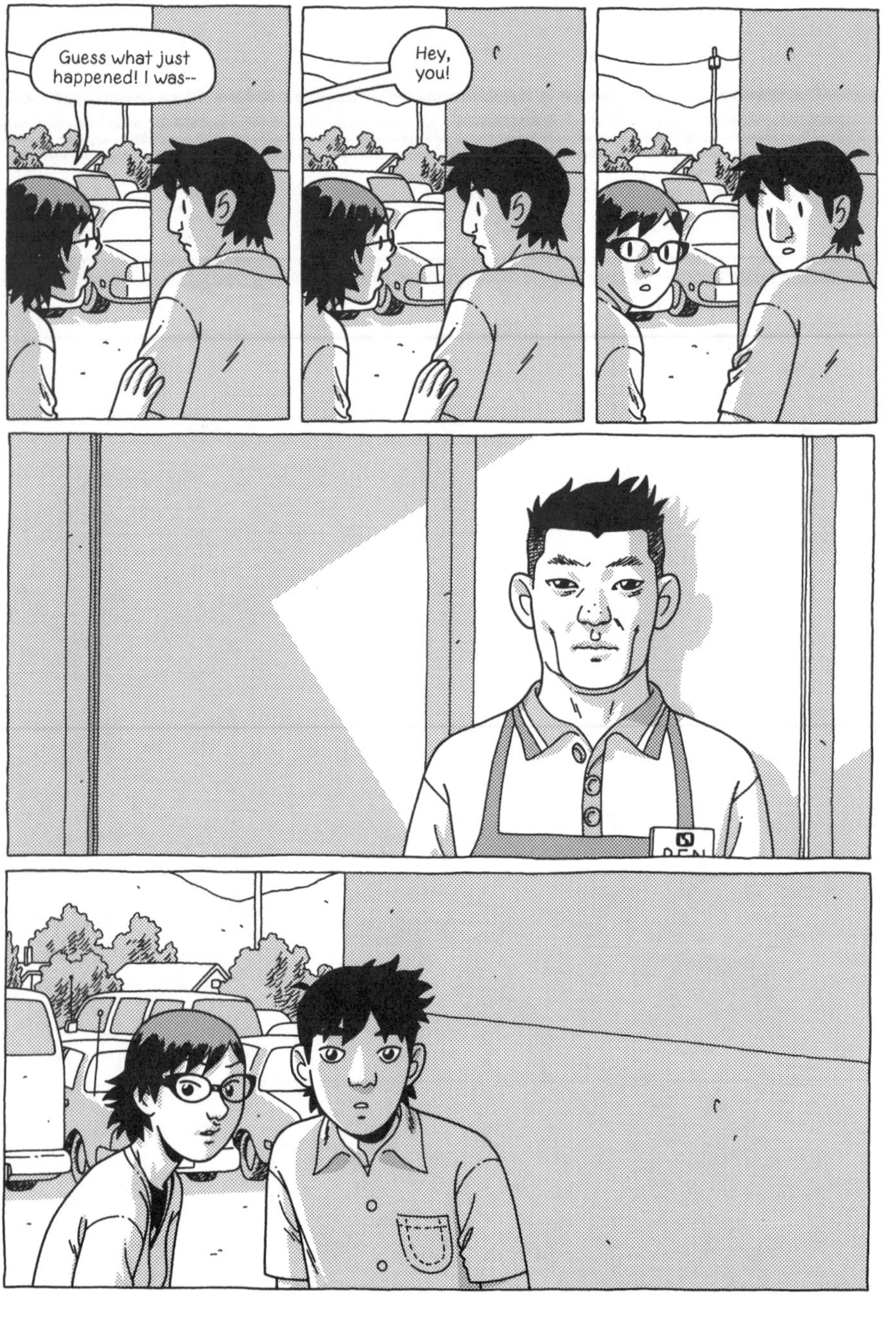
Guess what just happened! I was--
Hey, you!

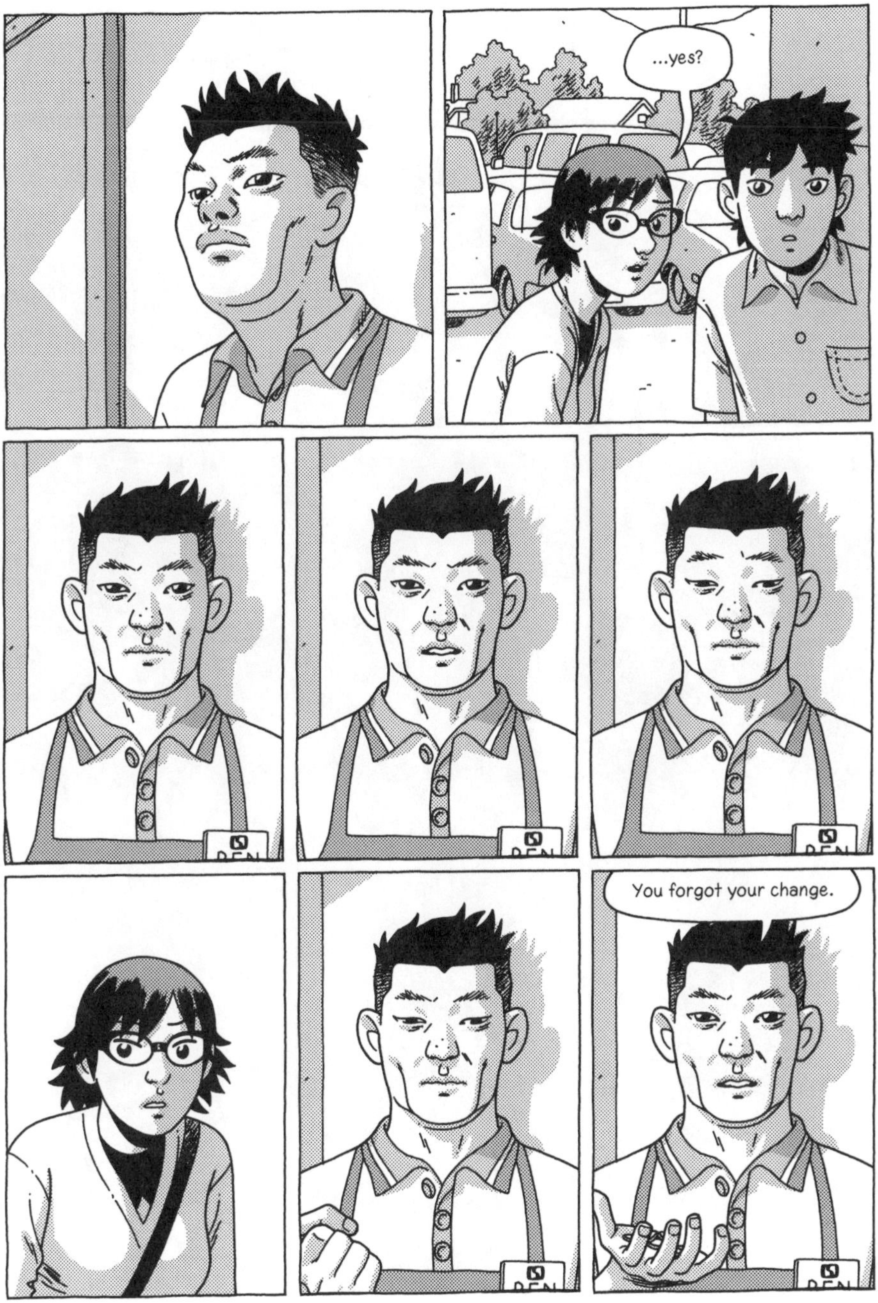
...yes?
You forgot your change.

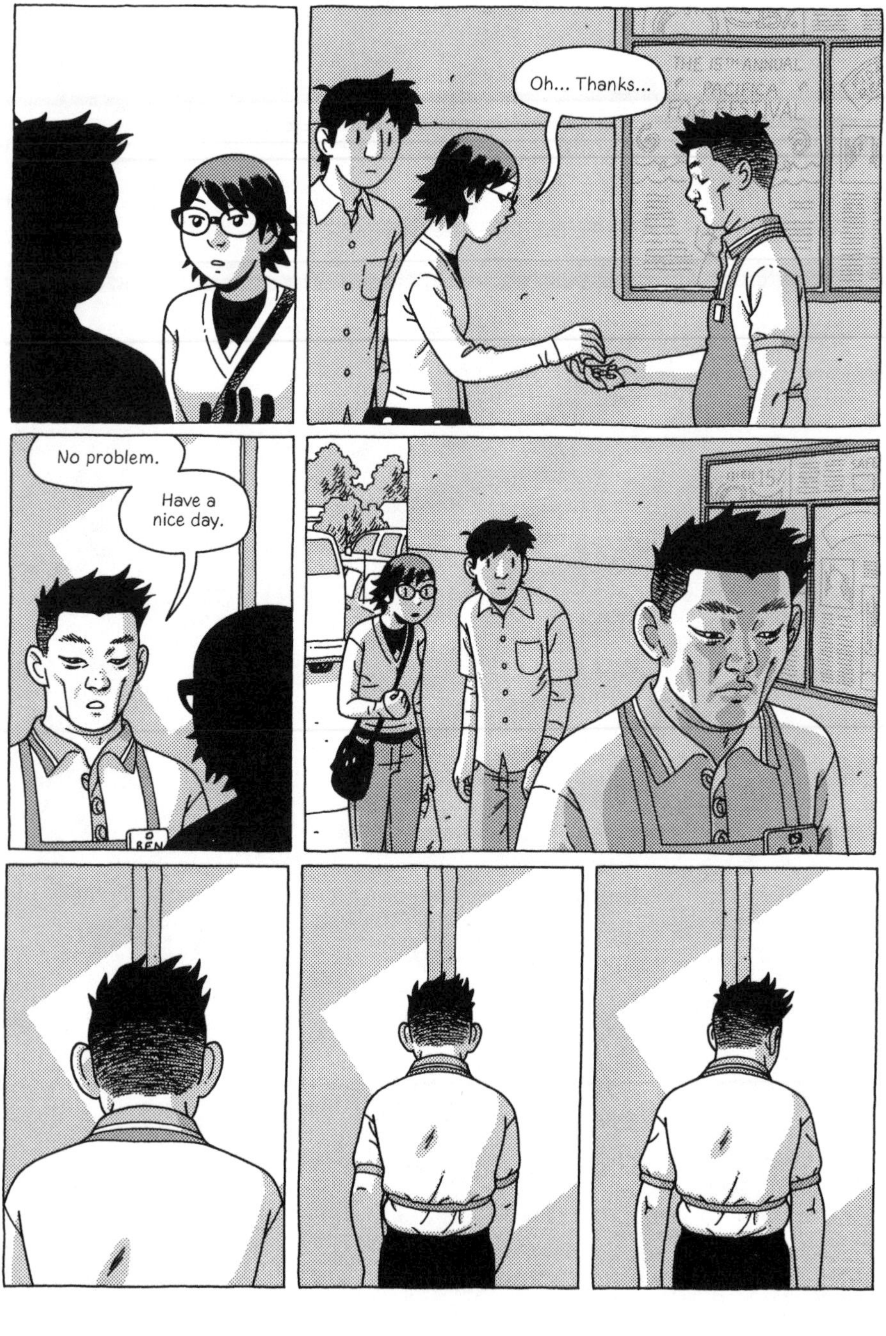

Oh... Thanks...
No problem.
Have a nice day.

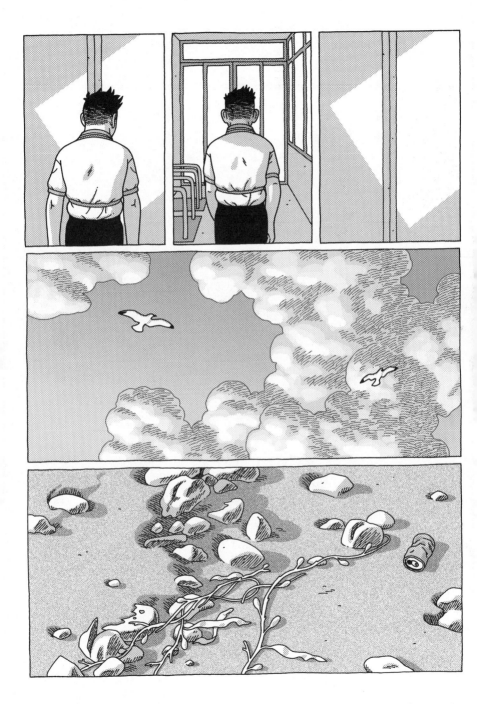

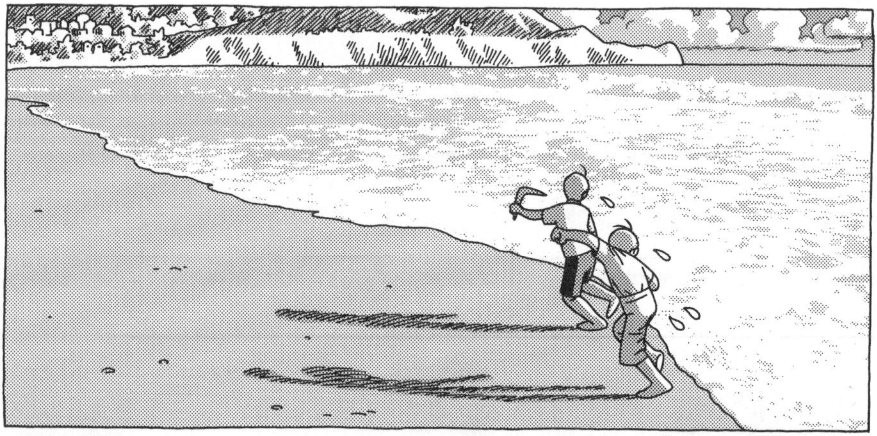

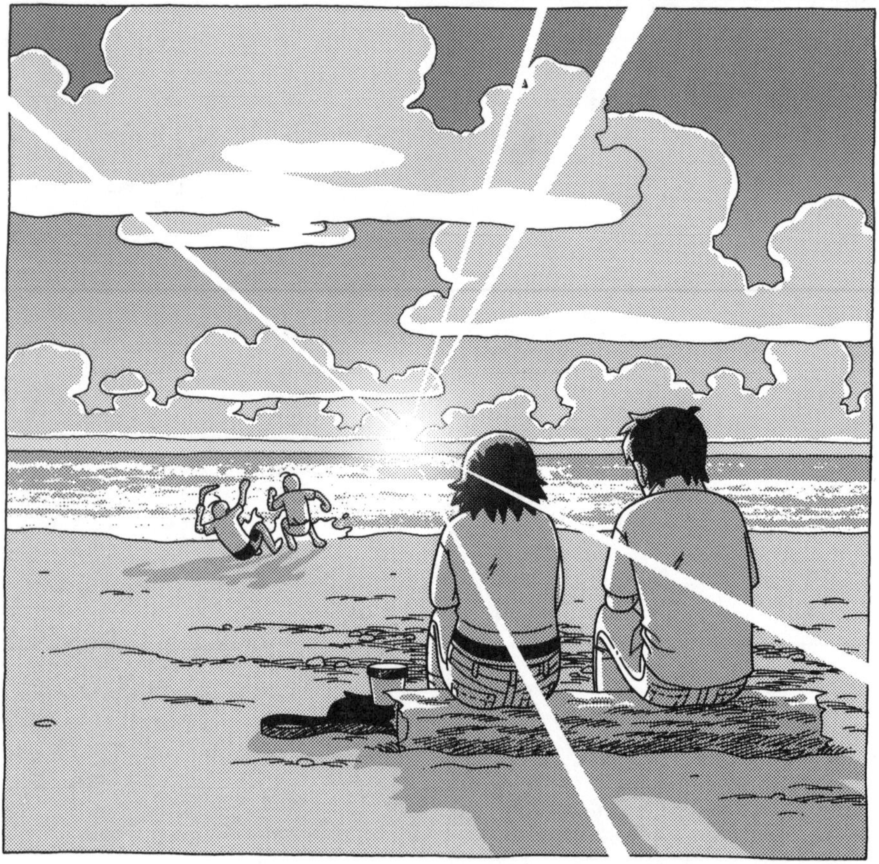

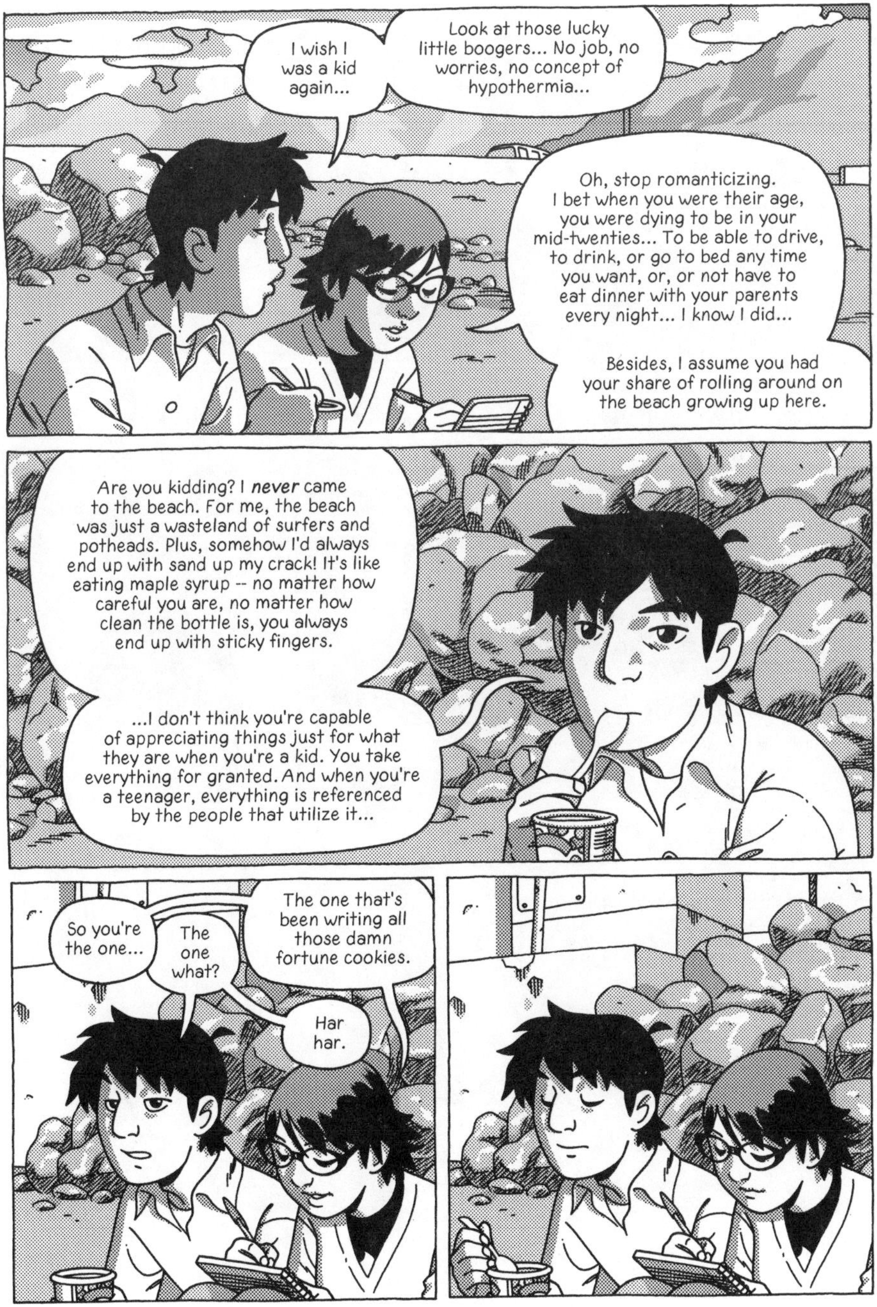
I wish I was a kid again...
Look at those lucky little boogers... No job, no worries, no concept of hypothermia...
Oh, stop romanticizing. I bet when you were their age, you were dying to be in your mid-twenties... To be able to drive, to drink, or go to bed any time you want, or, or not have to eat dinner with your parents every night... I know I did...
Besides, I assume you had your share of rolling around on the beach growing up here.
Are you kidding? I *never* came to the beach. For me, the beach was just a wasteland of surfers and potheads. Plus, somehow I'd always end up with sand up my crack! It's like eating maple syrup -- no matter how careful you are, no matter how clean the bottle is, you always end up with sticky fingers.
...I don't think you're capable of appreciating things just for what they are when you're a kid. You take everything for granted. And when you're a teenager, everything is referenced by the people that utilize it...
So you're the one...
The one what?
The one that's been writing all those damn fortune cookies.
Har har.

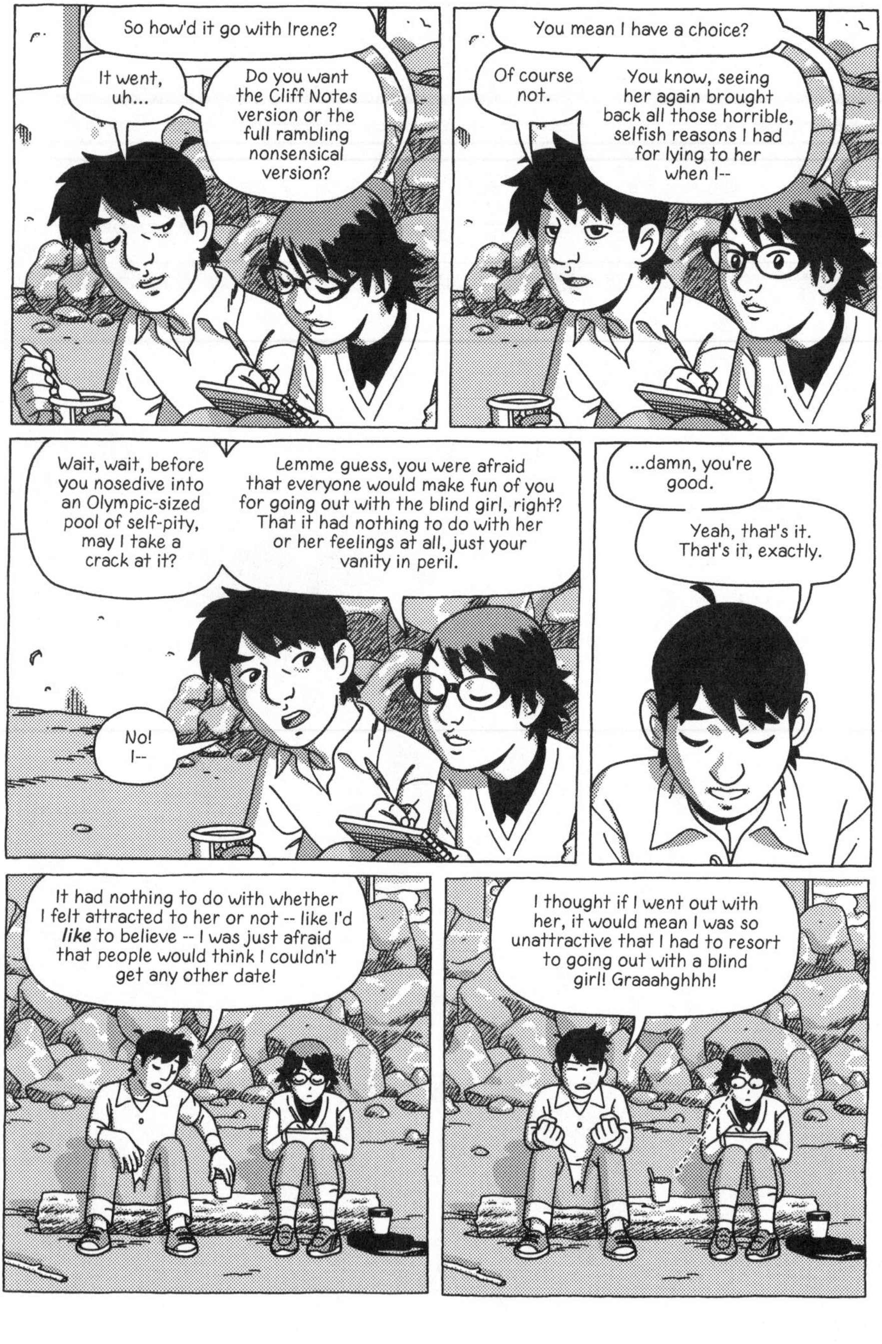
So how'd it go with Irene?
It went, uh...
Do you want the Cliff Notes version or the full rambling nonsensical version?
You mean I have a choice?
Of course not.
You know, seeing her again brought back all those horrible, selfish reasons I had for lying to her when I--
Wait, wait, before you nosedive into an Olympic-sized pool of self-pity, may I take a crack at it?
Lemme guess, you were afraid that everyone would make fun of you for going out with the blind girl, right? That it had nothing to do with her or her feelings at all, just your vanity in peril.
No! I--
...damn, you're good.
Yeah, that's it. That's it, exactly.
It had nothing to do with whether I felt attracted to her or not -- like I'd *like* to believe -- I was just afraid that people would think I couldn't get any other date!
I thought if I went out with her, it would mean I was so unattractive that I had to resort to going out with a blind girl! Graaahghhh!

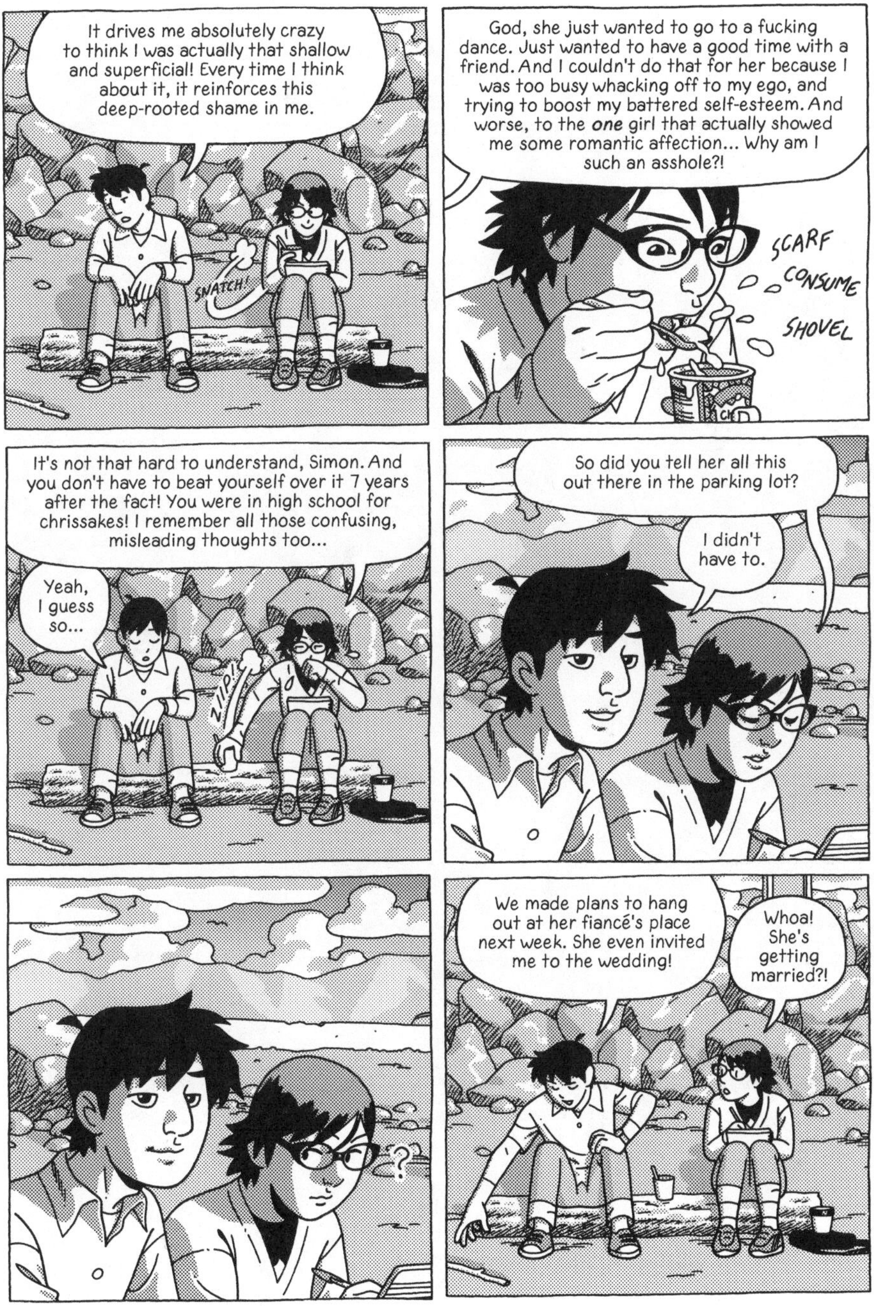

It drives me absolutely crazy to think I was actually that shallow and superficial! Every time I think about it, it reinforces this deep-rooted shame in me.
SNATCH!
God, she just wanted to go to a fucking dance. Just wanted to have a good time with a friend. And I couldn't do that for her because I was too busy whacking off to my ego, and trying to boost my battered self-esteem. And worse, to the *one* girl that actually showed me some romantic affection... Why am I such an asshole?!
SCARF
CONSUME
SHOVEL
It's not that hard to understand, Simon. And you don't have to beat yourself over it 7 years after the fact! You were in high school for chrissakes! I remember all those confusing, misleading thoughts too...
Yeah, I guess so...
ZIIP!
So did you tell her all this out there in the parking lot?
I didn't have to.
We made plans to hang out at her fiancé's place next week. She even invited me to the wedding!
Whoa! She's getting married?!

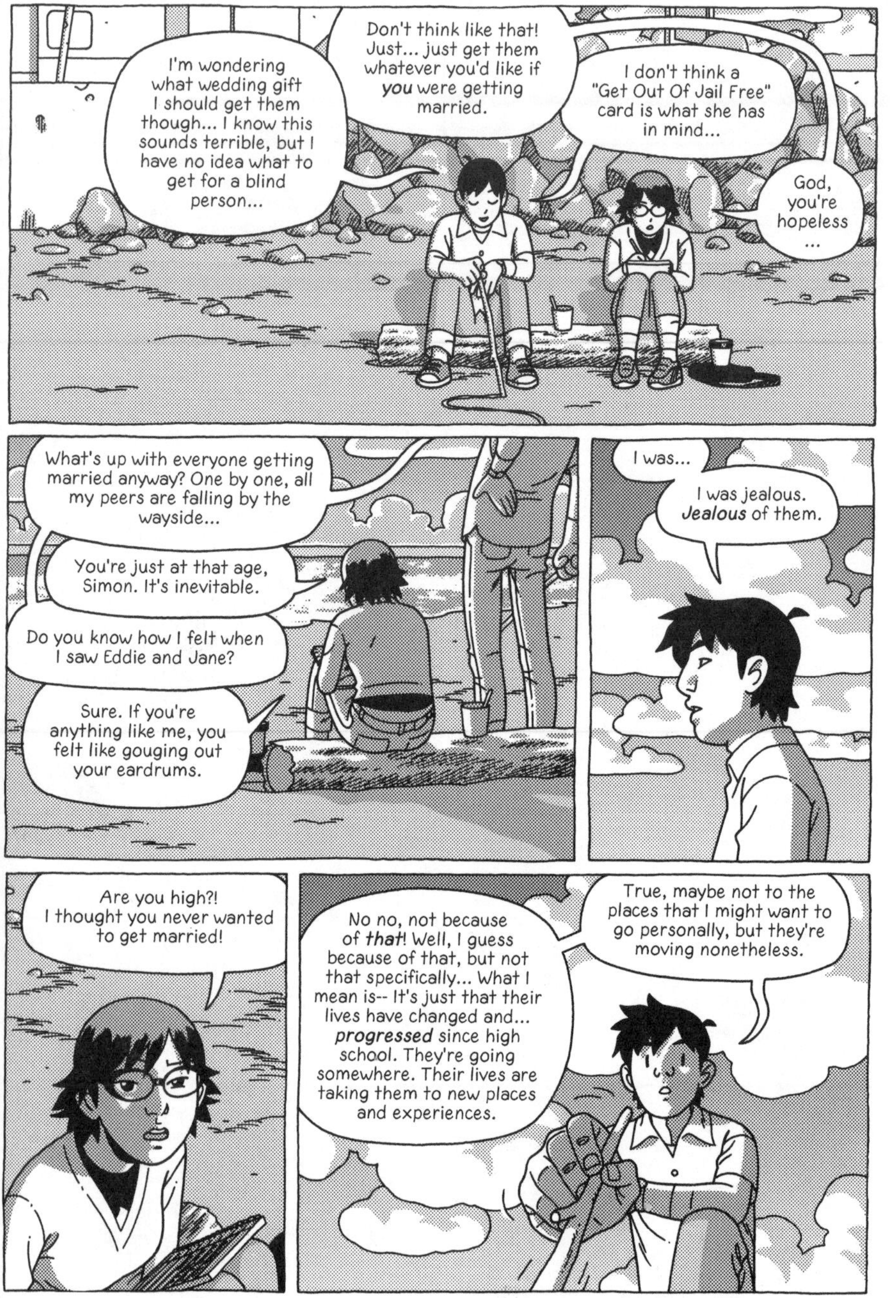
I'm wondering what wedding gift I should get them though... I know this sounds terrible, but I have no idea what to get for a blind person...
Don't think like that! Just... just get them whatever you'd like if *you* were getting married.
I don't think a "Get Out Of Jail Free" card is what she has in mind...
God, you're hopeless ...
What's up with everyone getting married anyway? One by one, all my peers are falling by the wayside...
You're just at that age, Simon. It's inevitable.
Do you know how I felt when I saw Eddie and Jane?
Sure. If you're anything like me, you felt like gouging out your eardrums.
I was...
I was jealous. *Jealous* of them.
Are you high?! I thought you never wanted to get married!
No no, not because of *that*! Well, I guess because of that, but not that specifically... What I mean is-- It's just that their lives have changed and... *progressed* since high school. They're going somewhere. Their lives are taking them to new places and experiences.
True, maybe not to the places that I might want to go personally, but they're moving nonetheless.

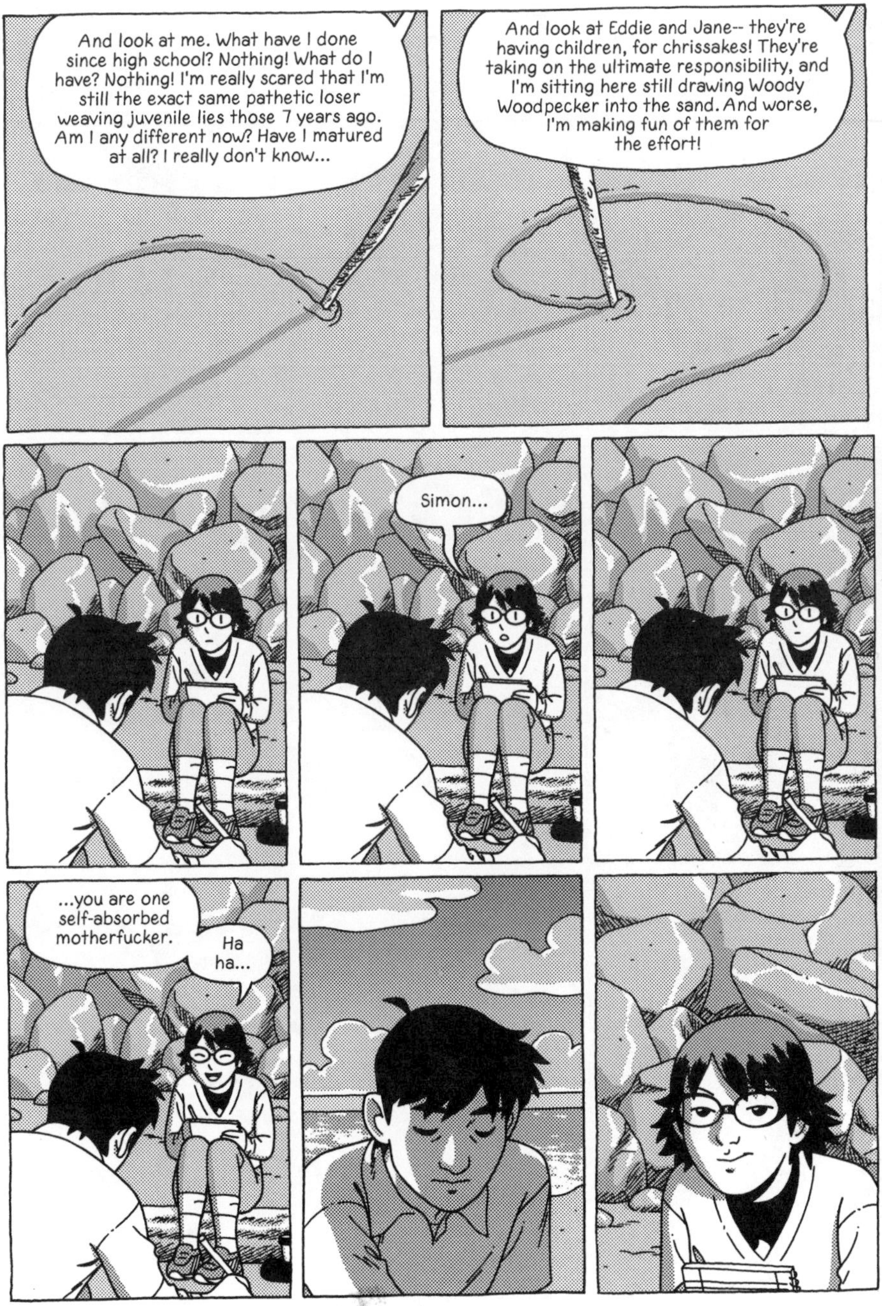

And look at me. What have I done since high school? Nothing! What do I have? Nothing! I'm really scared that I'm still the exact same pathetic loser weaving juvenile lies those 7 years ago. Am I any different now? Have I matured at all? I really don't know...
And look at Eddie and Jane-- they're having children, for chrissakes! They're taking on the ultimate responsibility, and I'm sitting here still drawing Woody Woodpecker into the sand. And worse, I'm making fun of them for the effort!
Simon...
...you are one self-absorbed motherfucker.
Ha ha...

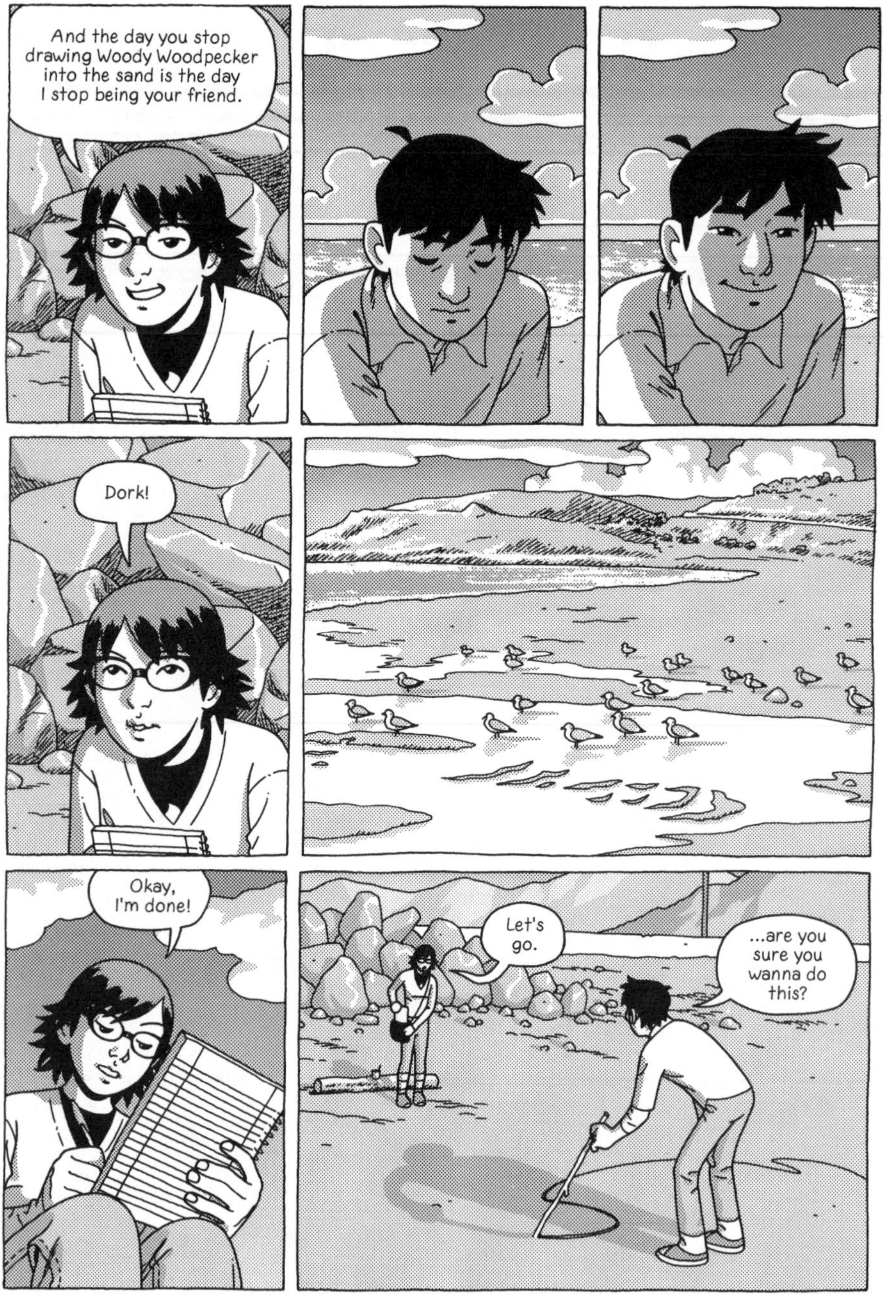
And the day you stop drawing Woody Woodpecker into the sand is the day I stop being your friend.
Dork!
Okay, I'm done!
Let's go.
...are you sure you wanna do this?

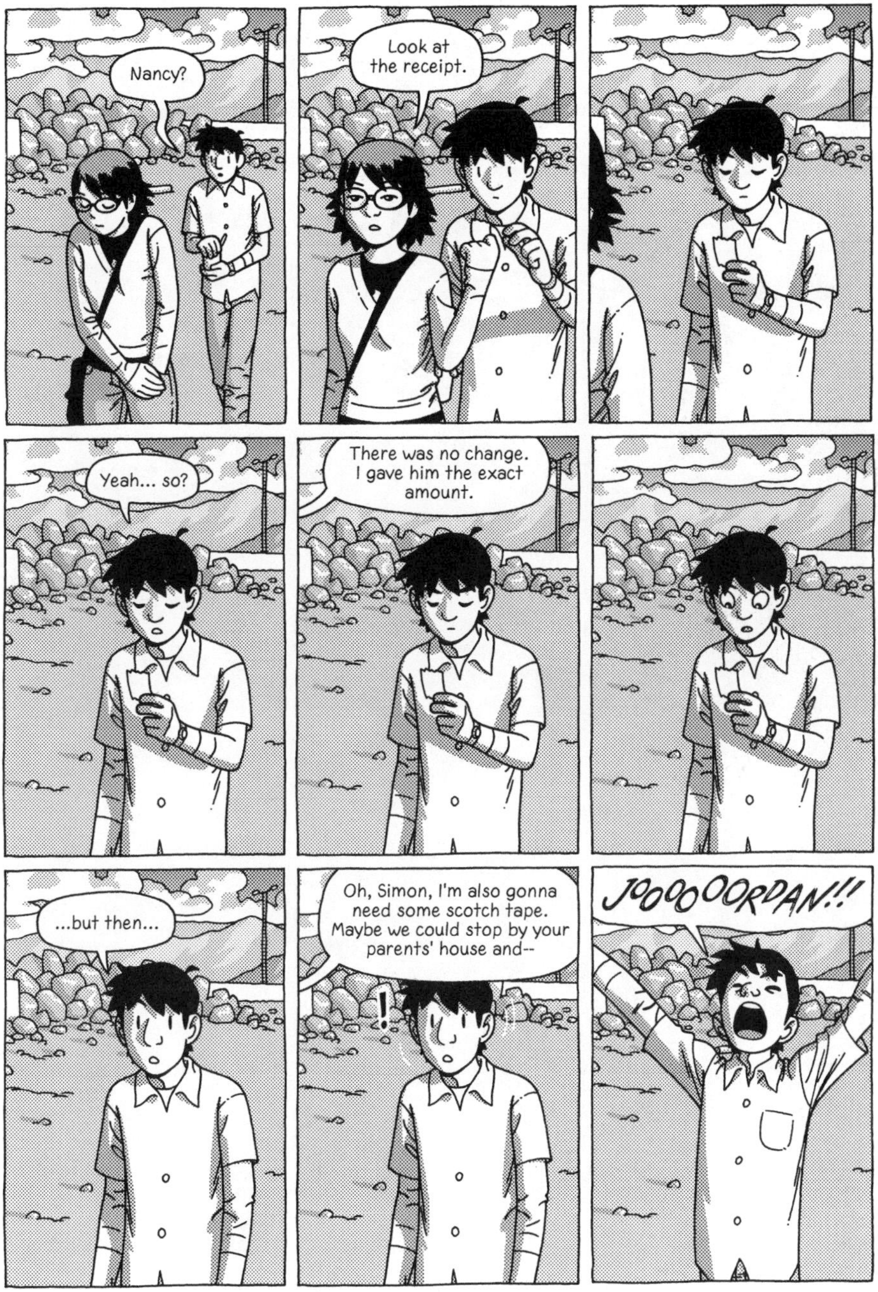
Nancy?
Look at the receipt.
Yeah... so?
There was no change. I gave him the exact amount.
...but then...
Oh, Simon, I'm also gonna need some scotch tape. Maybe we could stop by your parents' house and--
!
JOOOOORDAN!!!

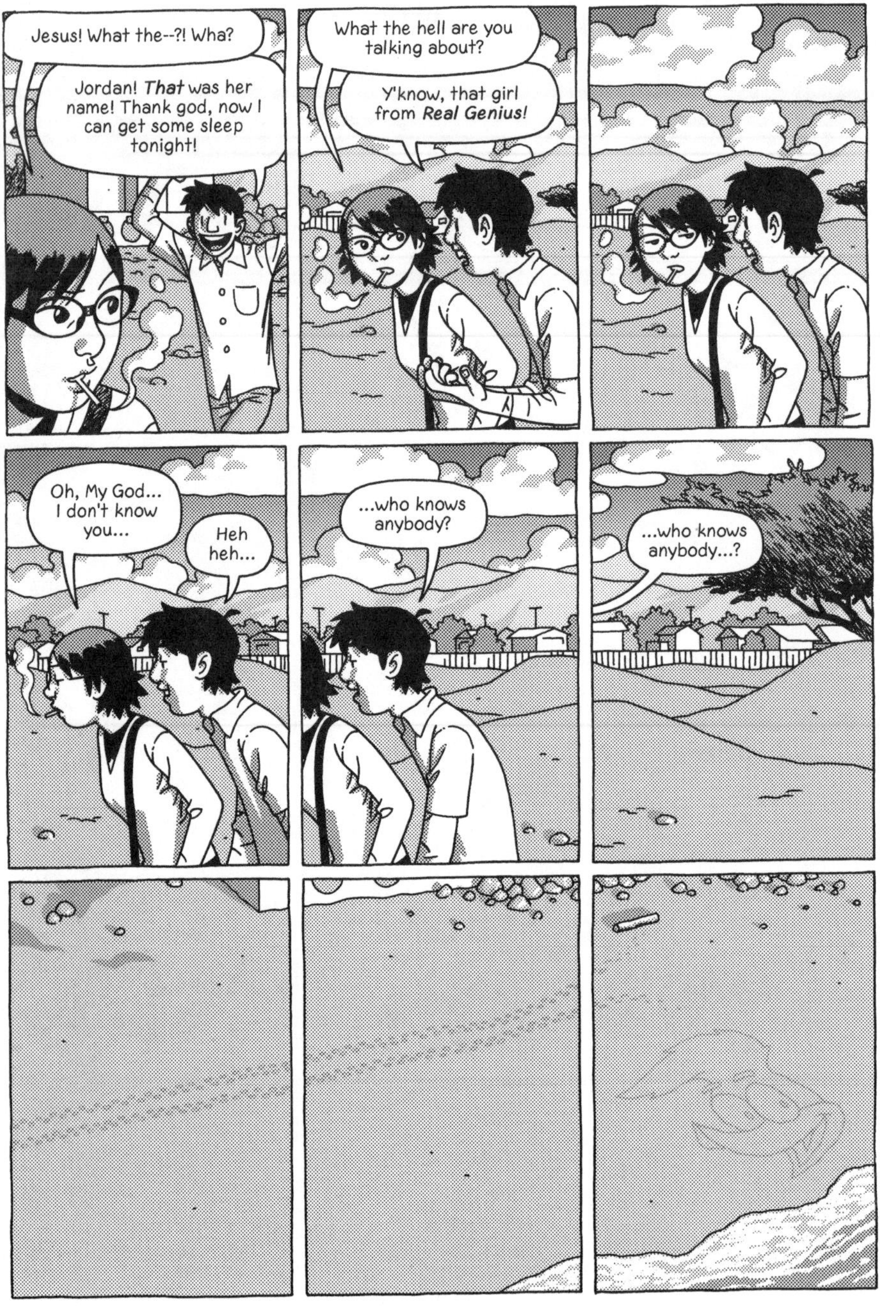
Jesus! What the--?! Wha?
Jordan! *That* was her name! Thank god, now I can get some sleep tonight!
What the hell are you talking about?
Y'know, that girl from ***Real Genius!***
Oh, My God... I don't know you...
Heh heh...
...who knows anybody?
...who knows anybody...?

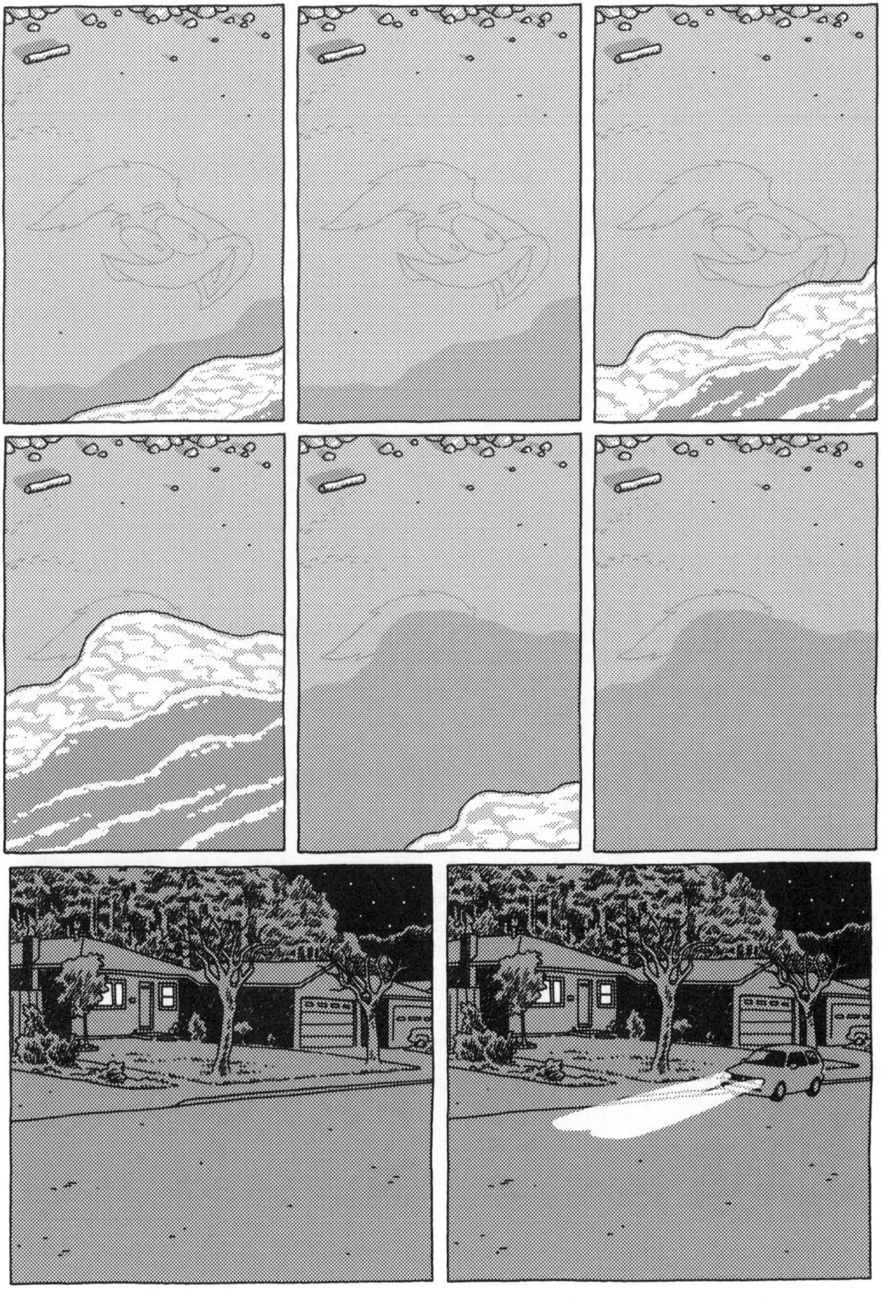

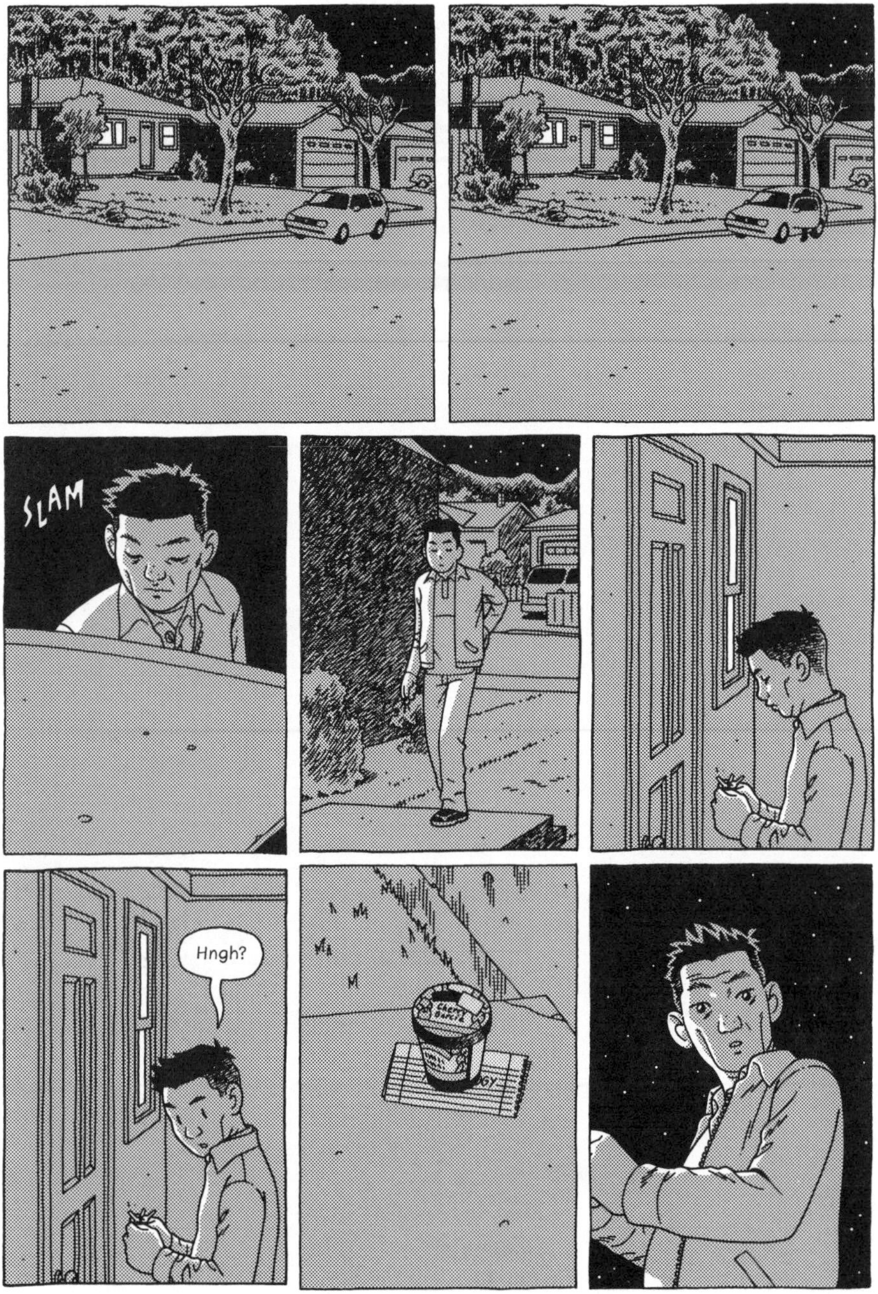
SLAM
Hngh?
Cherry Garcia

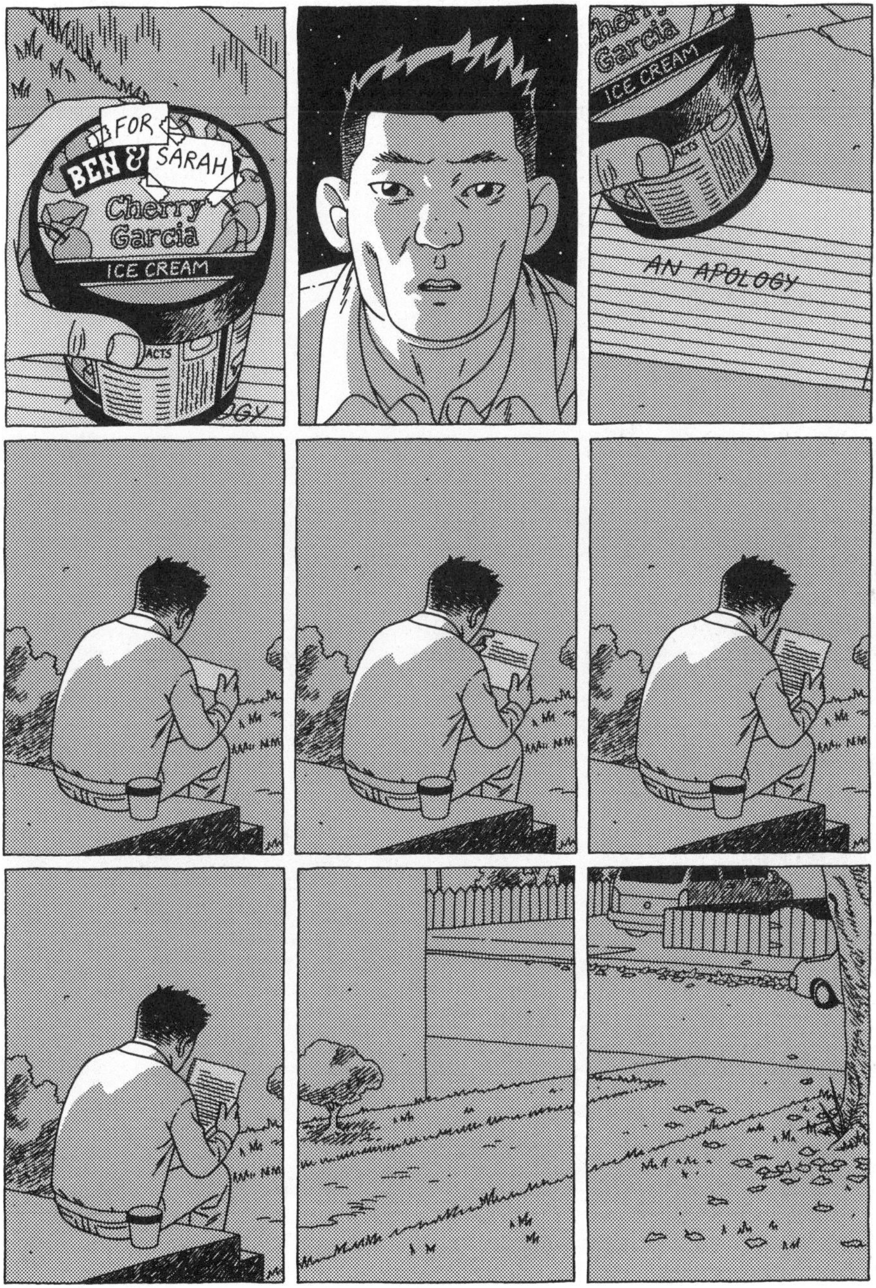
FOR
BEN &
SARAH
Cherry Garcia
ICE CREAM
AN APOLOGY

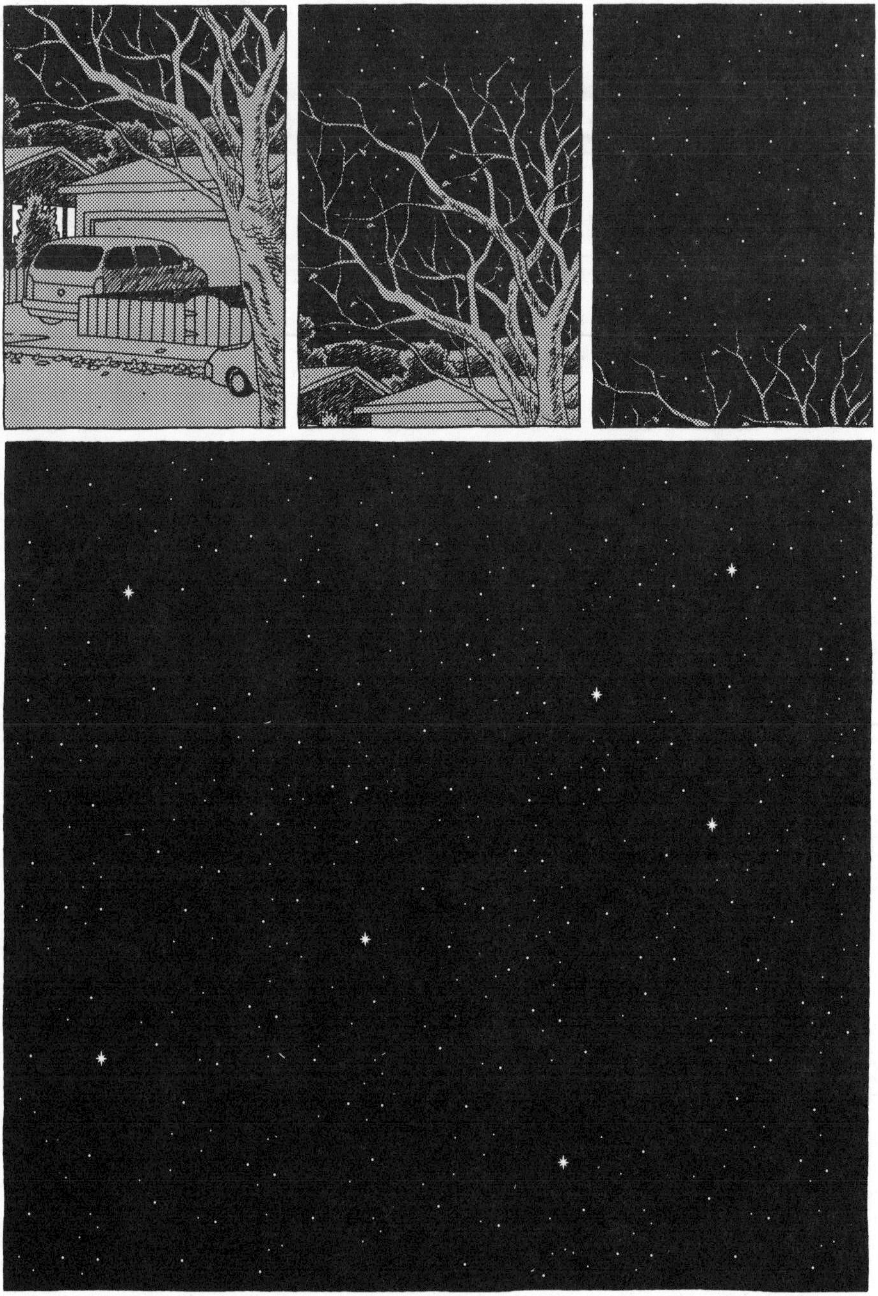

Short
Stories

HURDLES

I jump hurdles every day. While everyone else on the track team runs straight through, my fellow hurdlers and I go up and down, up and down. Some hurdlers jump over the hurdles, and others kick them down. I jump over them.

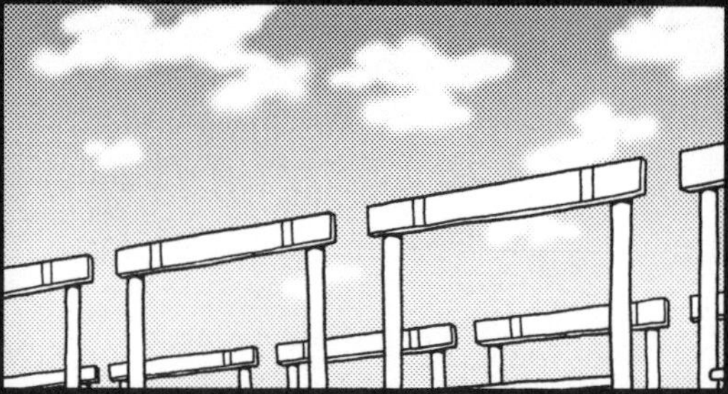

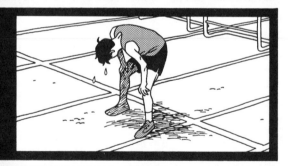

Sometimes I'd like to just kick them out of my way, but I guess I'm just too polite. But who cares, I can cross the finish line and that's all that matters. Besides, my coach says either way is just fine.

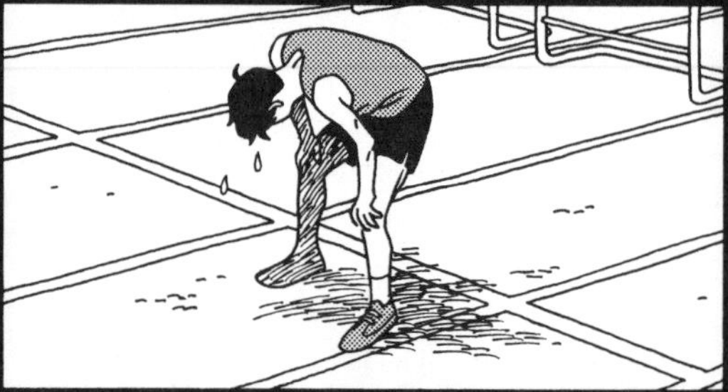

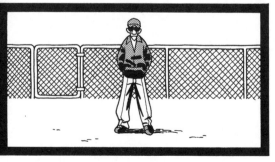

We call our coach "Pear-Nose". There's always a pair of black sunglasses atop that nose of his. And he always stands with his hands behind his back. Now that I think about it, I've never seen his hands. Maybe he doesn't have any hands, I don't know.

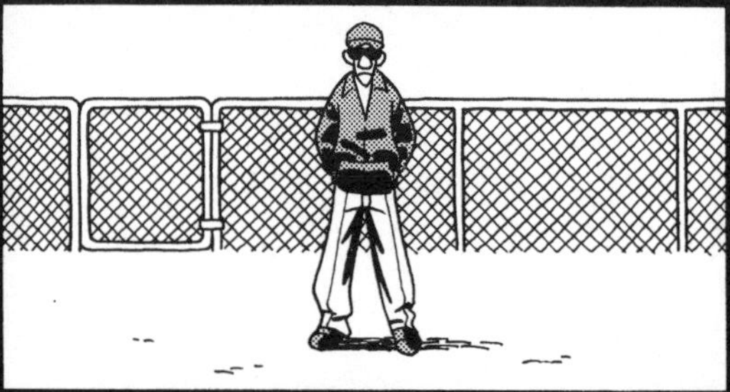

He drove us especially hard this one particular practice before a track meet with a rival high school. We circled the track, around and around, endlessly. Anyone who stepped off that beaten track was punished with more laps.

Finally, I couldn't go on anymore without water, so I parted from my lane and ran to the drinking fountain.

When I turned around, Pear-Nose was staring down at me.

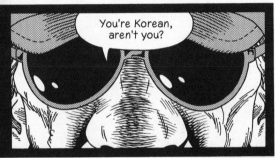

You're Korean, aren't you?

Yes.

How did you know?

Because the Chinese are smart.

Then he told me to run back onto the track. I started to run. I ran through the grass, past the baseball field, out of the main gate, and straight to my house.

I jump hurdles every day.

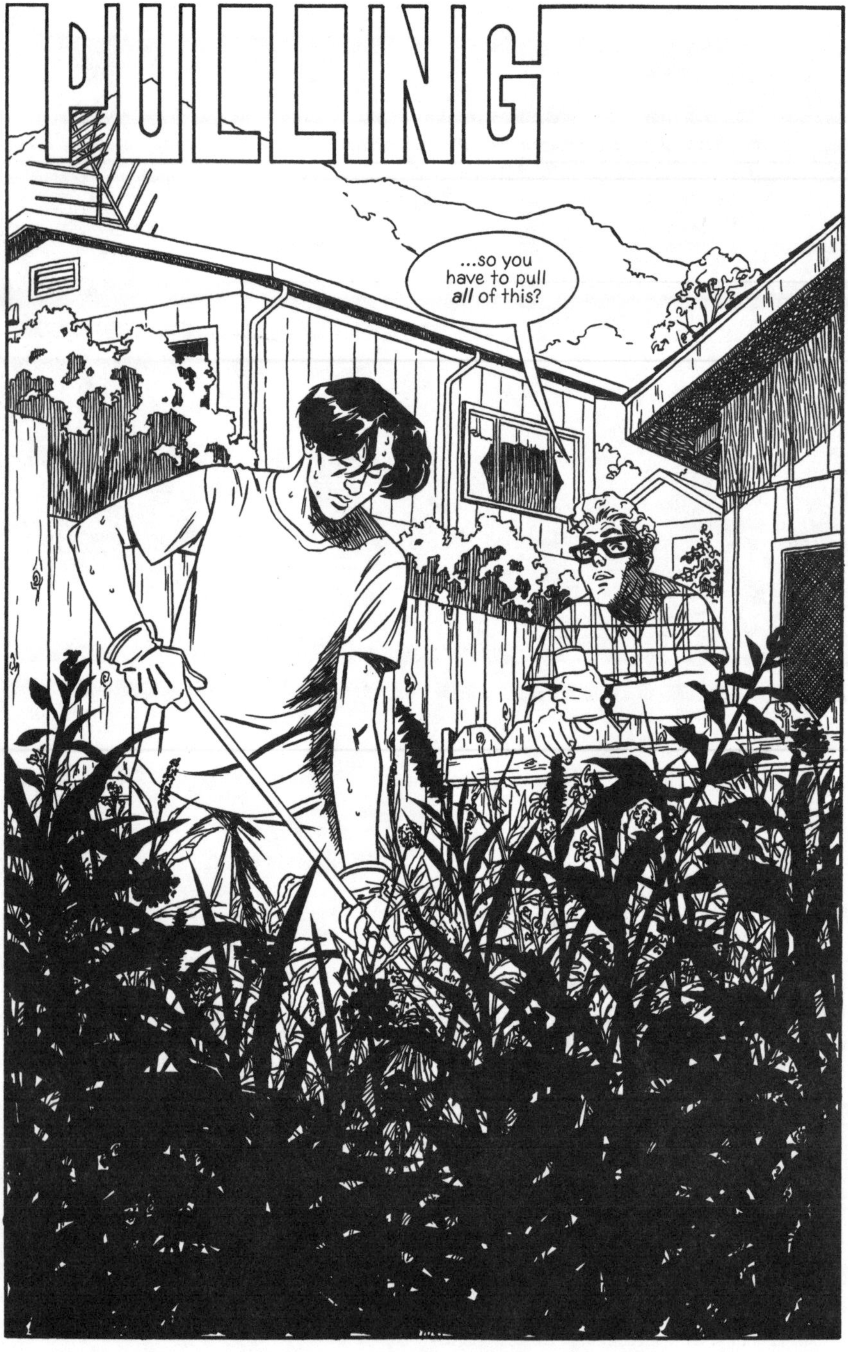
PULLING
...so you have to pull *all* of this?

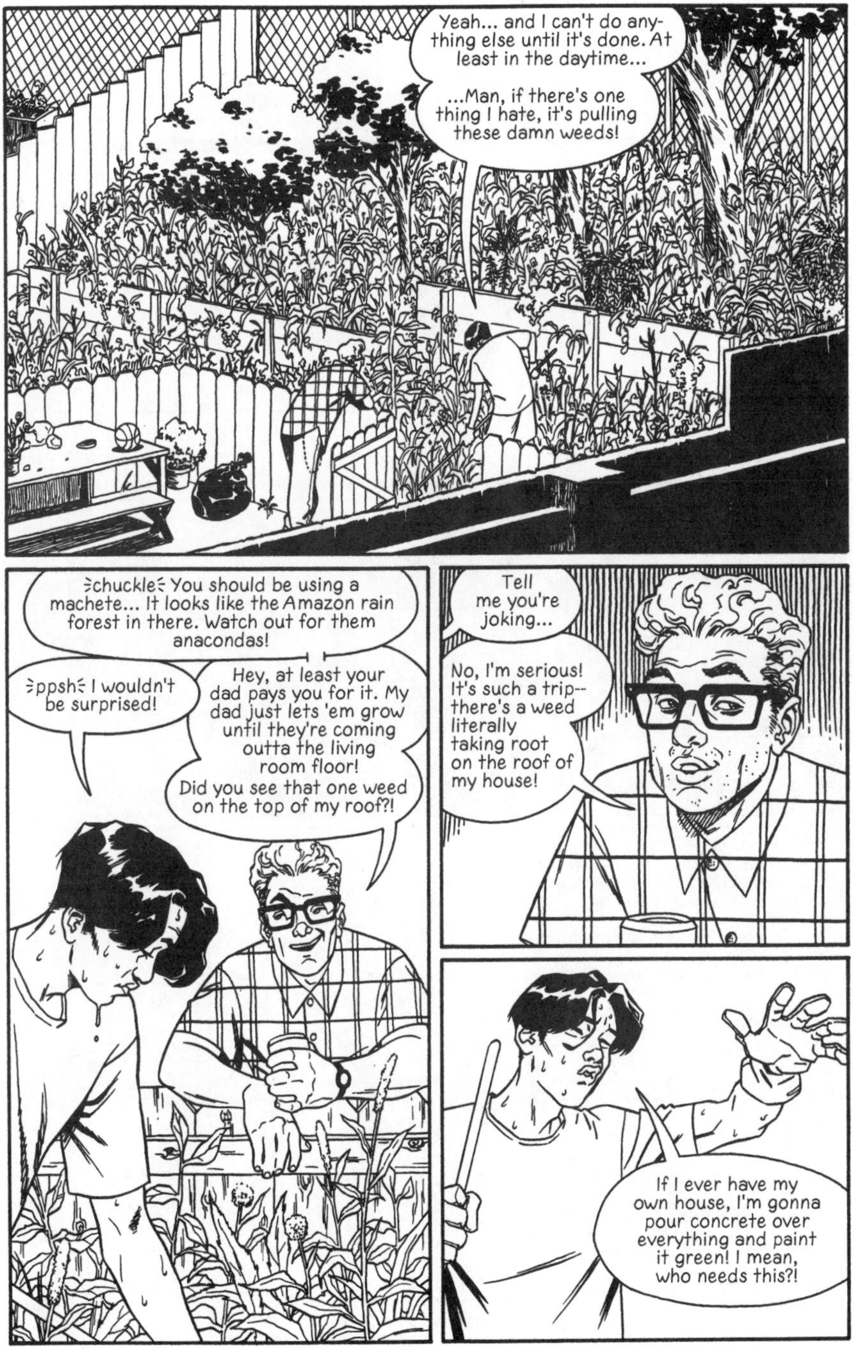
Yeah... and I can't do anything else until it's done. At least in the daytime...
...Man, if there's one thing I hate, it's pulling these damn weeds!
≡chuckle≡ You should be using a machete... It looks like the Amazon rain forest in there. Watch out for them anacondas!
≡ppsh≡ I wouldn't be surprised!
Hey, at least your dad pays you for it. My dad just lets 'em grow until they're coming outta the living room floor!
Did you see that one weed on the top of my roof?!
Tell me you're joking...
No, I'm serious! It's such a trip-- there's a weed literally taking root on the roof of my house!
If I ever have my own house, I'm gonna pour concrete over everything and paint it green! I mean, who needs this?!

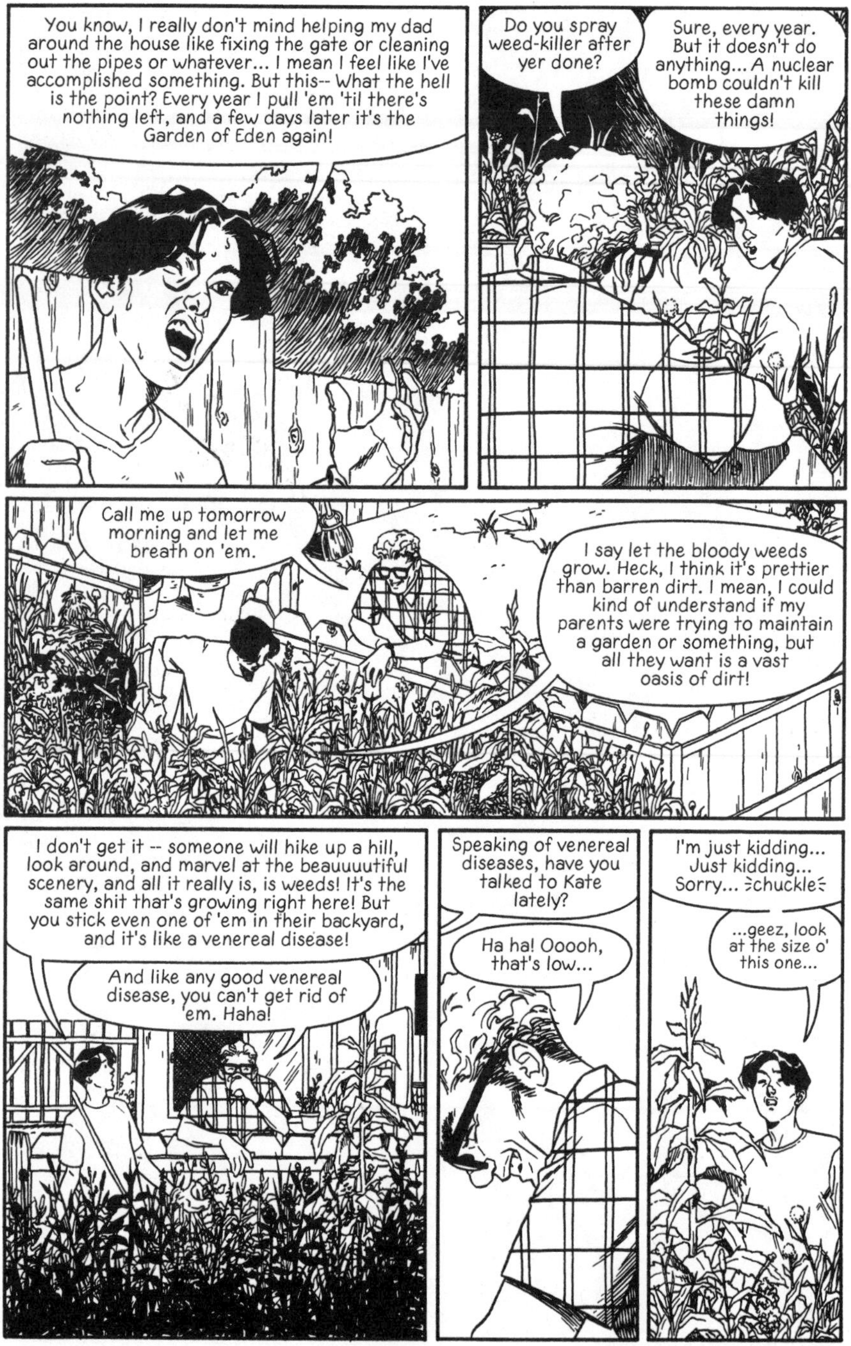
You know, I really don't mind helping my dad around the house like fixing the gate or cleaning out the pipes or whatever... I mean I feel like I've accomplished something. But this-- What the hell is the point? Every year I pull 'em 'til there's nothing left, and a few days later it's the Garden of Eden again!
Do you spray weed-killer after yer done?
Sure, every year. But it doesn't do anything... A nuclear bomb couldn't kill these damn things!
Call me up tomorrow morning and let me breath on 'em.
I say let the bloody weeds grow. Heck, I think it's prettier than barren dirt. I mean, I could kind of understand if my parents were trying to maintain a garden or something, but all they want is a vast oasis of dirt!
I don't get it -- someone will hike up a hill, look around, and marvel at the beauuuutiful scenery, and all it really is, is weeds! It's the same shit that's growing right here! But you stick even one of 'em in their backyard, and it's like a venereal disease!
And like any good venereal disease, you can't get rid of 'em. Haha!
Speaking of venereal diseases, have you talked to Kate lately?
Ha ha! Ooooh, that's low...
I'm just kidding... Just kidding... Sorry... ≷chuckle≶
...geez, look at the size o' this one...

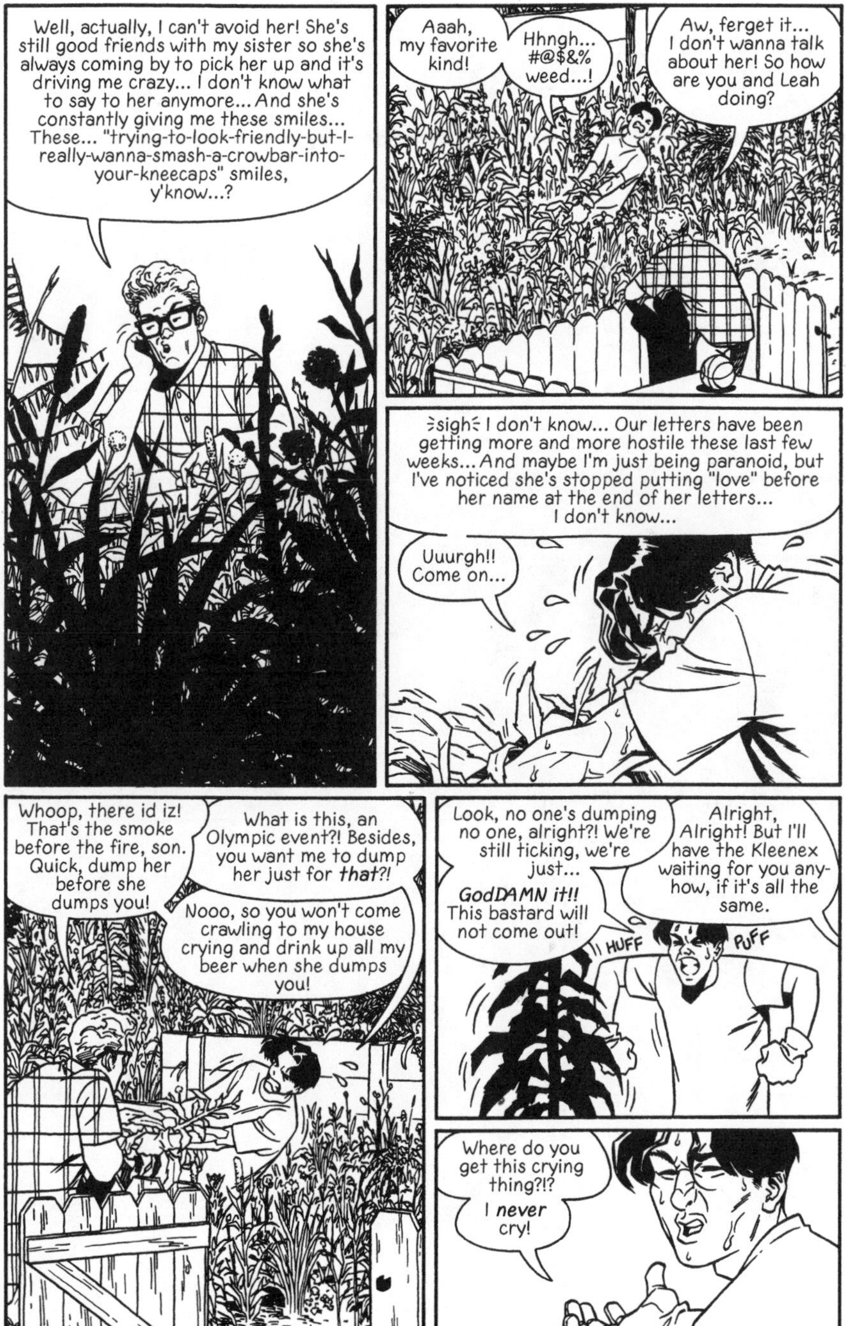
Well, actually, I can't avoid her! She's still good friends with my sister so she's always coming by to pick her up and it's driving me crazy... I don't know what to say to her anymore... And she's constantly giving me these smiles... These... "trying-to-look-friendly-but-I-really-wanna-smash-a-crowbar-into-your-kneecaps" smiles, y'know...?
Aaah, my favorite kind!
Hhngh... #@$&% weed...!
Aw, ferget it... I don't wanna talk about her! So how are you and Leah doing?
sigh I don't know... Our letters have been getting more and more hostile these last few weeks... And maybe I'm just being paranoid, but I've noticed she's stopped putting "love" before her name at the end of her letters... I don't know...
Uuurgh!! Come on...
Whoop, there id iz! That's the smoke before the fire, son. Quick, dump her before she dumps you!
What is this, an Olympic event?! Besides, you want me to dump her just for *that*?!
Nooo, so you won't come crawling to my house crying and drink up all my beer when she dumps you!
Look, no one's dumping no one, alright?! We're still ticking, we're just...
GodDAMN it!! This bastard will not come out!
Alright, Alright! But I'll have the Kleenex waiting for you anyhow, if it's all the same.
HUFF
PUFF
Where do you get this crying thing?!?
I ***never*** cry!

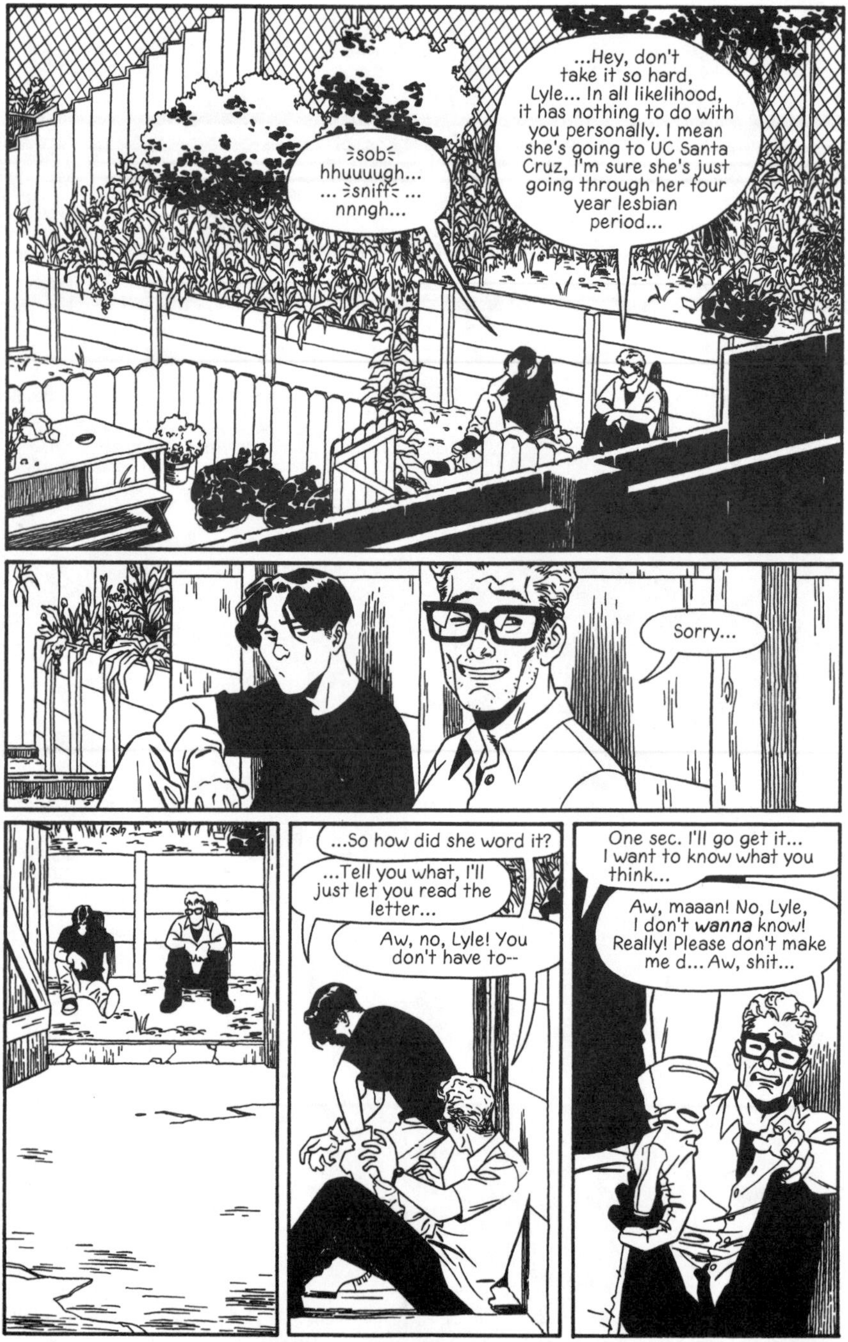

⩶sob⩶ hhuuuugh... ... ⩶sniff⩶ ... nnngh...
...Hey, don't take it so hard, Lyle... In all likelihood, it has nothing to do with you personally. I mean she's going to UC Santa Cruz, I'm sure she's just going through her four year lesbian period...
Sorry...
...So how did she word it?
...Tell you what, I'll just let you read the letter...
Aw, no, Lyle! You don't have to--
One sec. I'll go get it... I want to know what you think...
Aw, maaan! No, Lyle, I don't *wanna* know! Really! Please don't make me d... Aw, shit...

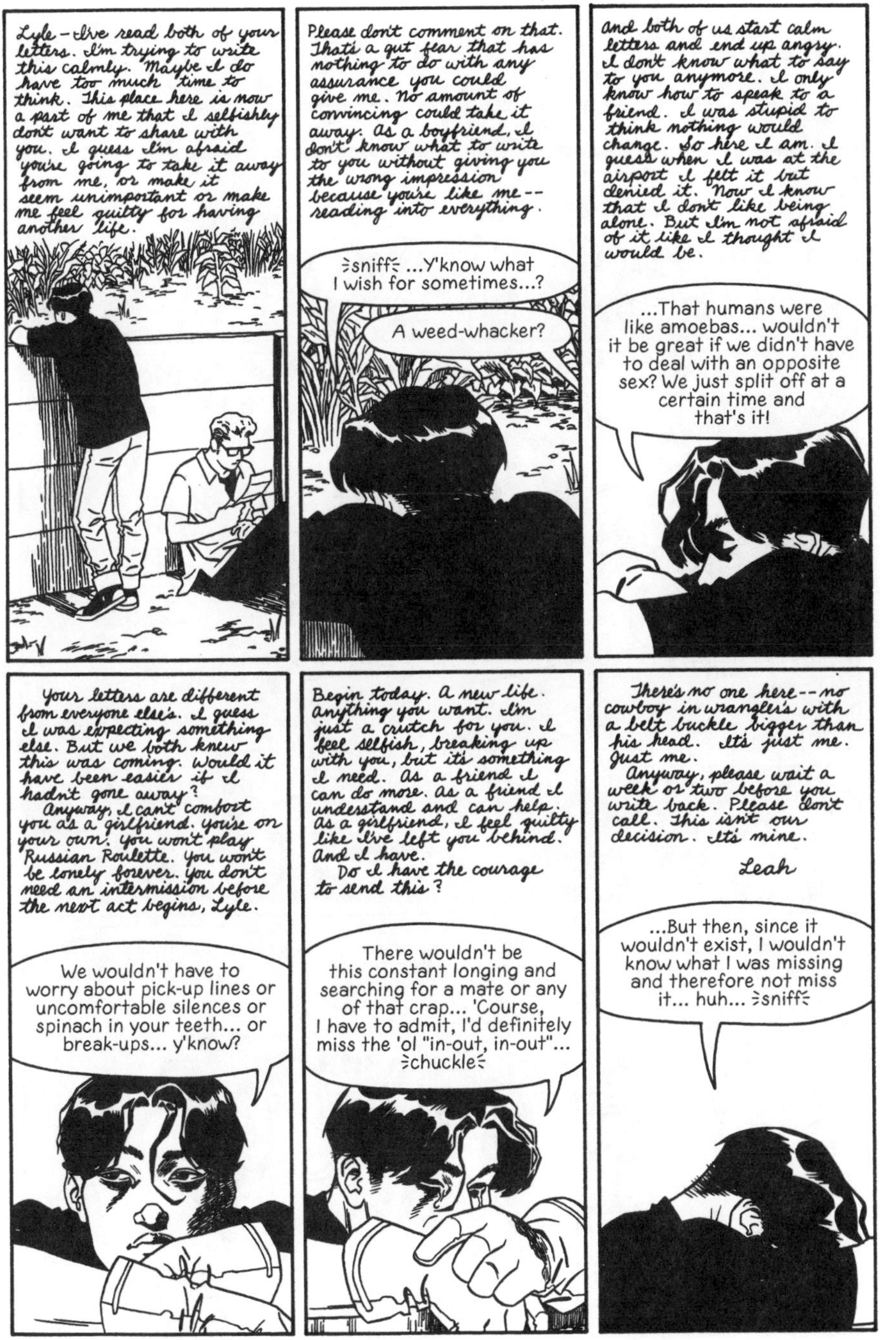
Lyle--I've read both of your letters. I'm trying to write this calmly. Maybe I do have too much time to think. This place here is now a part of me that I selfishly don't want to share with you. I guess I'm afraid you're going to take it away from me, or make it seem unimportant or make me feel guilty for having another life.
Please don't comment on that. That's a gut fear that has nothing to do with any assurance you could give me. No amount of convincing could take it away. As a boyfriend, I don't know what to write to you without giving you the wrong impression because you're like me-- reading into everything.
≷sniff≶ ...Y'know what I wish for sometimes...?
A weed-whacker?
and both of us start calm letters and end up angry. I don't know what to say to you anymore. I only know how to speak to a friend. I was stupid to think nothing would change. So here I am. I guess when I was at the airport I felt it but denied it. Now I know that I don't like being alone. But I'm not afraid of it like I thought I would be.
...That humans were like amoebas... wouldn't it be great if we didn't have to deal with an opposite sex? We just split off at a certain time and that's it!
Your letters are different from everyone else's. I guess I was expecting something else. But we both knew this was coming. Would it have been easier if I hadn't gone away?
Anyway, I can't comfort you as a girlfriend. You're on your own. You won't play Russian Roulette. You won't be lonely forever. You don't need an intermission before the next act begins, Lyle.
We wouldn't have to worry about pick-up lines or uncomfortable silences or spinach in your teeth... or break-ups... y'know?
Begin today. A new life. Anything you want. I'm just a crutch for you. I feel selfish, breaking up with you, but it's something I need. As a friend I can do more. As a friend I understand and can help. As a girlfriend, I feel guilty like I've left you behind. And I have.
Do I have the courage to send this?
There wouldn't be this constant longing and searching for a mate or any of that crap... 'Course, I have to admit, I'd definitely miss the 'ol "in-out, in-out"... ≷chuckle≶
There's no one here--no cowboy in wrangler's with a belt buckle bigger than his head. It's just me. Just me.
Anyway, please wait a week or two before you write back. Please don't call. This isn't our decision. It's mine.
Leah
...But then, since it wouldn't exist, I wouldn't know what I was missing and therefore not miss it... huh... ≷sniff≶

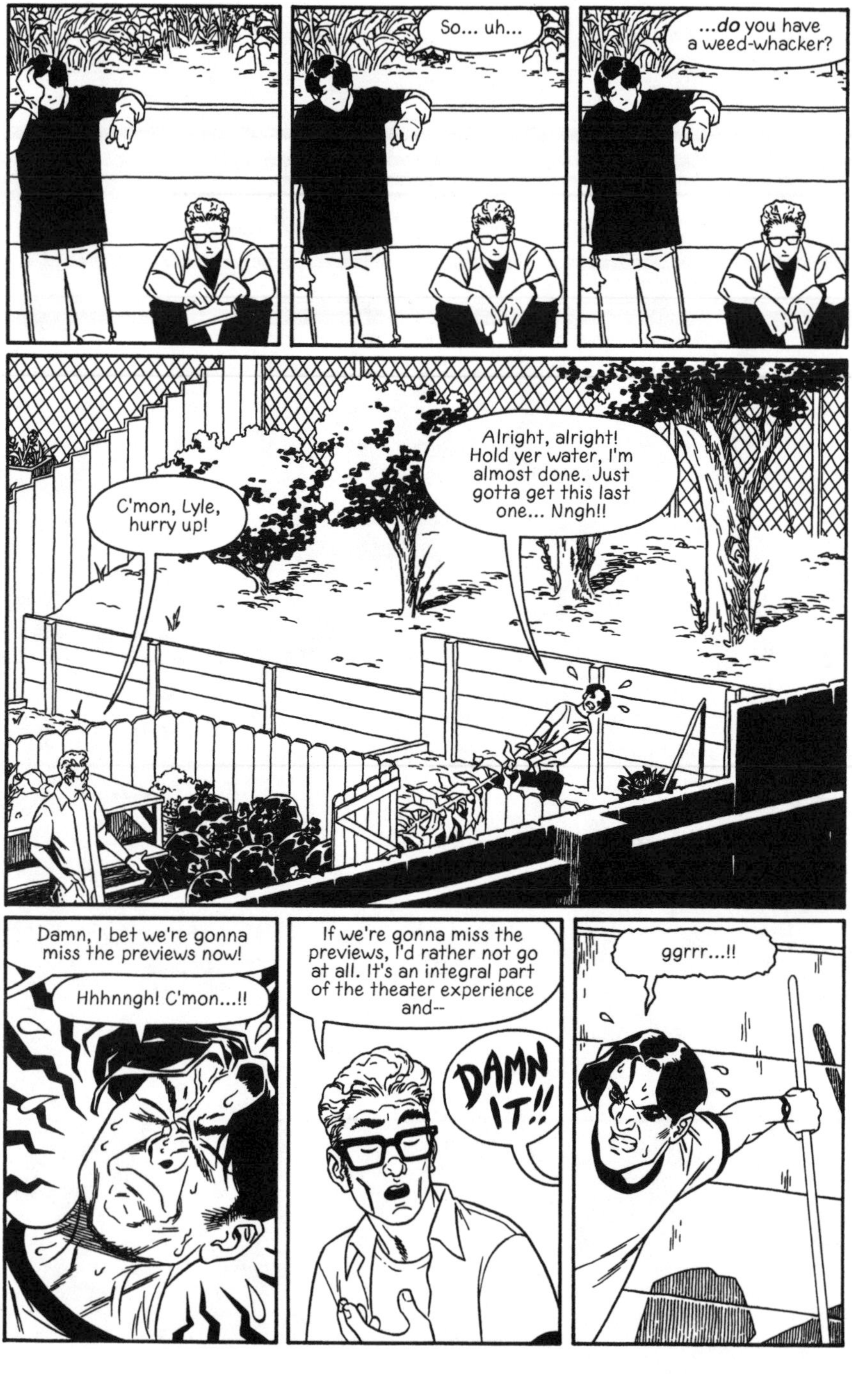
So... uh...
...*do* you have a weed-whacker?
C'mon, Lyle, hurry up!
Alright, alright! Hold yer water, I'm almost done. Just gotta get this last one... Nngh!!
Damn, I bet we're gonna miss the previews now!
Hhhnngh! C'mon...!!
If we're gonna miss the previews, I'd rather not go at all. It's an integral part of the theater experience and--
DAMN IT!!
ggrrr...!!

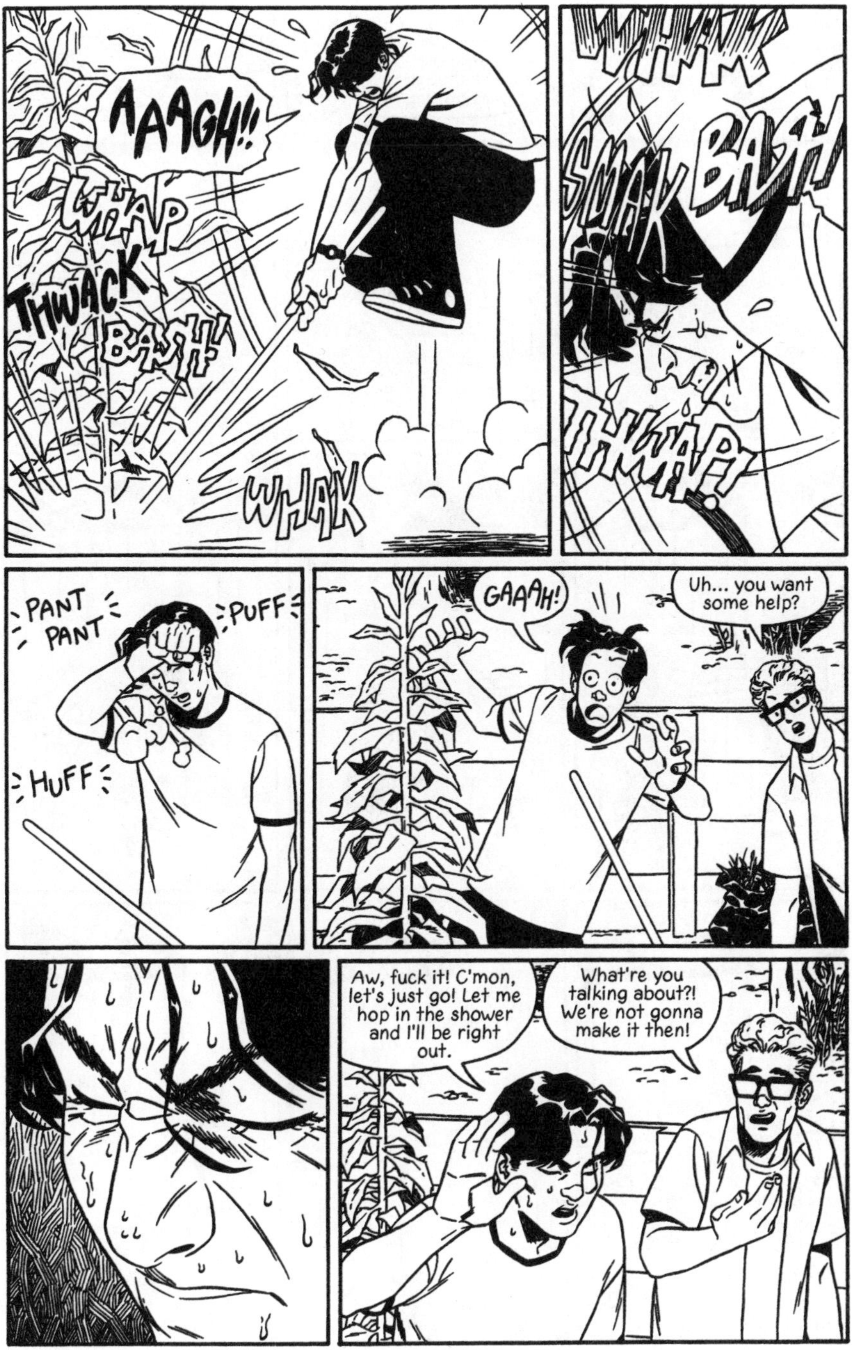
AAAGH!!
WHAP
THWACK
BASH!
WHAK
SMAK
BASH
THWAP!
PANT PANT
PUFF
HUFF
GAAAH!
Uh... you want some help?
Aw, fuck it! C'mon, let's just go! Let me hop in the shower and I'll be right out.
What're you talking about?! We're not gonna make it then!

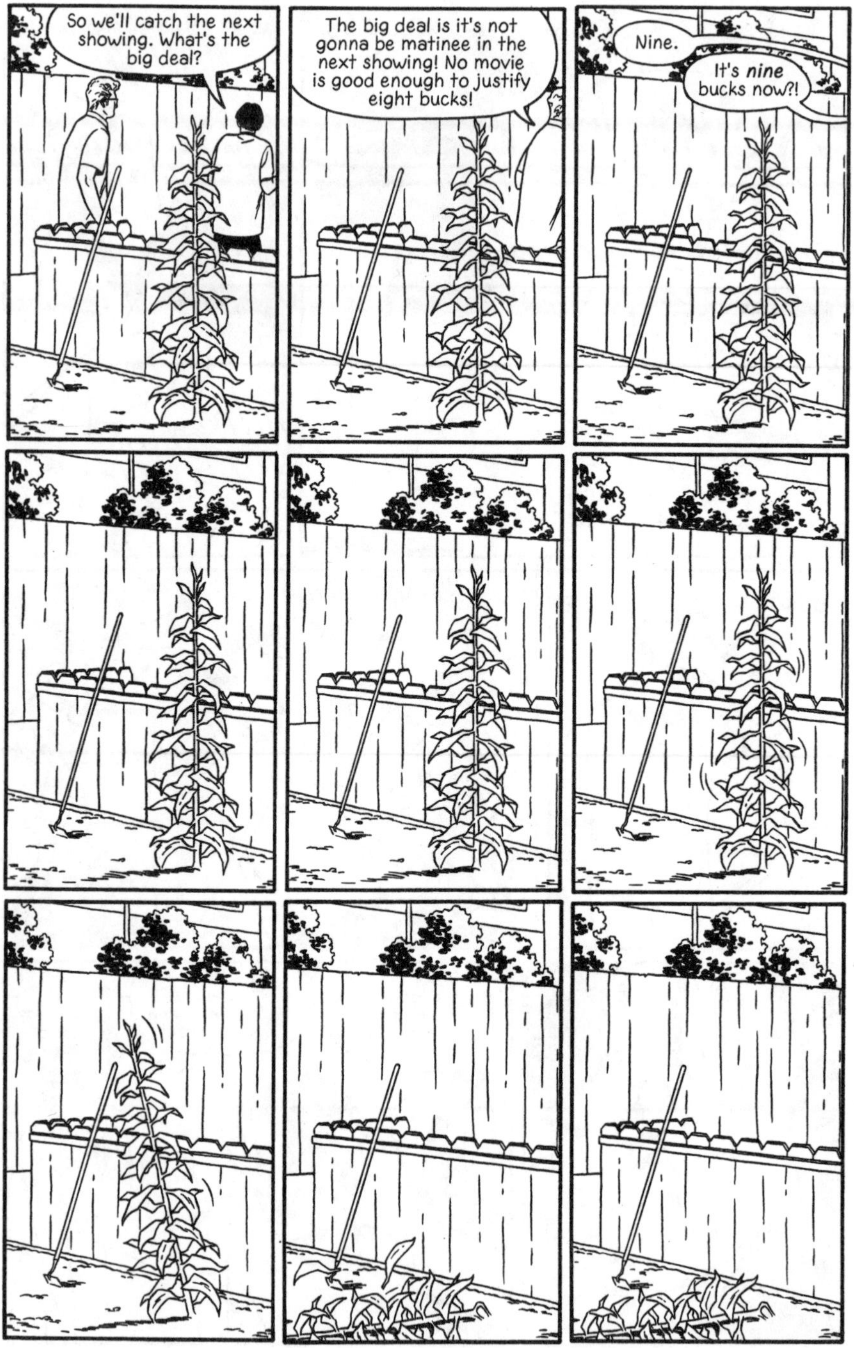
So we'll catch the next showing. What's the big deal?
The big deal is it's not gonna be matinee in the next showing! No movie is good enough to justify eight bucks!
Nine.
It's *nine* bucks now?!

SUPER UNLEADED

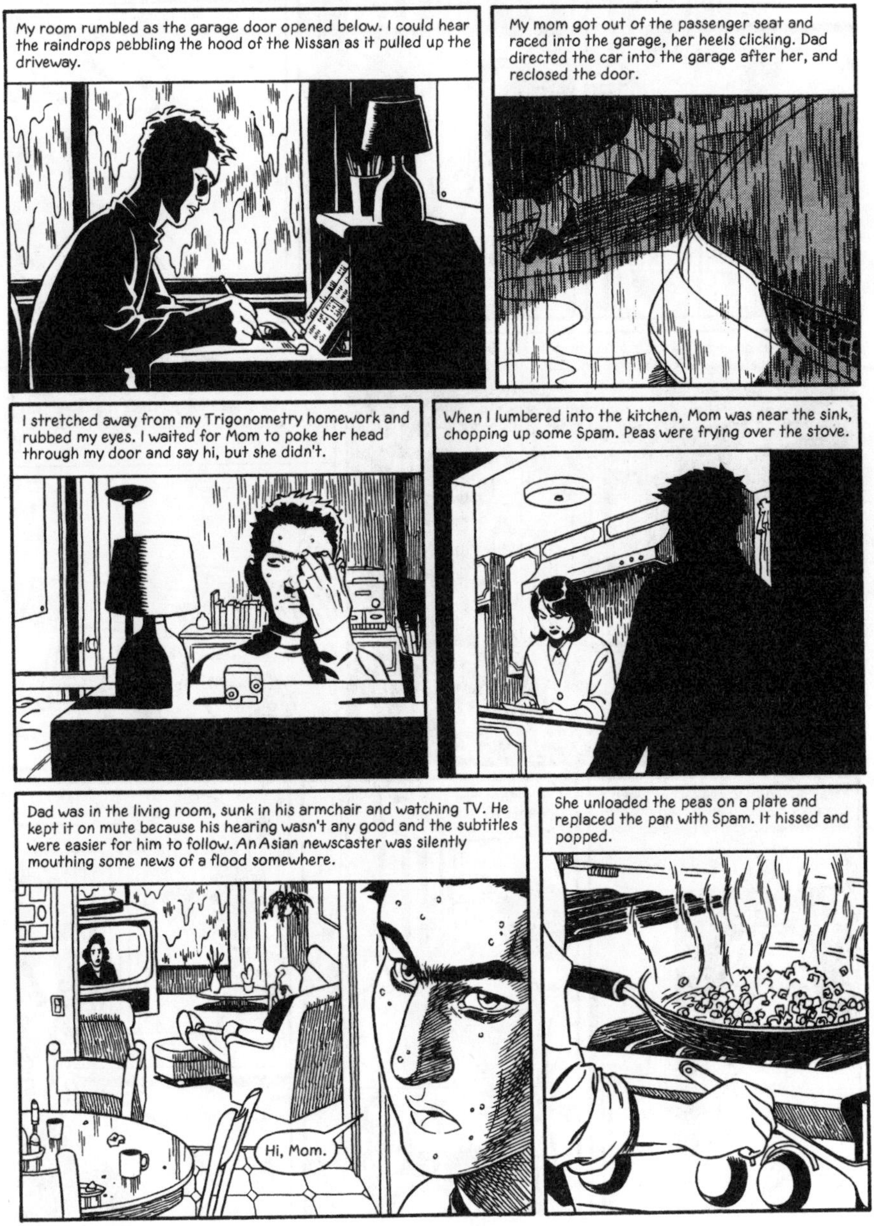

My room rumbled as the garage door opened below. I could hear the raindrops pebbling the hood of the Nissan as it pulled up the driveway.
My mom got out of the passenger seat and raced into the garage, her heels clicking. Dad directed the car into the garage after her, and reclosed the door.
I stretched away from my Trigonometry homework and rubbed my eyes. I waited for Mom to poke her head through my door and say hi, but she didn't.
When I lumbered into the kitchen, Mom was near the sink, chopping up some Spam. Peas were frying over the stove.
Dad was in the living room, sunk in his armchair and watching TV. He kept it on mute because his hearing wasn't any good and the subtitles were easier for him to follow. An Asian newscaster was silently mouthing some news of a flood somewhere.
Hi, Mom.
She unloaded the peas on a plate and replaced the pan with Spam. It hissed and popped.

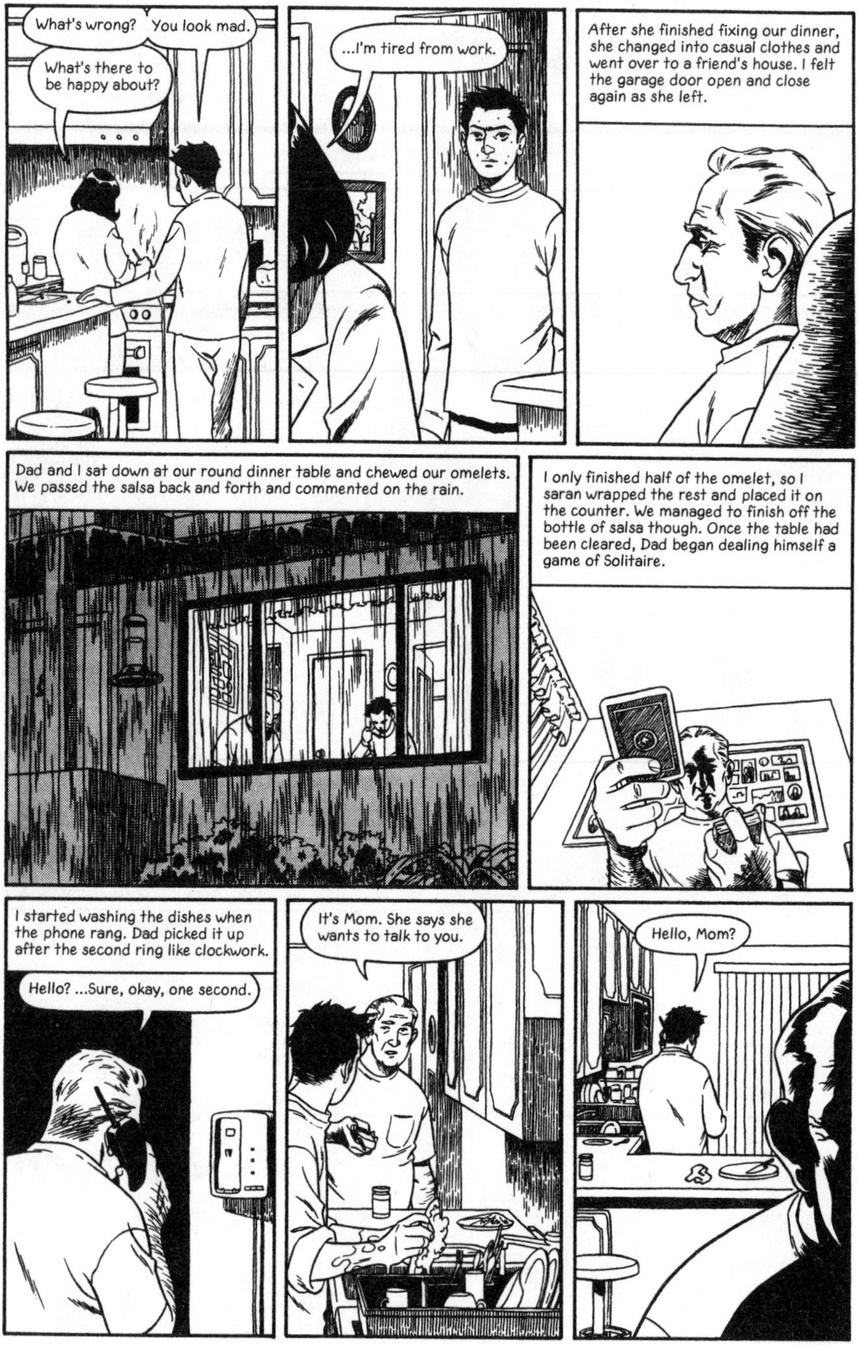
What's wrong?
You look mad.
What's there to be happy about?
...I'm tired from work.
After she finished fixing our dinner, she changed into casual clothes and went over to a friend's house. I felt the garage door open and close again as she left.
Dad and I sat down at our round dinner table and chewed our omelets. We passed the salsa back and forth and commented on the rain.
I only finished half of the omelet, so I saran wrapped the rest and placed it on the counter. We managed to finish off the bottle of salsa though. Once the table had been cleared, Dad began dealing himself a game of Solitaire.
I started washing the dishes when the phone rang. Dad picked it up after the second ring like clockwork.
Hello? ...Sure, okay, one second.
It's Mom. She says she wants to talk to you.
Hello, Mom?

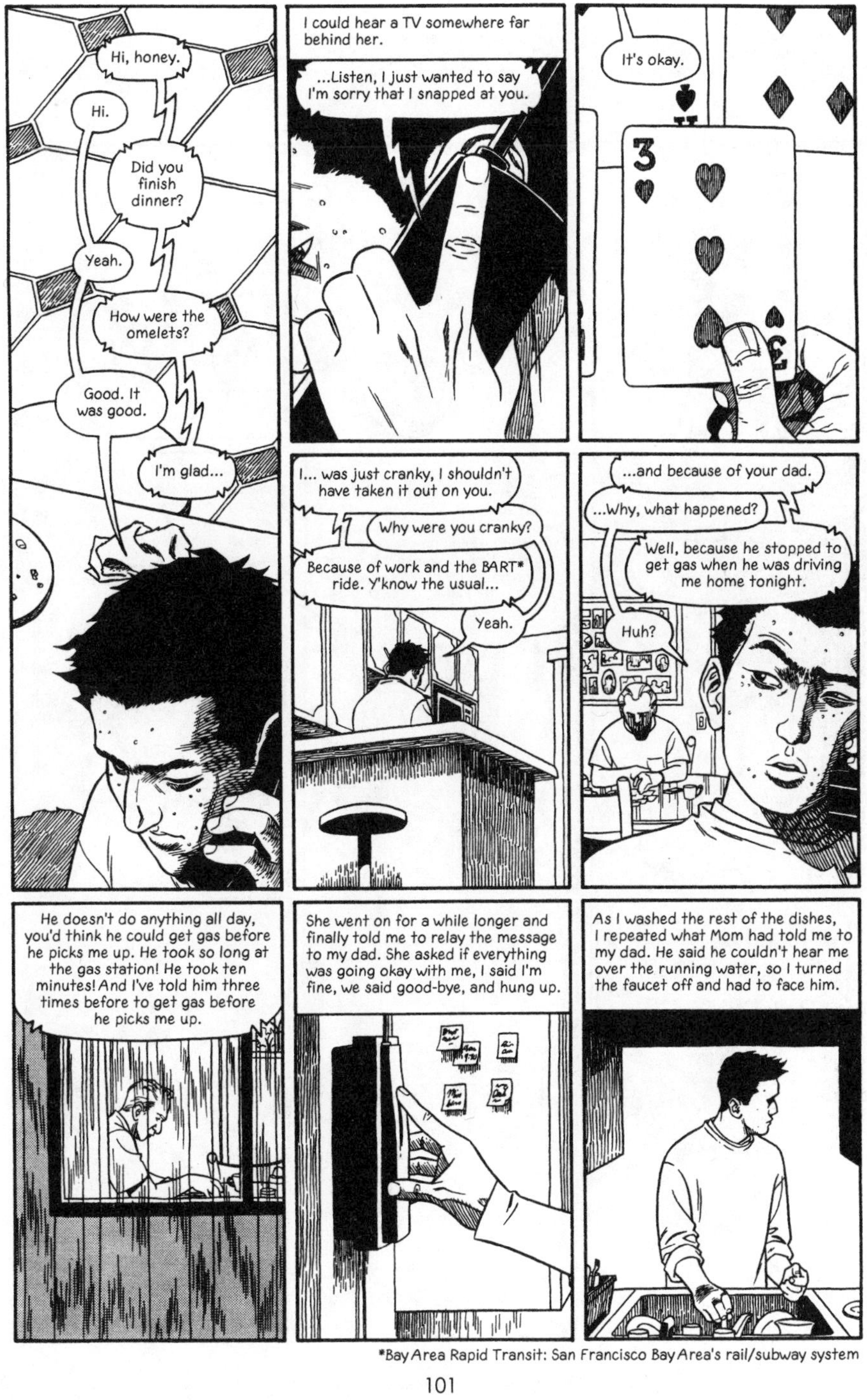
Hi, honey.
Hi.
Did you finish dinner?
Yeah.
How were the omelets?
Good. It was good.
I'm glad...
I could hear a TV somewhere far behind her.
...Listen, I just wanted to say I'm sorry that I snapped at you.
It's okay.
I... was just cranky, I shouldn't have taken it out on you.
Why were you cranky?
Because of work and the BART* ride. Y'know the usual...
Yeah.
...and because of your dad.
...Why, what happened?
Well, because he stopped to get gas when he was driving me home tonight.
Huh?
He doesn't do anything all day, you'd think he could get gas before he picks me up. He took so long at the gas station! He took ten minutes! And I've told him three times before to get gas before he picks me up.
She went on for a while longer and finally told me to relay the message to my dad. She asked if everything was going okay with me, I said I'm fine, we said good-bye, and hung up.
As I washed the rest of the dishes, I repeated what Mom had told me to my dad. He said he couldn't hear me over the running water, so I turned the faucet off and had to face him.

*Bay Area Rapid Transit: San Francisco Bay Area's rail/subway system

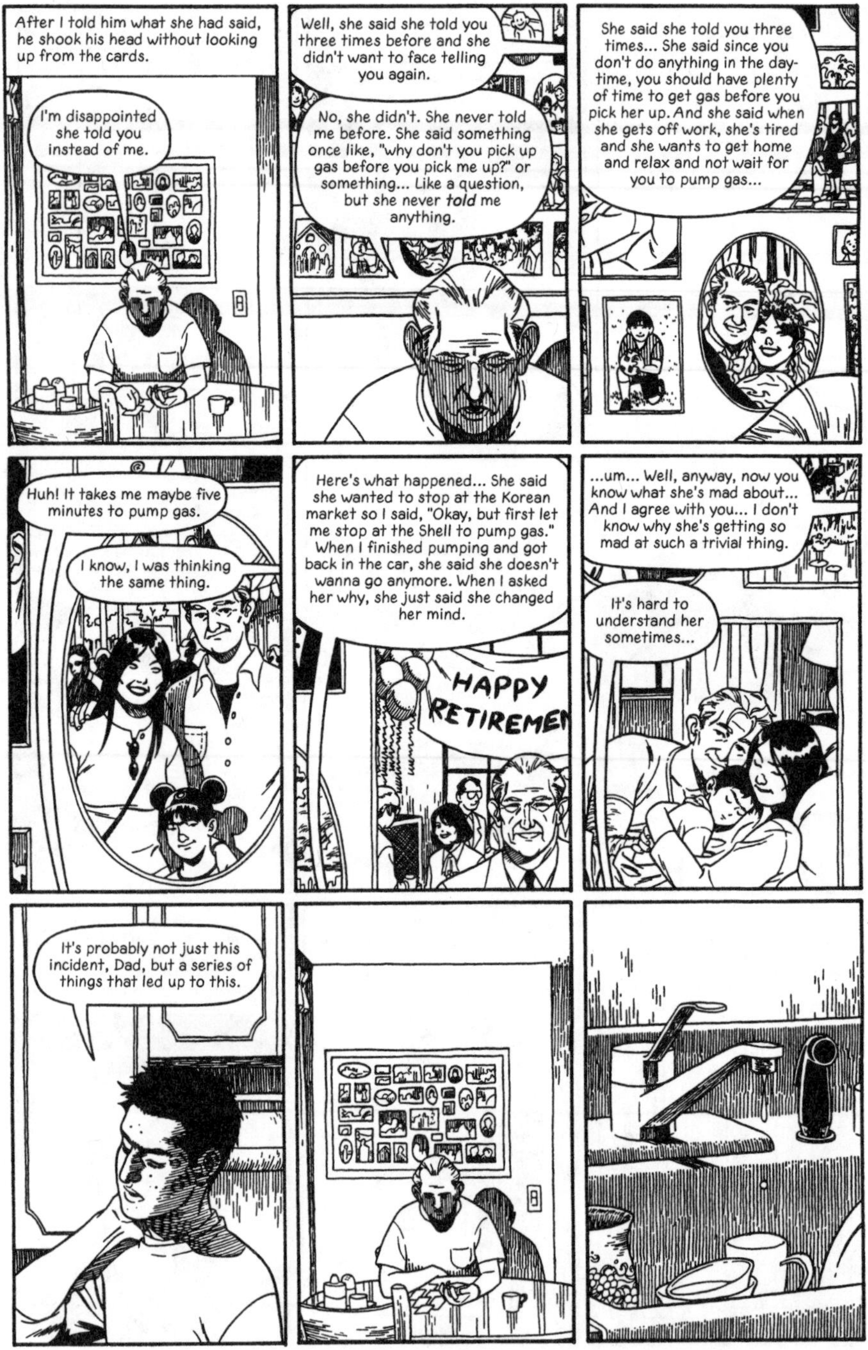

After I told him what she had said, he shook his head without looking up from the cards.
I'm disappointed she told you instead of me.
Well, she said she told you three times before and she didn't want to face telling you again.
No, she didn't. She never told me before. She said something once like, "why don't you pick up gas before you pick me up?" or something... Like a question, but she never *told* me anything.
She said she told you three times... She said since you don't do anything in the day-time, you should have plenty of time to get gas before you pick her up. And she said when she gets off work, she's tired and she wants to get home and relax and not wait for you to pump gas...
Huh! It takes me maybe five minutes to pump gas.
I know, I was thinking the same thing.
Here's what happened... She said she wanted to stop at the Korean market so I said, "Okay, but first let me stop at the Shell to pump gas." When I finished pumping and got back in the car, she said she doesn't wanna go anymore. When I asked her why, she just said she changed her mind.
HAPPY RETIREMEN
...um... Well, anyway, now you know what she's mad about... And I agree with you... I don't know why she's getting so mad at such a trivial thing.
It's hard to understand her sometimes...
It's probably not just this incident, Dad, but a series of things that led up to this.

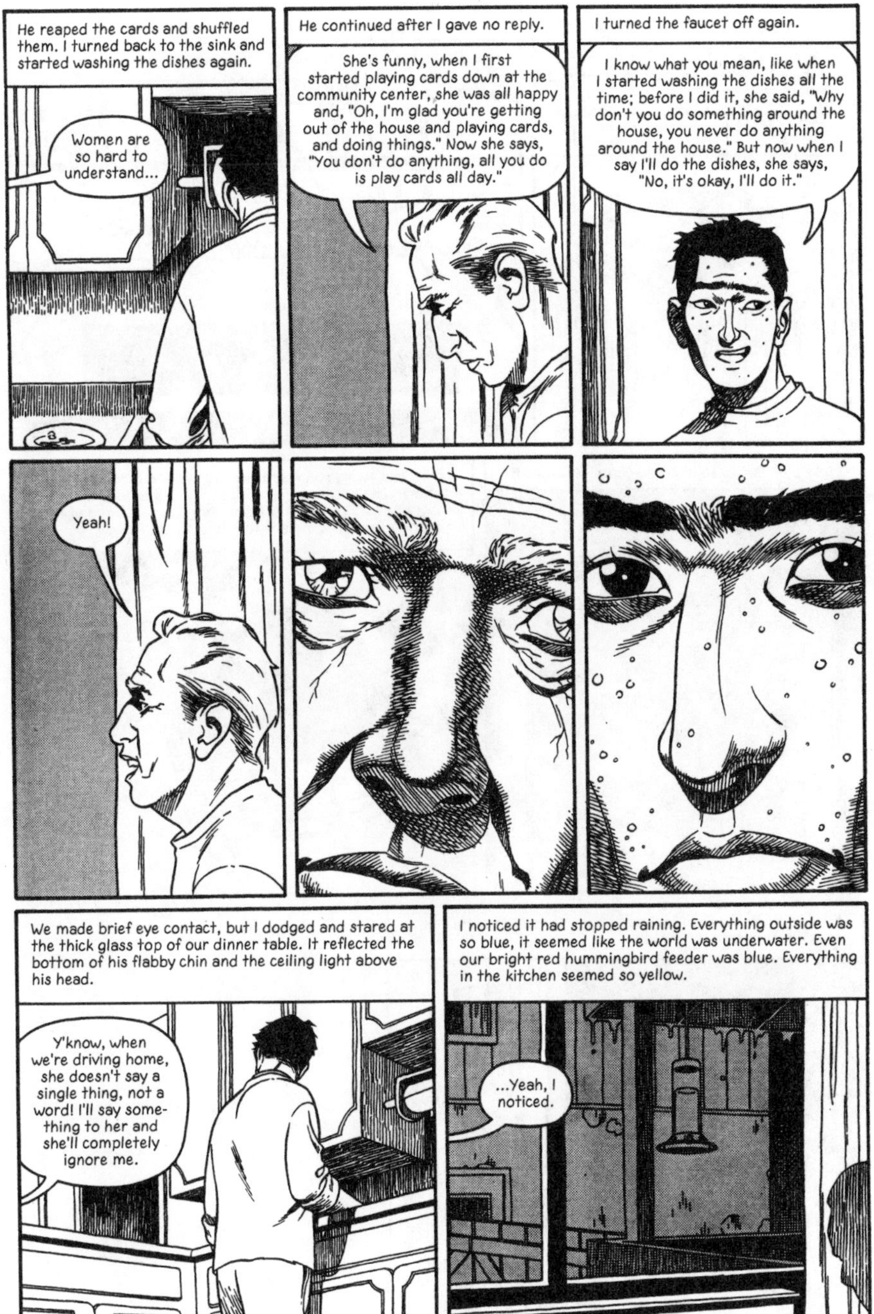
He reaped the cards and shuffled them. I turned back to the sink and started washing the dishes again.
Women are so hard to understand...
He continued after I gave no reply.
She's funny, when I first started playing cards down at the community center, she was all happy and, "Oh, I'm glad you're getting out of the house and playing cards, and doing things." Now she says, "You don't do anything, all you do is play cards all day."
I turned the faucet off again.
I know what you mean, like when I started washing the dishes all the time; before I did it, she said, "Why don't you do something around the house, you never do anything around the house." But now when I say I'll do the dishes, she says, "No, it's okay, I'll do it."
Yeah!
We made brief eye contact, but I dodged and stared at the thick glass top of our dinner table. It reflected the bottom of his flabby chin and the ceiling light above his head.
Y'know, when we're driving home, she doesn't say a single thing, not a word! I'll say something to her and she'll completely ignore me.
I noticed it had stopped raining. Everything outside was so blue, it seemed like the world was underwater. Even our bright red hummingbird feeder was blue. Everything in the kitchen seemed so yellow.
...Yeah, I noticed.

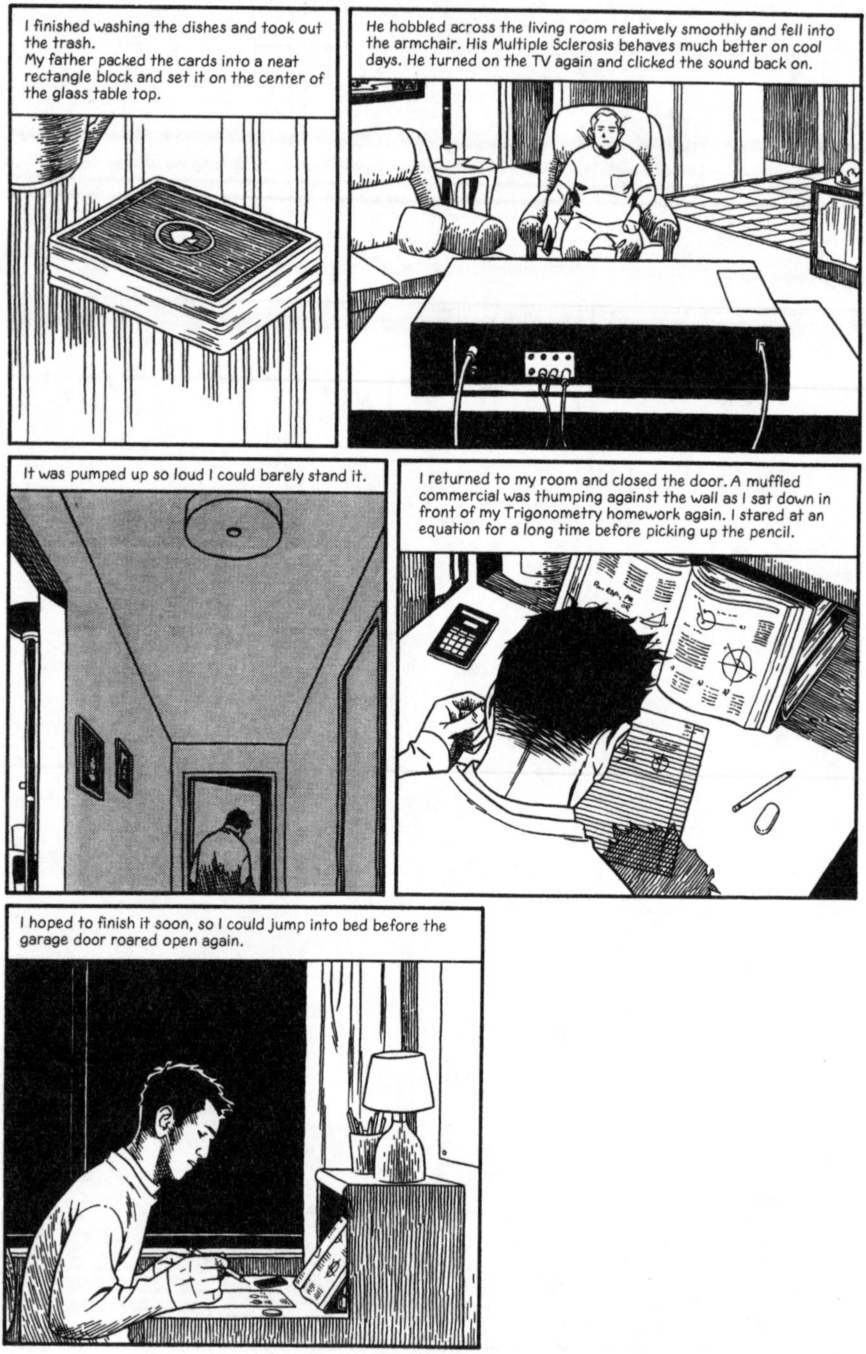
I finished washing the dishes and took out the trash.
My father packed the cards into a neat rectangle block and set it on the center of the glass table top.
He hobbled across the living room relatively smoothly and fell into the armchair. His Multiple Sclerosis behaves much better on cool days. He turned on the TV again and clicked the sound back on.
It was pumped up so loud I could barely stand it.
I returned to my room and closed the door. A muffled commercial was thumping against the wall as I sat down in front of my Trigonometry homework again. I stared at an equation for a long time before picking up the pencil.
I hoped to finish it soon, so I could jump into bed before the garage door roared open again.

interview with a human

Welcome back to *Xelix Live!* If you're just joining us, we're talking to President Doe all the way from the outer edge of the Milky Way galaxy via intergalactic satellite. President Doe is the leader of the human race, the latest species to join the IFS (Intergalactic Federation of Sentients).

So President Doe, to continue our discussion on human society and culture, isn't it true that your species has recently migrated to yet another planet? That would make it the fifth planet you've inhabited in the last two millennia.

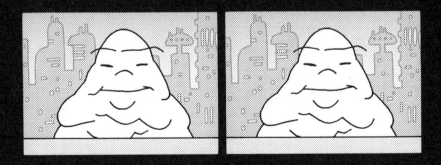

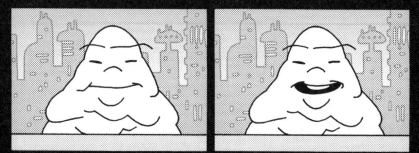

Yes, Xelix, that is true.

President Doe, for the last time, could you please turn off your holovision? I can hear it in the background...

Oh, haha, sorry about that... Never been on holovision before... Haha...

Mr. President, I couldn't help but notice that you simply turned the HV off with your mind. I didn't realize humans had telekinetic abilities...

Oh, we don't. Ever since the 22nd century, everyone has a remote control, cell phone, internet connection, and a complete set of Tony Robbins self-help tapes implanted right into our brains the minute we're born. As well as circumcision for the males, of course.

Of course. And didn't your species used to have limbs?

Yes, I hate to admit it, but during ancient times, we had to rely on those clumsy things for everything from transportation to sexual pleasure. Thanks to the development of antigravitational and brain-implant technology, we slowly weaned off of our obsolete arms and legs. Gradually evolution took its course and now you see the beautiful form before you. Ha ha!

Uh, yes... haha... Now then, back to our discussion on your species' frequent change of home planets... Many of our viewers are appalled at how quickly humans use up a planet's resources and destroy its environment. What can you tell us about that?

I take offense to that accusation. Not only does that statement border on speciesism, but it's completely inaccurate. The last two planets we inhabited were obliterated by our constant warfare, and had nothing to do with environmental abuse.

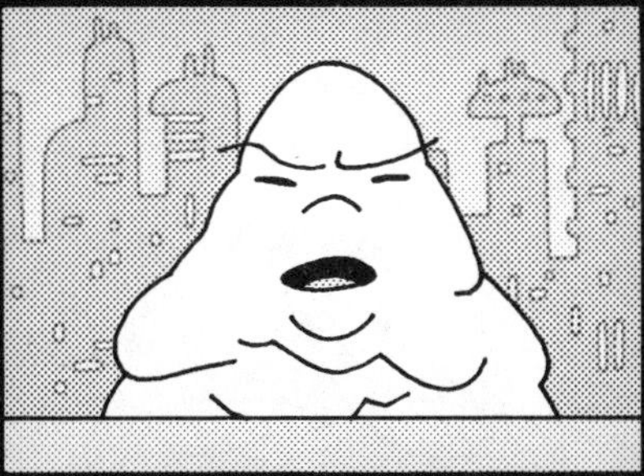

And speaking of your species' tendency toward senseless violence, investigative reports seem to confirm that much of these "wars", as you call them, were ignited by an ancient inane practice called, "religion". Would you care to elaborate on that, Mr. President?

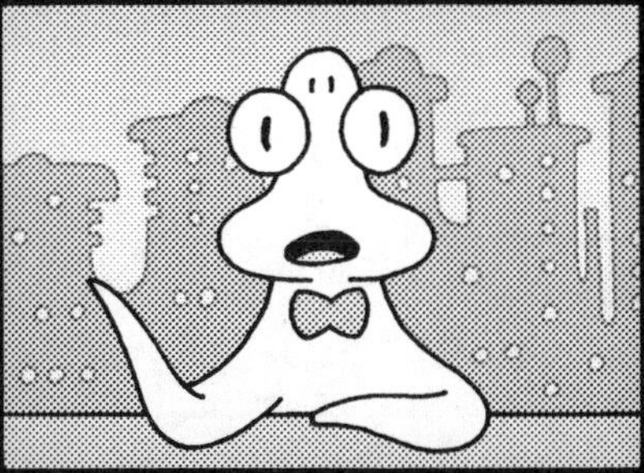

That is a complete lie!! Human beings never practiced such a thing. That's sheer fabrication by our enemies in the Snickers galaxy simply to make us look stupid and gullible! Do you think we just crawled out of primordial snot?!

Religion! The nerve!

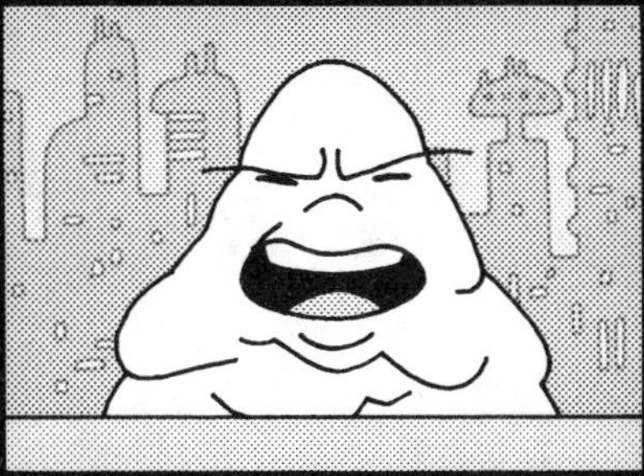

Then would you care to explain this, President Doe? Our investigative reporters found this digital book called, "The Bible" which contain some silly notions of some unseen omnipotent being who judges humans -- after they're dead, no less! -- as well as someone who ***rises*** from the dead and-- Ha ha ha, I'm sorry, President D-- hoo ha-- I'm sorry, I just can't-- haha-- continue this... Bwahahahahaaa!!

(studio audience laughs)

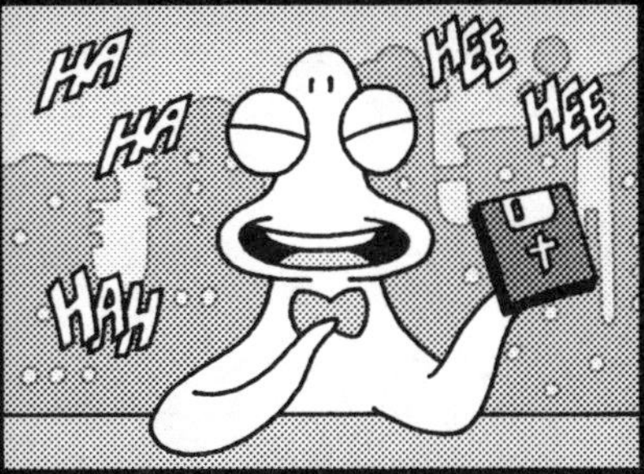
HA
HA
HAH
HEE
HEE

Um, th--that's... uh... it... I...
That book was... um... Th-That thing was
planted by our enemies in the Snickers
galaxy!! Isn't it obvious that--

Coincidentally though, Mr. President,
our culture has a book that's strangely
similar to your Bible entitled,
The Happy Neighbor.

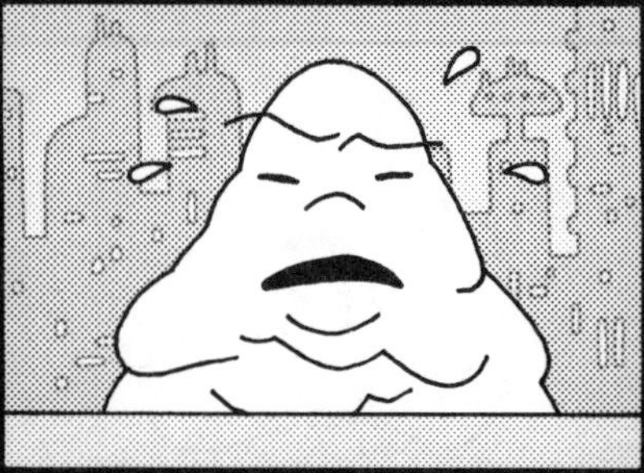

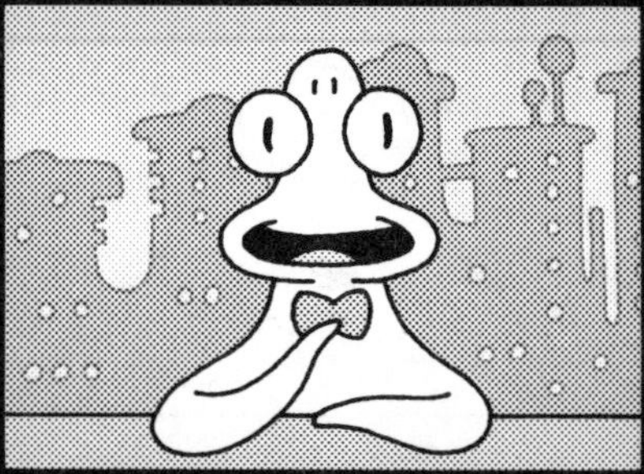

Really?

Yes, but ours only contain pictures and
the pages are made out of cardboard.
Hahahahahahaha!!

(studio audience laughs)

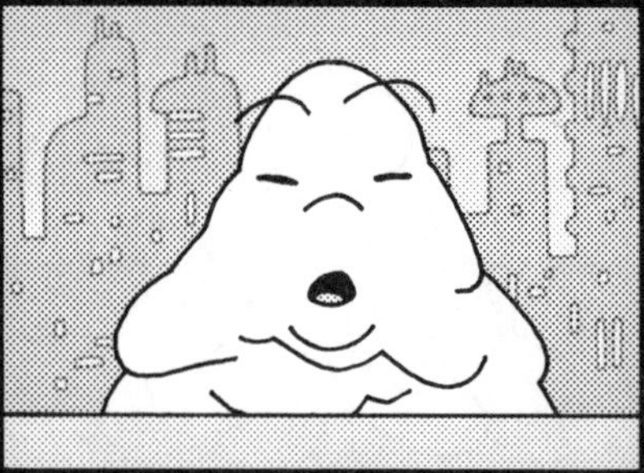

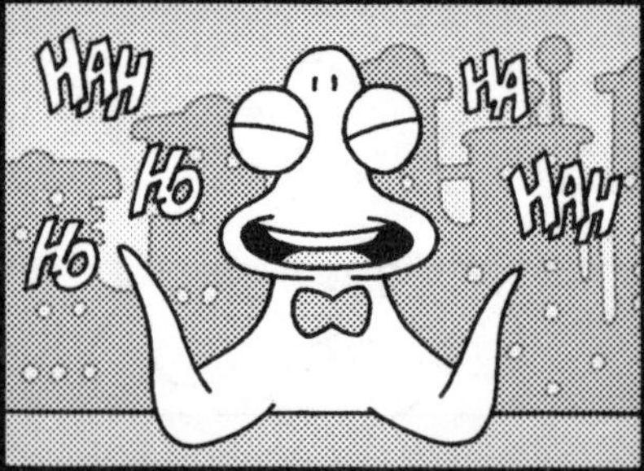
HAH
HA
HO
HAH
HO

Alright, I confess, religion is very important to our species. But *that* ancient rhetoric has been wiped off the face of all five Earths many many millennia ago! Most humans don't even remember it! We've evolved as a species and have a true God to which we focus our morality.

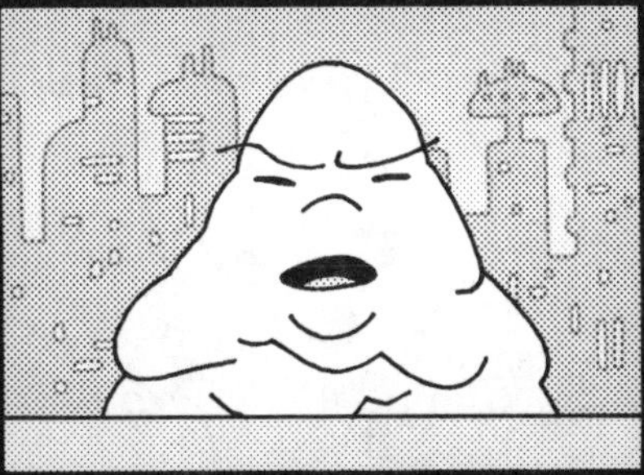

Surely you don't mean this absurd "Santa Claus"?!

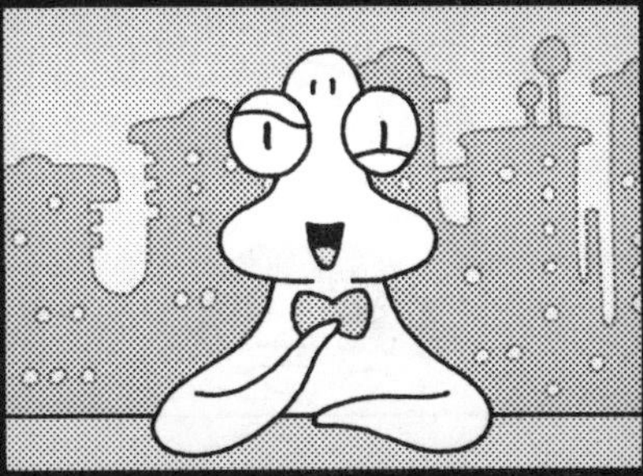

How dare you! By spitting on our God, you have spit on the entire human race!!

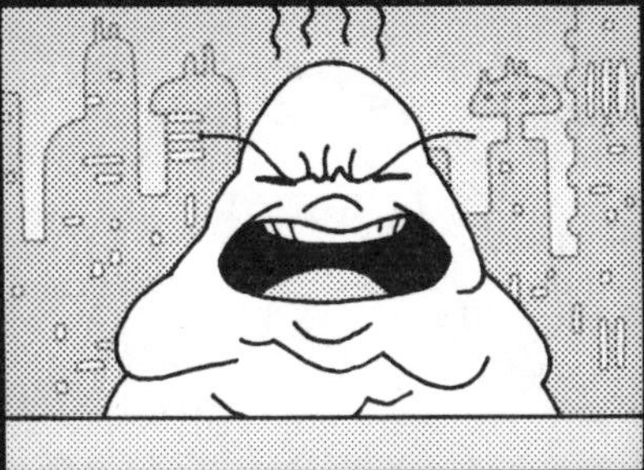

I'm-- haha-- sorry, President Doe, it's just that, just th-- Hahahahahaha!!

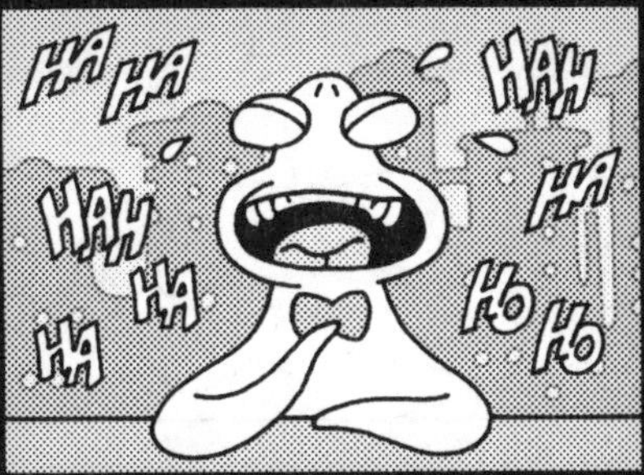
HA HA
HAH
HAH
HA
HA
HA
HO
HO

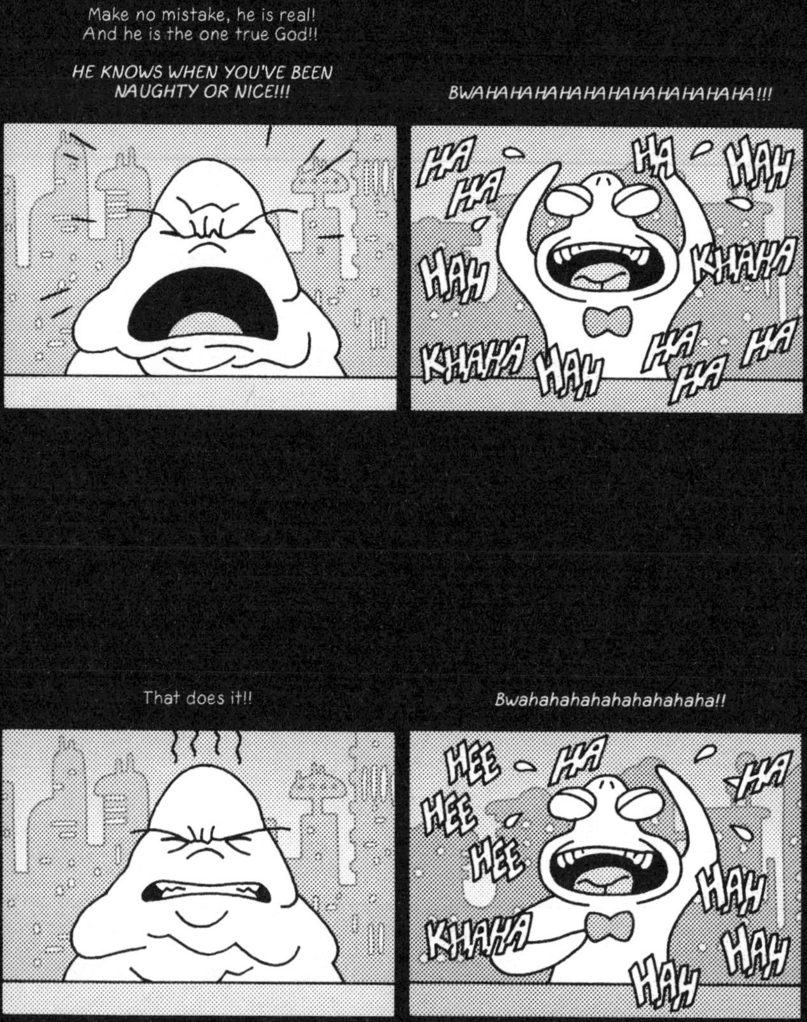
Make no mistake, he is real!
And he is the one true God!!
HE KNOWS WHEN YOU'VE BEEN NAUGHTY OR NICE!!!
BWAHAHAHAHAHAHAHAHAHAHAHAHA!!!
HA HA
HA
HAH
HAH
KHAHA
KHAHA
HAH
HA HA
HA
That does it!!
Bwahahahahahahahahaha!!
HEE
HA
HEE
HA
HEE
HAH
KHAHA
HAH
HAH

Oooohwahahahahahaha-- huh?

This just in, ladies and gentlemen!
A special report! Satellites have detected
dozens of unidentified projectiles
rocketing toward our pla--

ξkkkkkkkkkkkkkhhhhhhhhhhξ

ξkkkkkkkkkkkkkhhhhhhhhhhξ

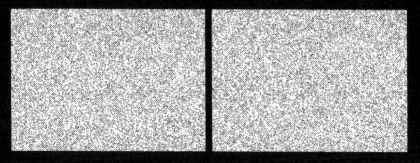

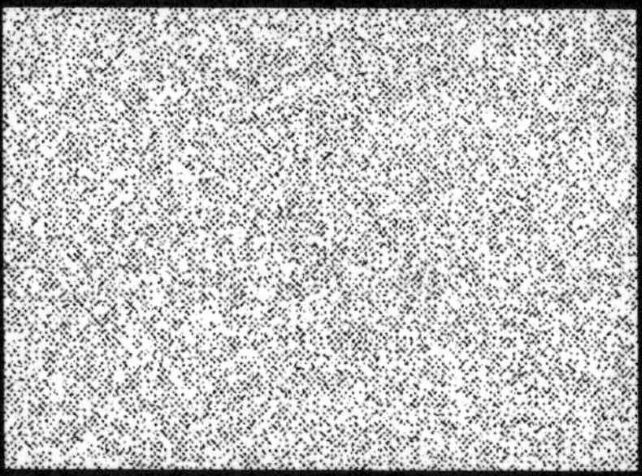

EMO ROCK HYUNG

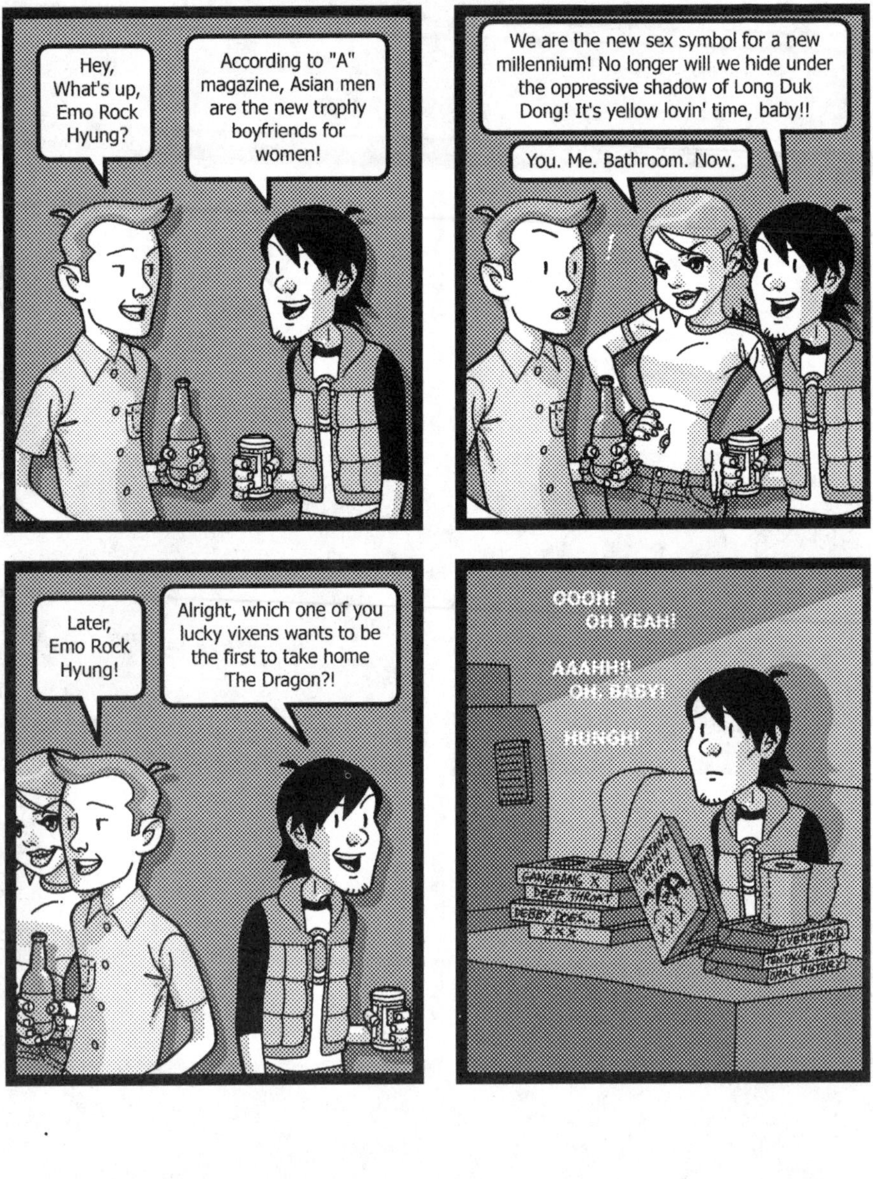
Hey, What's up, Emo Rock Hyung?
According to "A" magazine, Asian men are the new trophy boyfriends for women!
We are the new sex symbol for a new millennium! No longer will we hide under the oppressive shadow of Long Duk Dong! It's yellow lovin' time, baby!!
You. Me. Bathroom. Now.
!
Later, Emo Rock Hyung!
Alright, which one of you lucky vixens wants to be the first to take home The Dragon?!
OOOH!
OH YEAH!
AAAHH!!
OH, BABY!
HUNGH!
GANGBANG X
DEEP THROAT
DEBBY DOES...
XXX
OVERFIEND
TENTACLE SEX
ORAL HISTORY

Oliver
Pikk

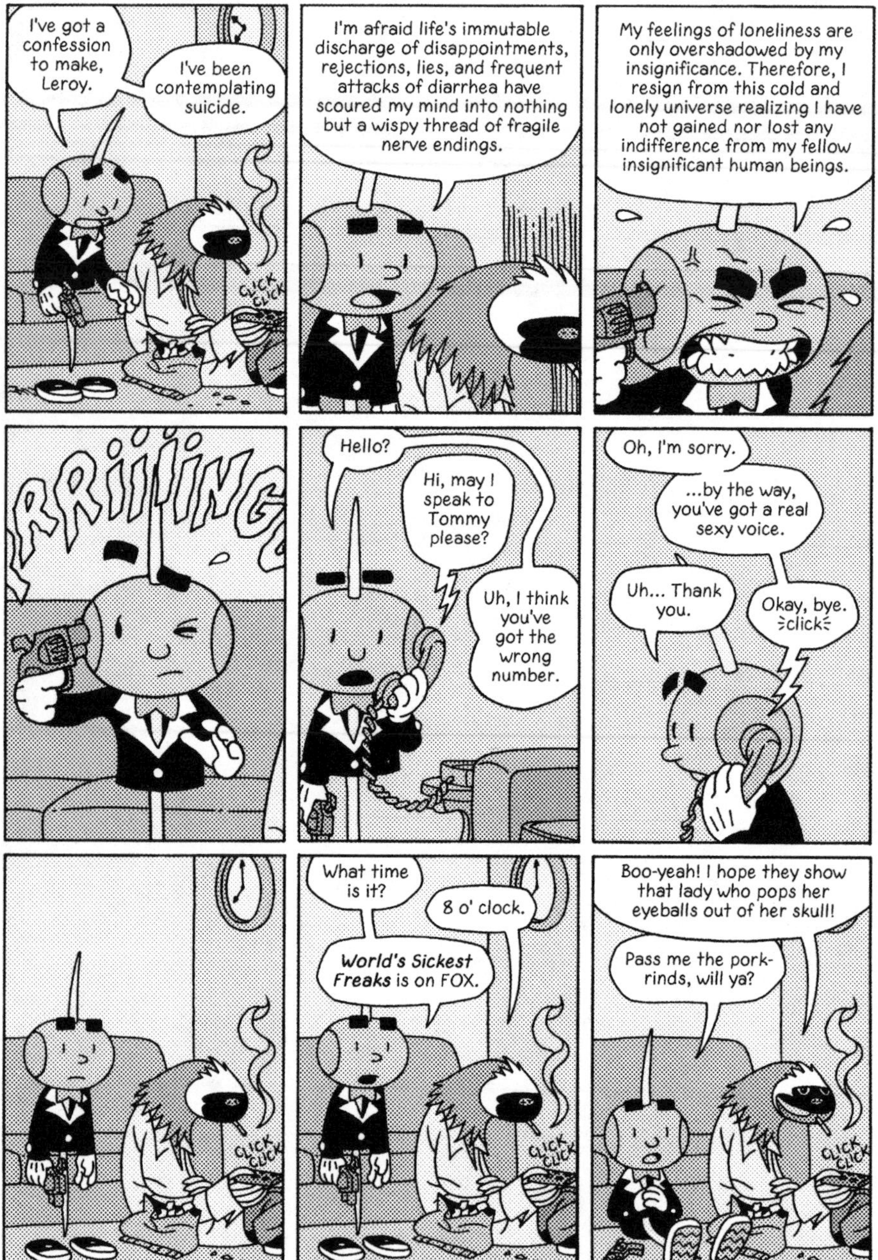
I've got a confession to make, Leroy.
I've been contemplating suicide.
CLICK CLICK
I'm afraid life's immutable discharge of disappointments, rejections, lies, and frequent attacks of diarrhea have scoured my mind into nothing but a wispy thread of fragile nerve endings.
My feelings of loneliness are only overshadowed by my insignificance. Therefore, I resign from this cold and lonely universe realizing I have not gained nor lost any indifference from my fellow insignificant human beings.
RRIIING
Hello?
Hi, may I speak to Tommy please?
Uh, I think you've got the wrong number.
Oh, I'm sorry.
...by the way, you've got a real sexy voice.
Uh... Thank you.
Okay, bye. click
CLICK CLICK
What time is it?
8 o' clock.
World's Sickest Freaks is on FOX.
CLICK CLICK
Boo-yeah! I hope they show that lady who pops her eyeballs out of her skull!
Pass me the pork-rinds, will ya?
CLICK CLICK

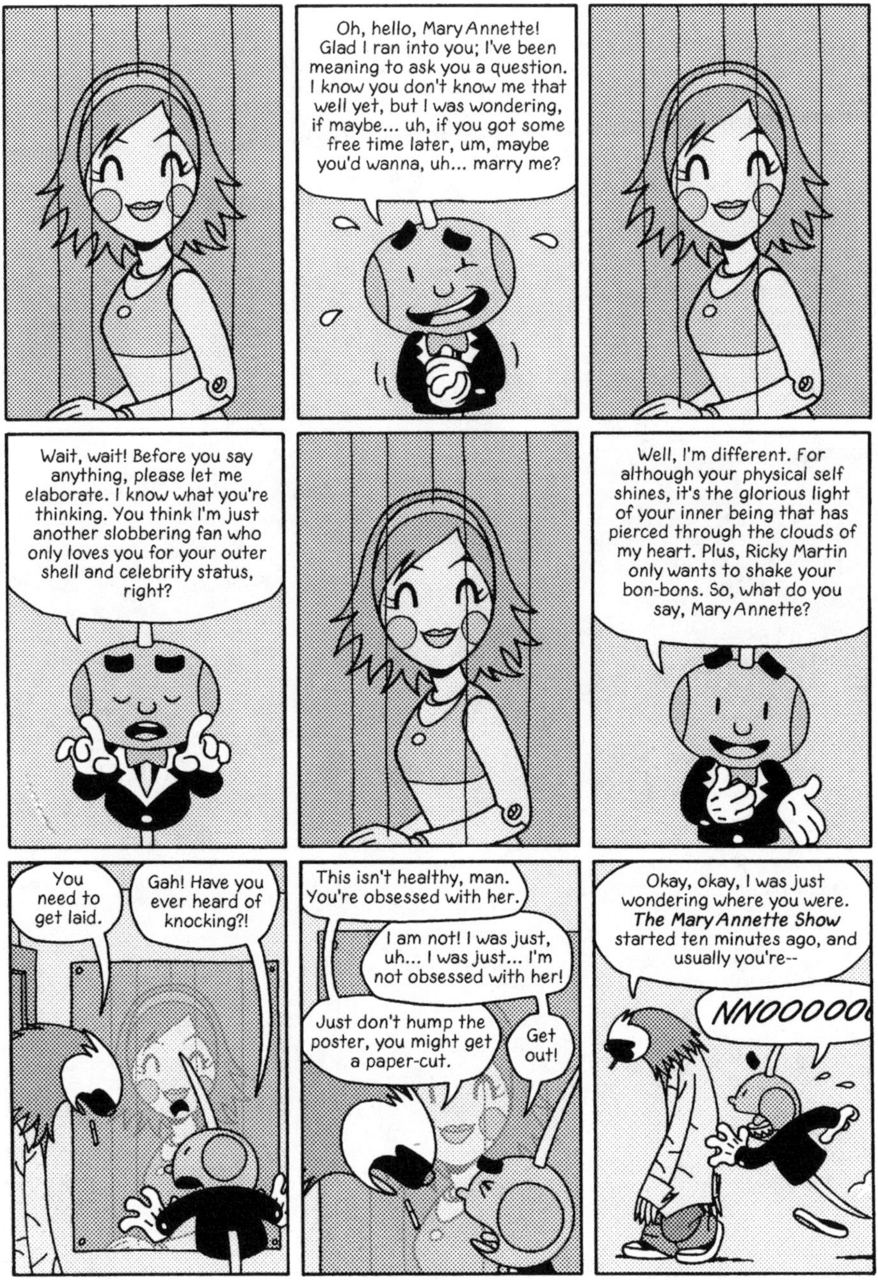
Oh, hello, Mary Annette! Glad I ran into you; I've been meaning to ask you a question. I know you don't know me that well yet, but I was wondering, if maybe... uh, if you got some free time later, um, maybe you'd wanna, uh... marry me?
Wait, wait! Before you say anything, please let me elaborate. I know what you're thinking. You think I'm just another slobbering fan who only loves you for your outer shell and celebrity status, right?
Well, I'm different. For although your physical self shines, it's the glorious light of your inner being that has pierced through the clouds of my heart. Plus, Ricky Martin only wants to shake your bon-bons. So, what do you say, Mary Annette?
You need to get laid.
Gah! Have you ever heard of knocking?!
This isn't healthy, man. You're obsessed with her.
I am not! I was just, uh... I was just... I'm not obsessed with her!
Just don't hump the poster, you might get a paper-cut.
Get out!
Okay, okay, I was just wondering where you were. *The Mary Annette Show* started ten minutes ago, and usually you're--
NNOOOOOO

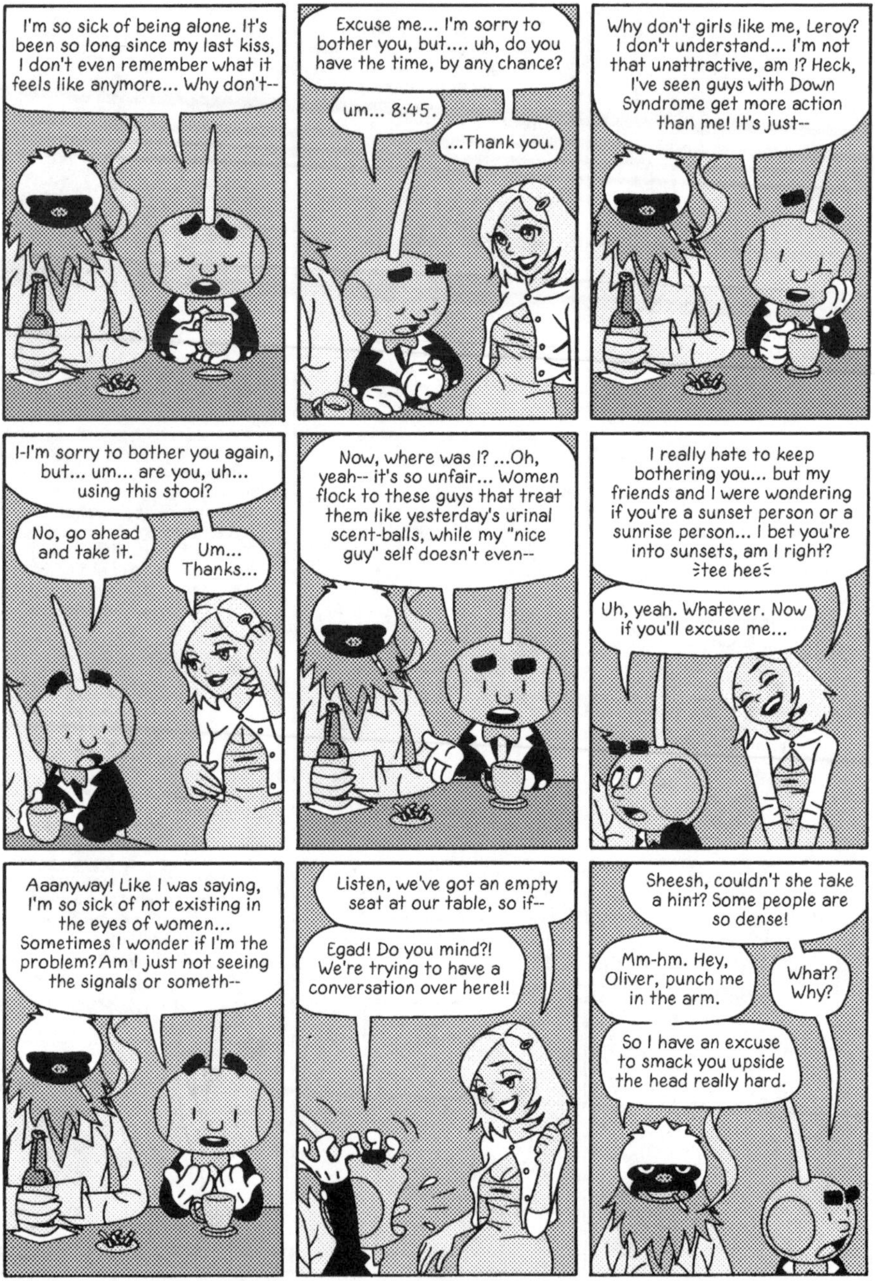
I'm so sick of being alone. It's been so long since my last kiss, I don't even remember what it feels like anymore... Why don't--
Excuse me... I'm sorry to bother you, but.... uh, do you have the time, by any chance?
um... 8:45.
...Thank you.
Why don't girls like me, Leroy? I don't understand... I'm not that unattractive, am I? Heck, I've seen guys with Down Syndrome get more action than me! It's just--
I-I'm sorry to bother you again, but... um... are you, uh... using this stool?
No, go ahead and take it.
Um... Thanks...
Now, where was I? ...Oh, yeah-- it's so unfair... Women flock to these guys that treat them like yesterday's urinal scent-balls, while my "nice guy" self doesn't even--
I really hate to keep bothering you... but my friends and I were wondering if you're a sunset person or a sunrise person... I bet you're into sunsets, am I right? tee hee
Uh, yeah. Whatever. Now if you'll excuse me...
Aaanyway! Like I was saying, I'm so sick of not existing in the eyes of women... Sometimes I wonder if I'm the problem? Am I just not seeing the signals or someth--
Listen, we've got an empty seat at our table, so if--
Egad! Do you mind?! We're trying to have a conversation over here!!
Sheesh, couldn't she take a hint? Some people are so dense!
Mm-hm. Hey, Oliver, punch me in the arm.
What? Why?
So I have an excuse to smack you upside the head really hard.

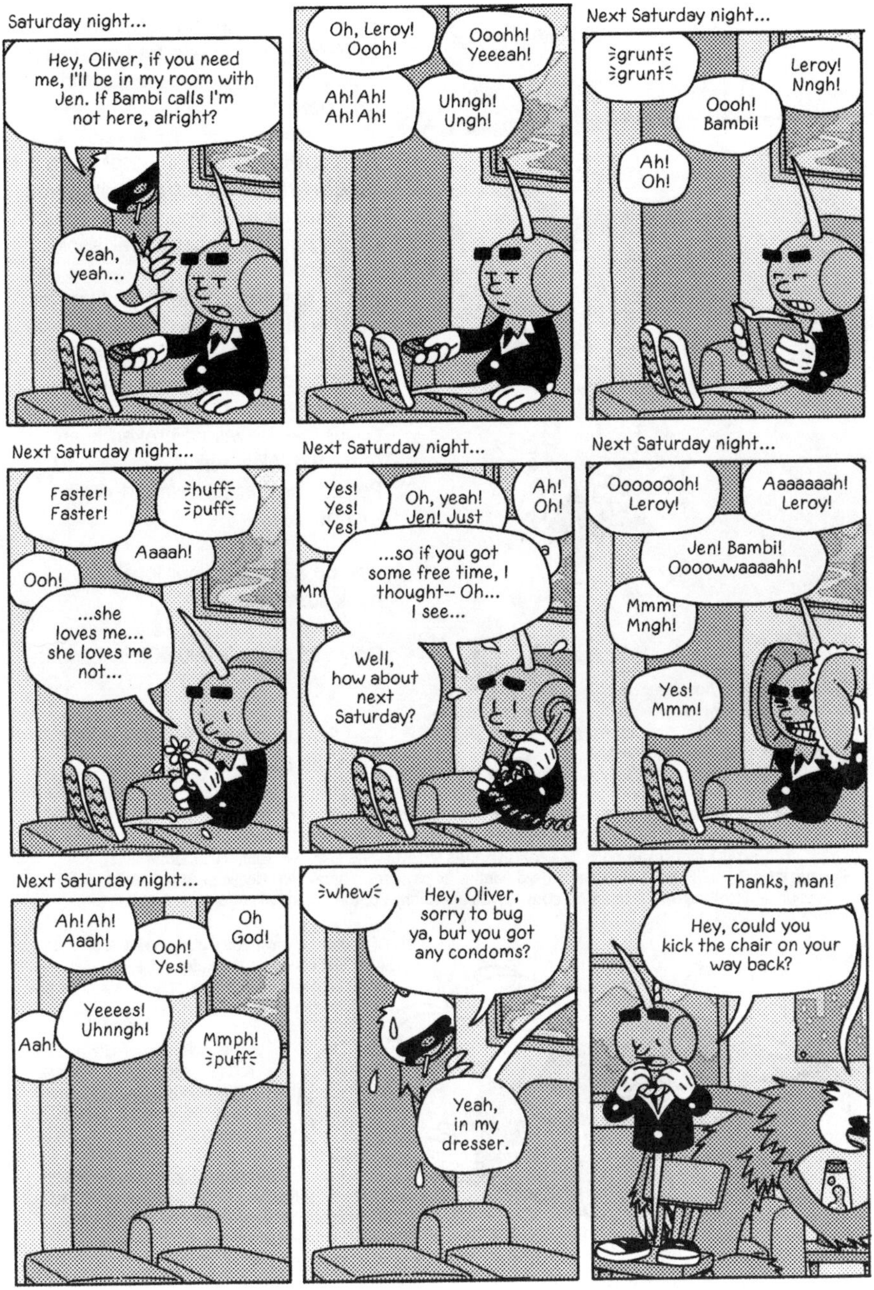
Saturday night...
Hey, Oliver, if you need me, I'll be in my room with Jen. If Bambi calls I'm not here, alright?
Yeah, yeah...
Oh, Leroy! Oooh!
Ooohh! Yeeeah!
Ah! Ah! Ah! Ah!
Uhngh! Ungh!
Next Saturday night...
grunt grunt
Leroy! Nngh!
Oooh! Bambi!
Ah! Oh!
Next Saturday night...
Faster! Faster!
huff puff
Aaaah!
Ooh!
...she loves me... she loves me not...
Next Saturday night...
Yes! Yes! Yes!
Oh, yeah! Jen! Just
Ah! Oh!
...so if you got some free time, I thought-- Oh... I see...
Well, how about next Saturday?
Next Saturday night...
Ooooooh! Leroy!
Aaaaaaah! Leroy!
Jen! Bambi! Oooowwaaaahh!
Mmm! Mngh!
Yes! Mmm!
Next Saturday night...
Ah! Ah! Aaah!
Ooh! Yes!
Oh God!
Yeeees! Uhnngh!
Aah!
Mmph! puff
whew
Hey, Oliver, sorry to bug ya, but you got any condoms?
Yeah, in my dresser.
Thanks, man!
Hey, could you kick the chair on your way back?

advertisement

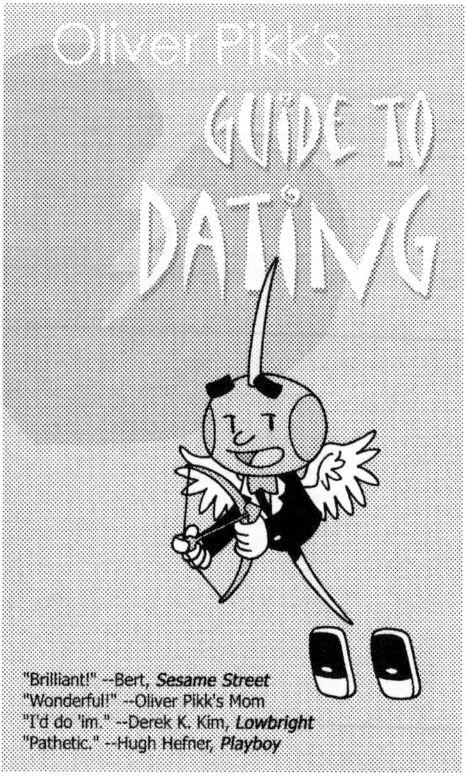
Oliver Pikk's
GUIDE TO DATING
"Brilliant!" --Bert, *Sesame Street*
"Wonderful!" --Oliver Pikk's Mom
"I'd do 'im." --Derek K. Kim, *Lowbright*
"Pathetic." --Hugh Hefner, *Playboy*

From the best-selling author of ***Self-loathing Made Easy*** comes a brand new book on romance and rejection!

Bottomline Press, in association with ***Lowbright Production,*** brings you the solution to all your dating troubles in one handsome hardcover book.

Full of tips and pointers, you'll never need another resource for your love life! That's right, with 22 exhausting chapters covering everything from genital hygiene to restraining orders, Oliver Pikk leaves no broken heart unturned. Also makes a great gift! Perfect for that 32-year old virgin friend!

Pick up a copy at your local book store today!

Only $25.95! ($1,000,000 in Canada)

See following page for an excerpt from the book!

You can also order online at **lowbright.com**. All major credit cards accepted. You must be 18 years or older to order. If you are female and attractive, please send a nude photo(s) of yourself to **oliverpikk@hotmail.com** for verification. As for everyone else, we believe you, order away. **Special offer!** The author also accepts used panties as payment if approved. Please send a nude photo(s) of yourself to **oliverpikk@hotmail.com**. If you are approved, the author will notify you immediately.

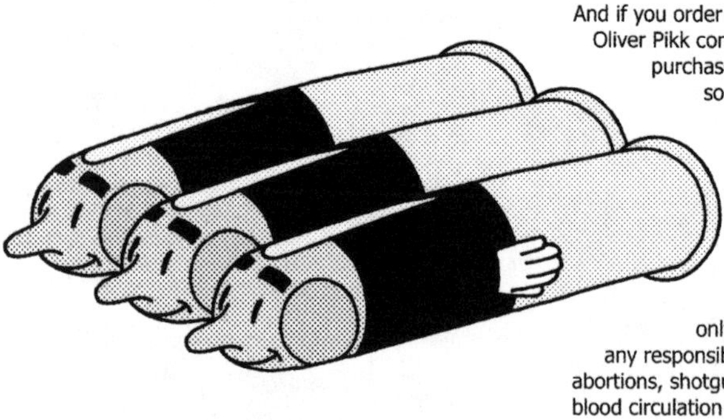

And if you order now, you'll also receive a pack of Oliver Pikk condoms absolutely free with each purchase! This offer is only for a limited time, so order today!

Leave them scattered around your room to show all your buddies that you are "getting some"! Particularly useful if you're ***not*** "getting some".

Warning: For display purposes only! The manufacturer does not accept any responsibility for unwanted pregnancies, abortions, shotgun weddings, or the loss of penile blood circulation in the use of this product.

advertisement

PROBLEM   SOLUTION

Can't decide on a gift for that special someone?

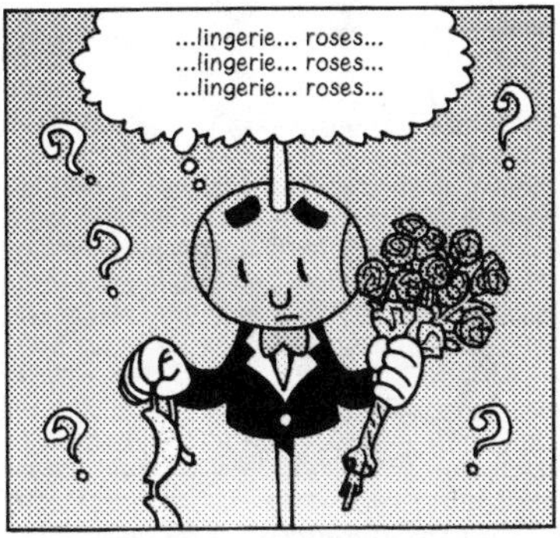
...lingerie... roses...
...lingerie... roses...
...lingerie... roses...

Get yourself porn instead!

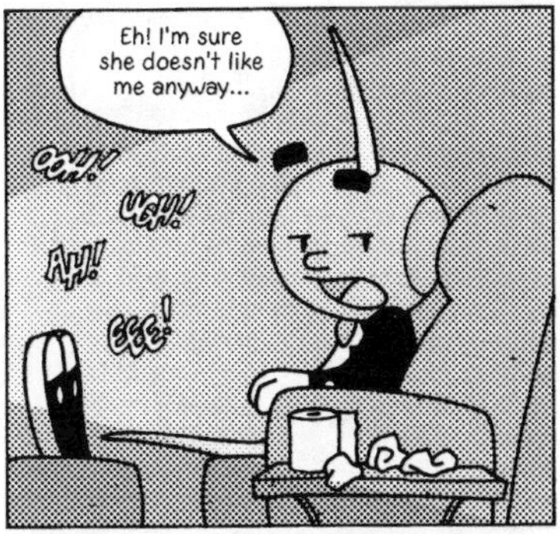
Eh! I'm sure she doesn't like me anyway...
OOH!
UGH!
AH!
EEE!

Having problems courting a stranger?

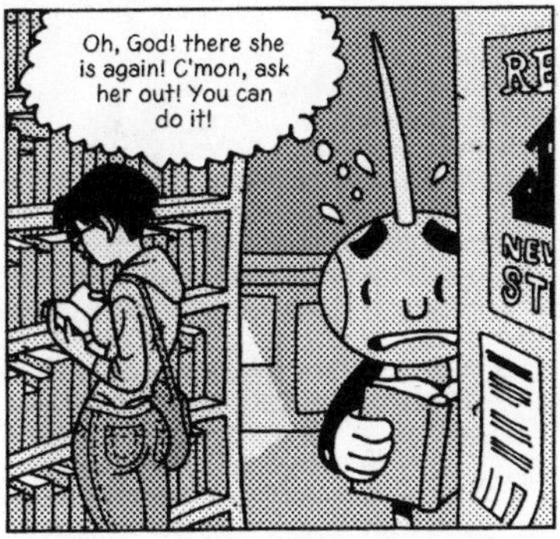
Oh, God! there she is again! C'mon, ask her out! You can do it!

Stalk her!

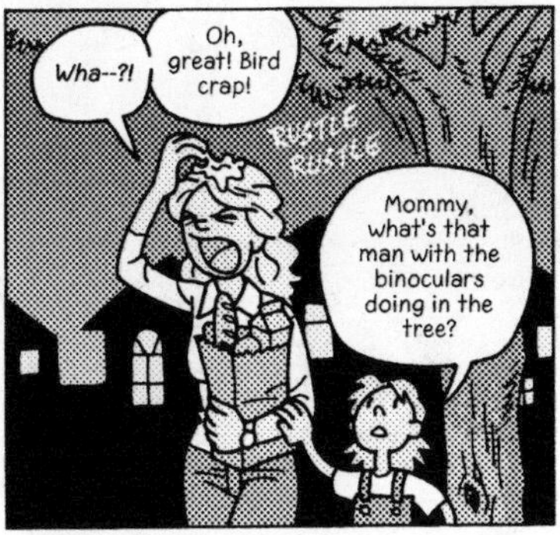
Wha--?!
Oh, great! Bird crap!
RUSTLE RUSTLE
Mommy, what's that man with the binoculars doing in the tree?

In love with someone who could care less?

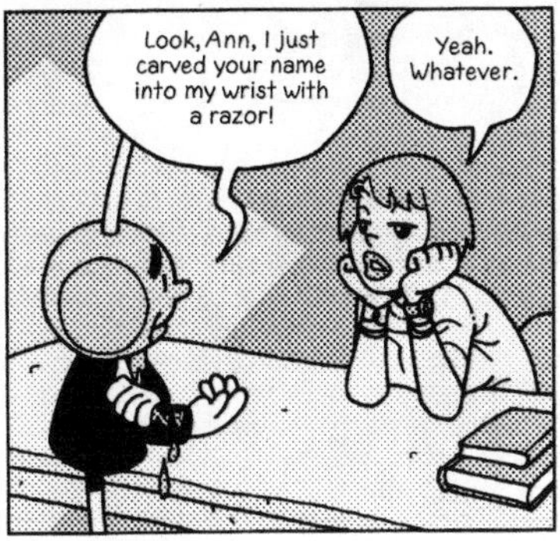
Look, Ann, I just carved your name into my wrist with a razor!
Yeah. Whatever.

Kill yourself!

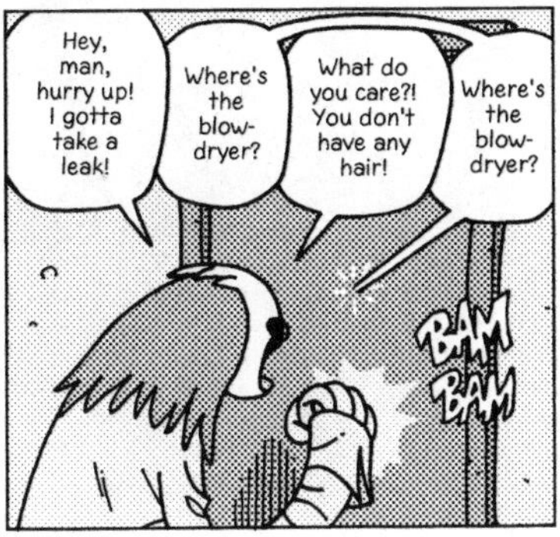
Hey, man, hurry up! I gotta take a leak!
Where's the blow-dryer?
What do you care?! You don't have any hair!
Where's the blow-dryer?
BAM
BAM

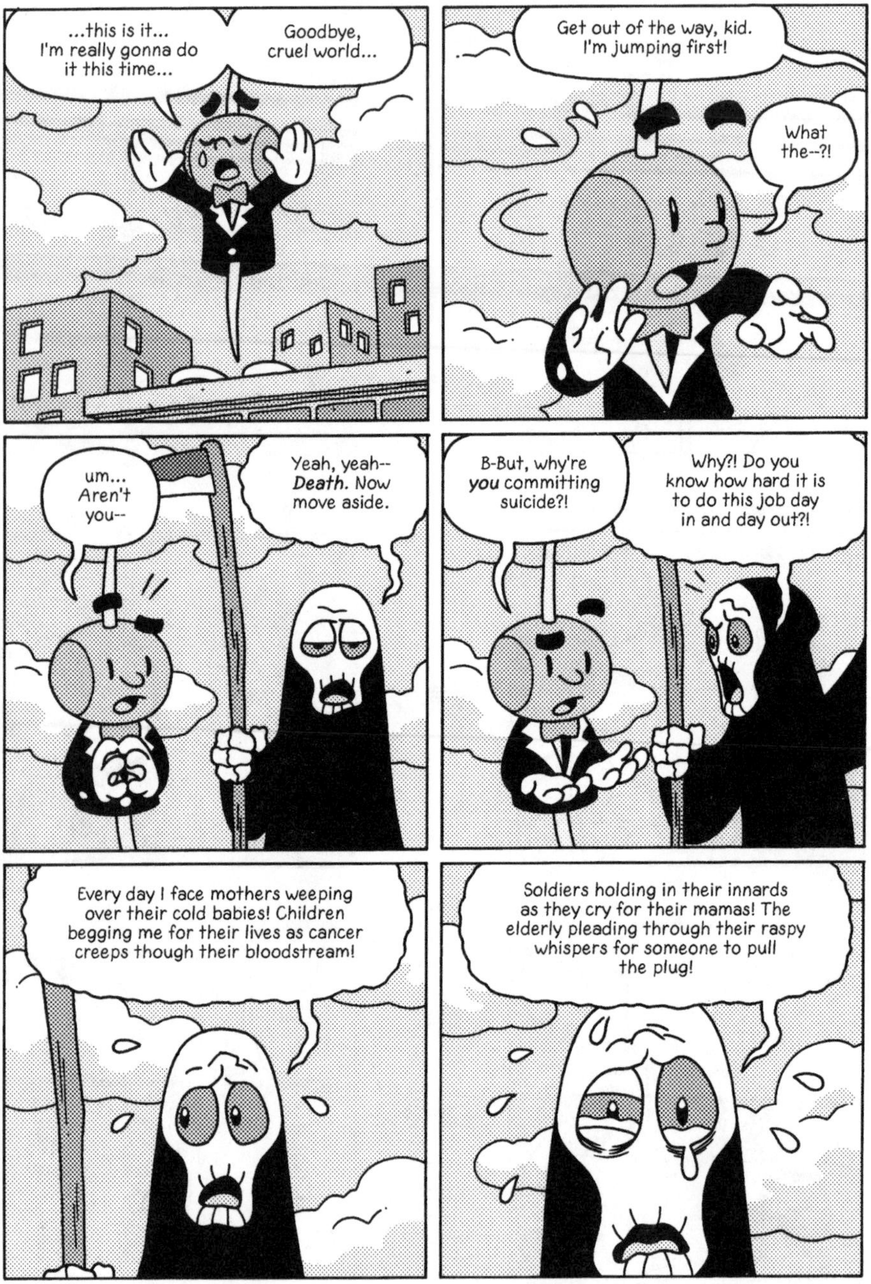

...this is it...
I'm really gonna do
it this time...
Goodbye,
cruel world...
Get out of the way, kid.
I'm jumping first!
What
the--?!
um...
Aren't
you--
Yeah, yeah--
Death. Now
move aside.
B-But, why're
you committing
suicide?!
Why?! Do you
know how hard it is
to do this job day
in and day out?!
Every day I face mothers weeping
over their cold babies! Children
begging me for their lives as cancer
creeps though their bloodstream!
Soldiers holding in their innards
as they cry for their mamas! The
elderly pleading through their raspy
whispers for someone to pull
the plug!

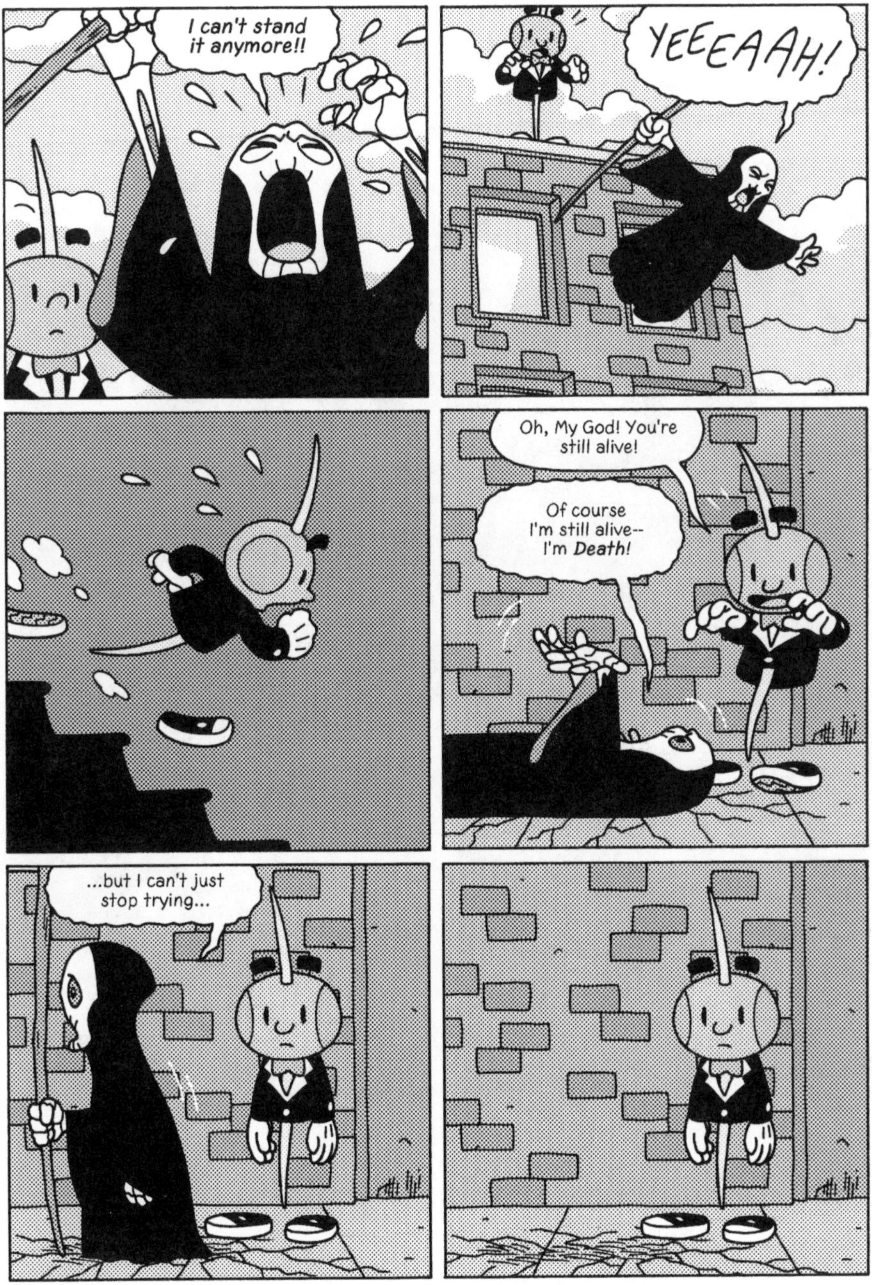
I can't stand it anymore!!
YEEEAAAH!
Oh, My God! You're still alive!
Of course I'm still alive-- I'm *Death!*
...but I can't just stop trying...

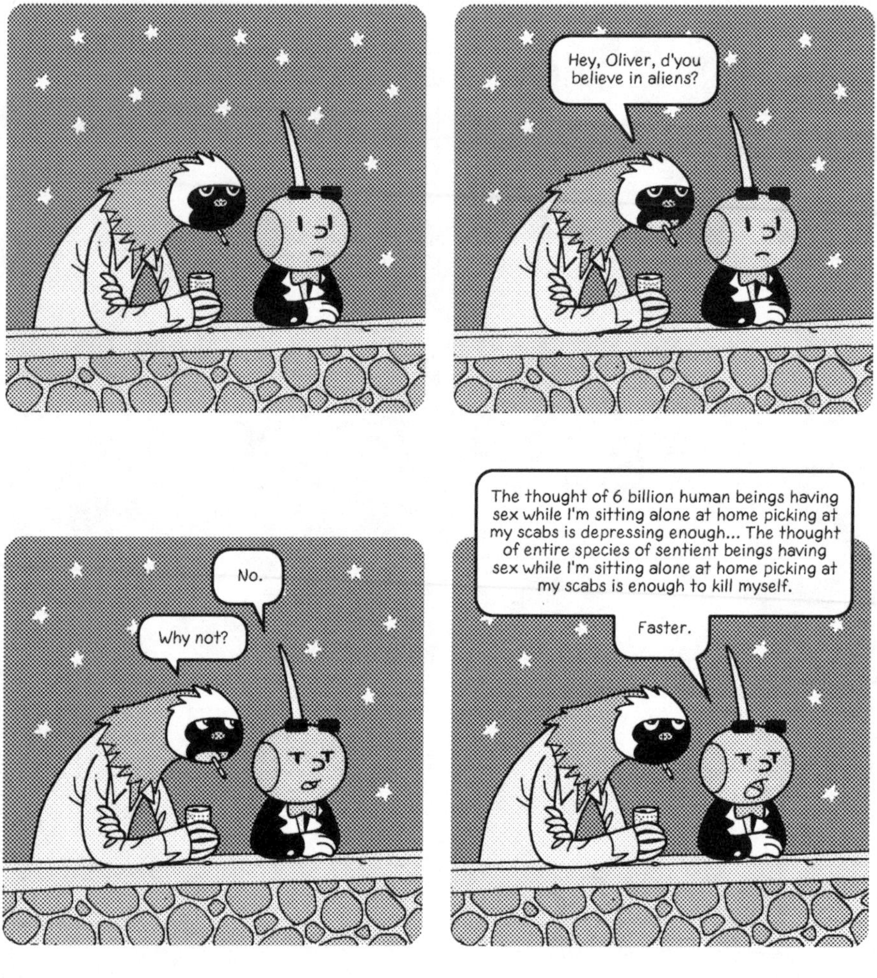

Hey, Oliver, d'you believe in aliens?
No.
Why not?
The thought of 6 billion human beings having sex while I'm sitting alone at home picking at my scabs is depressing enough... The thought of entire species of sentient beings having sex while I'm sitting alone at home picking at my scabs is enough to kill myself.
Faster.

Autobio
Stories

Valentine's Day

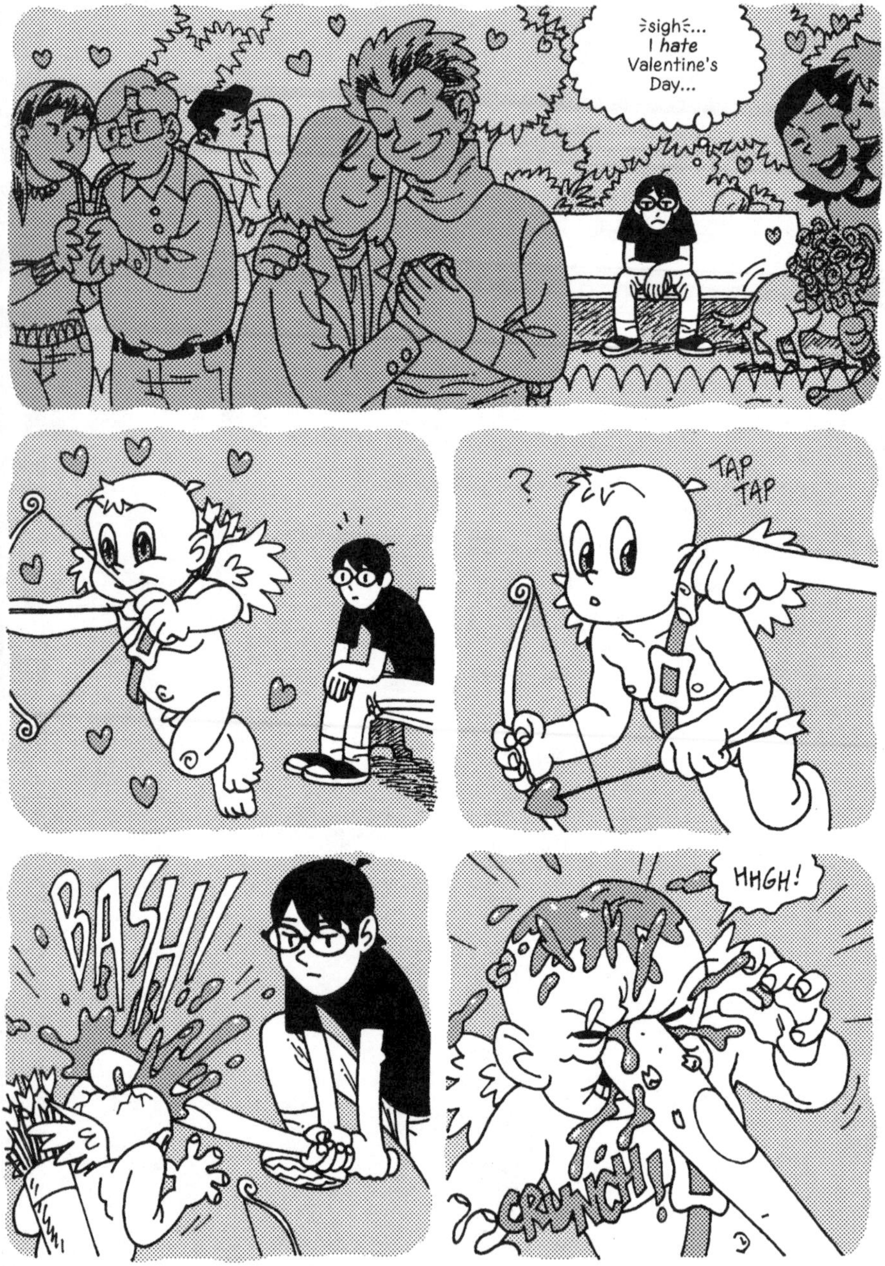

≡sigh≡...
I *hate*
Valentine's
Day...
TAP
TAP
BASH!
HHGH!
CRUNCH!

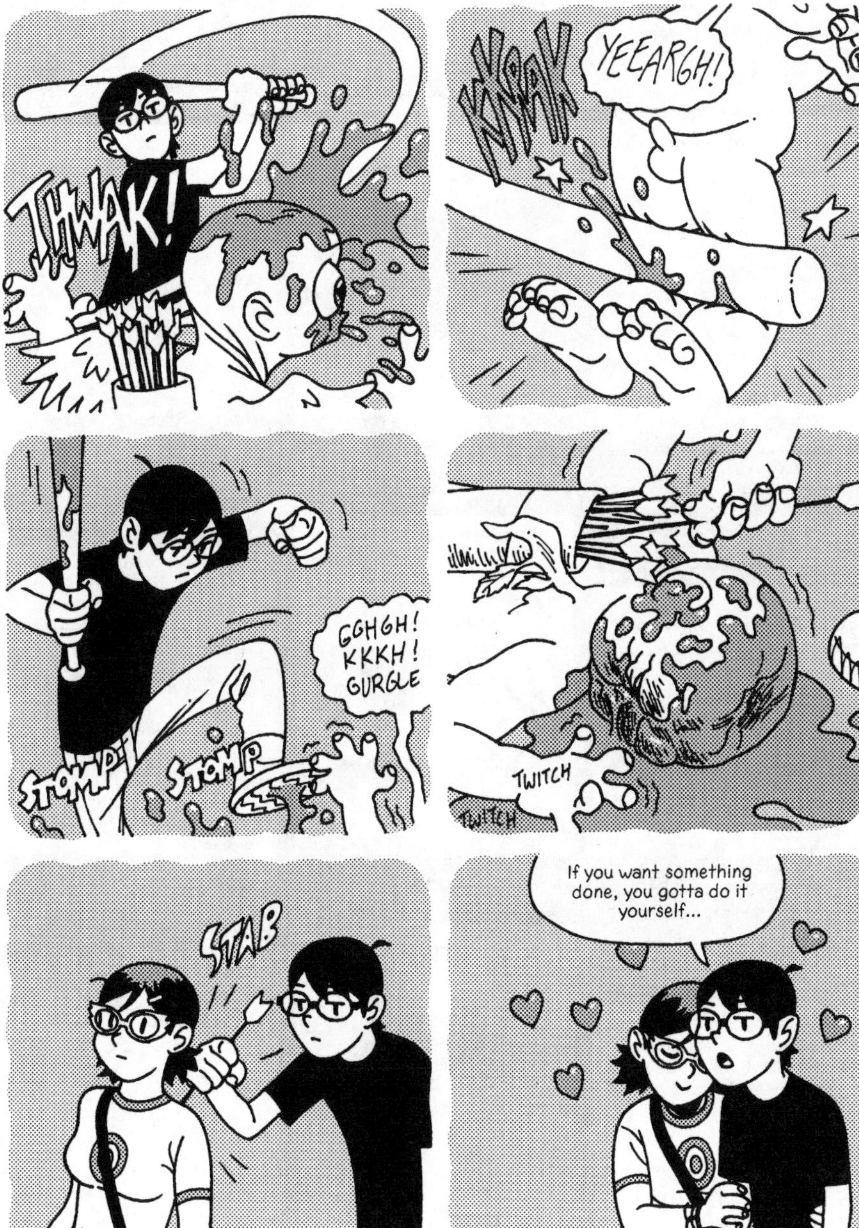
THWAK!
YEEARGH!
GGHGH! KKKH! GURGLE
STOMP
STOMP
TWITCH
TWITCH
STAB
If you want something done, you gotta do it yourself...

My Sistine Chapel

Being "the artist" in my class wasn't always peaches and cream. Sure, I always got the flattering line, "remember me when you're famous", in my yearbook...

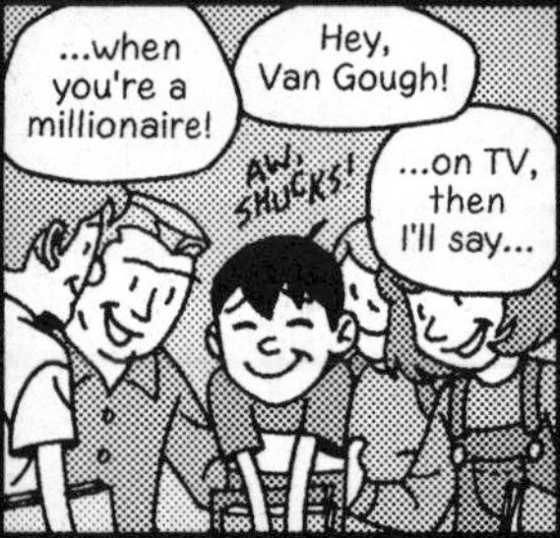
...when you're a millionaire!
Hey, Van Gough!
AW, SHUCKS!
...on TV, then I'll say...

...but at the same time, I was forced into drawing Garfield or Woody Woodpecker into a hundred other yearbooks.

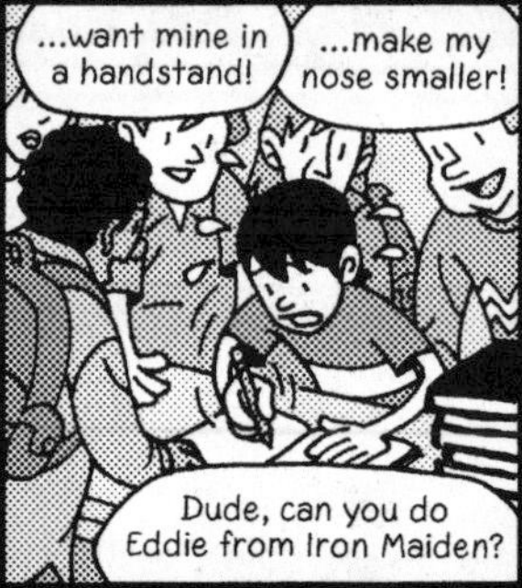
...want mine in a handstand!
...make my nose smaller!
Dude, can you do Eddie from Iron Maiden?

I was heinously exploited in 8th grade... One day, my English teacher assigned each student to write and draw his or her very own children's book.

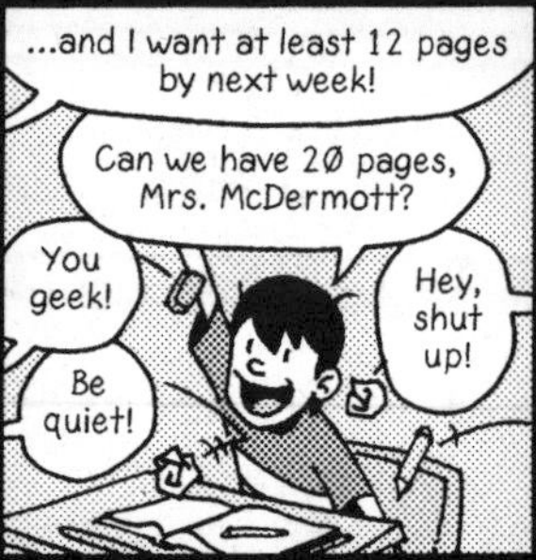
...and I want at least 12 pages by next week!
Can we have 2Ø pages, Mrs. McDermott?
You geek!
Hey, shut up!
Be quiet!

After class, Kathy Witherland, one of the prettiest and most popular girls in school, asked to speak with me-- someone whom she had never even looked in the direction of.

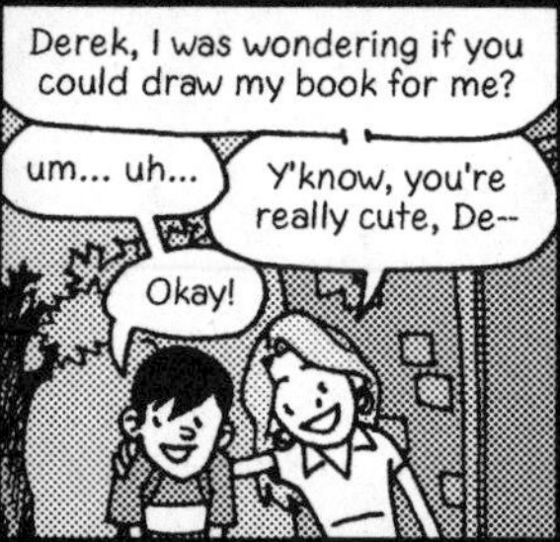
Derek, I was wondering if you could draw my book for me?
um... uh...
Y'know, you're really cute, De--
Okay!

Needless to say, my overactive imagination got the best of me.

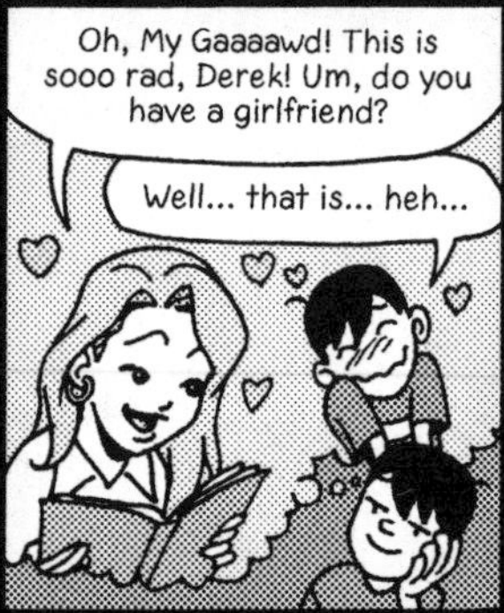
Oh, My Gaaaawd! This is sooo rad, Derek! Um, do you have a girlfriend?
Well... that is... heh...

On the night before it was due, I stayed up all night feverishly painting what I thought was going to be my *Sistine Chapel.*

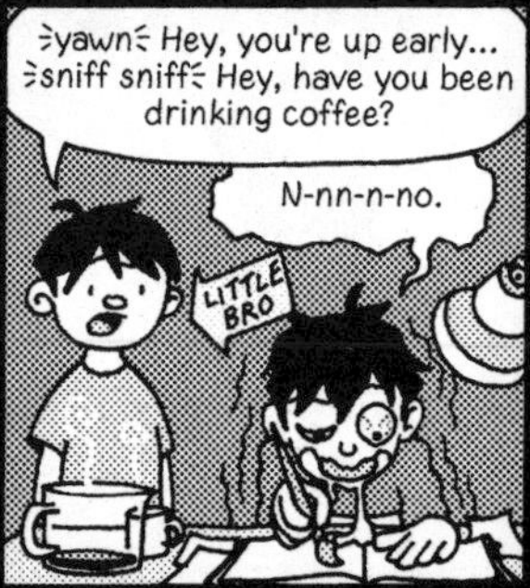
≈yawn≈ Hey, you're up early... ≈sniff sniff≈ Hey, have you been drinking coffee?
N-nn-n-no.
LITTLE BRO

The prospect of looking through the book together in my room later that day filled me with nervous excitement! When she finally arrived...

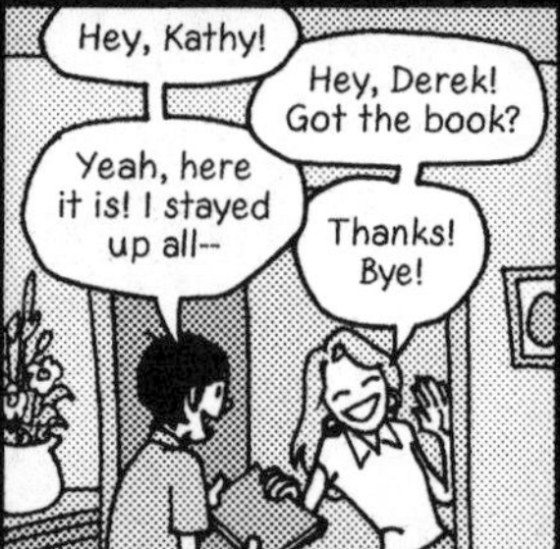
Hey, Kathy!
Hey, Derek! Got the book?
Yeah, here it is! I stayed up all--
Thanks! Bye!

She never spoke to me again.

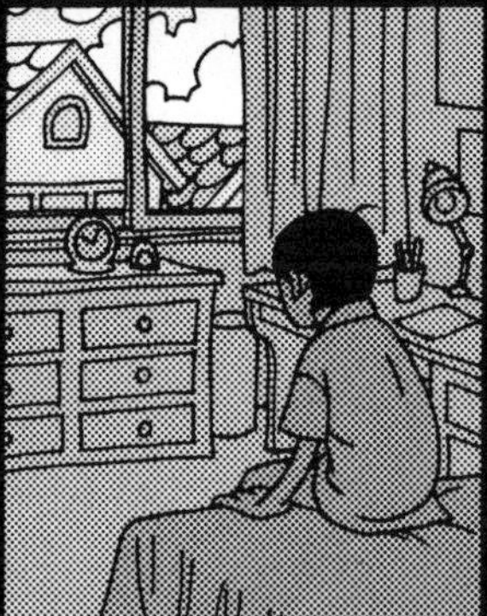

...until the end of the school year. She asked me to draw Garfield in her yearbook. I still chuckle every once in a while wondering how she liked her "Garfield".

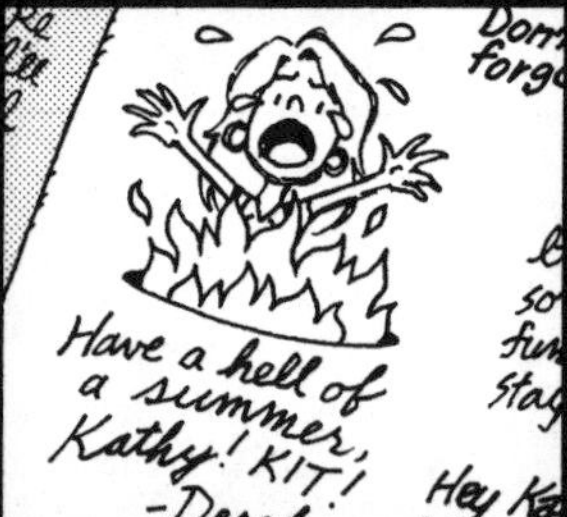
Have a hell of a summer, Kathy! KIT! -Derek

THE SHAFT

(Sorry about this, folks, but I've gotta get this off my chest!)

Ever since I moved to Korea two months ago, I've been plagued with the worst fucking luck!

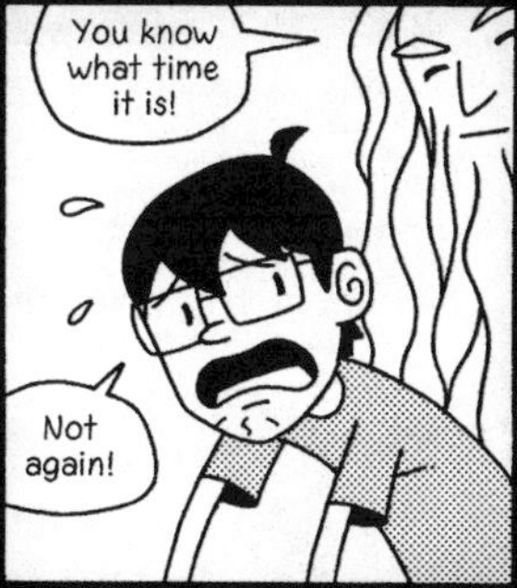
You know what time it is!
Not again!

Well, at least I can take dumps really easily now, thanks to all the splintered shafting I've been getting lately.

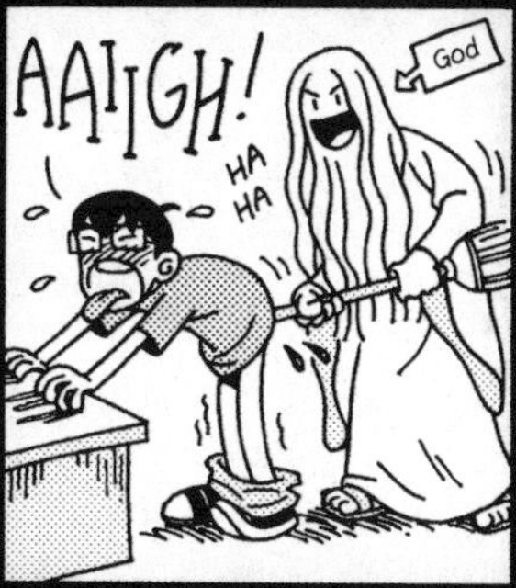
AAIIGH!
HA HA
God

First off, my brother, Brent, and I have been constantly getting into petty fights, putting our friendship on very thin ice numerous times.

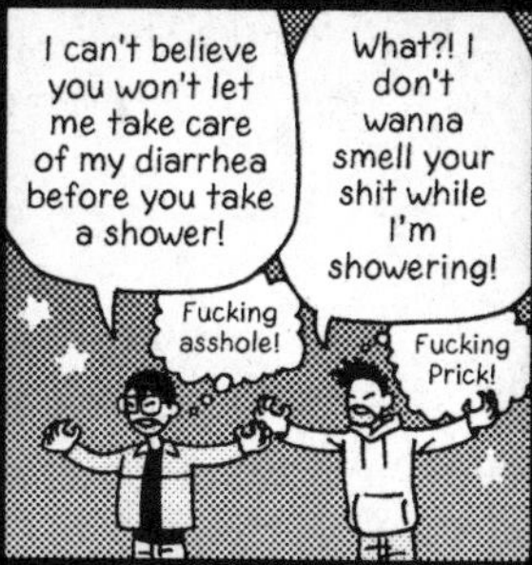
I can't believe you won't let me take care of my diarrhea before you take a shower!
What?! I don't wanna smell your shit while I'm showering!
Fucking asshole!
Fucking Prick!

Then for whatever reason, Brent's computer, which was working fine before I got here, decided it didn't like me and refused to work.

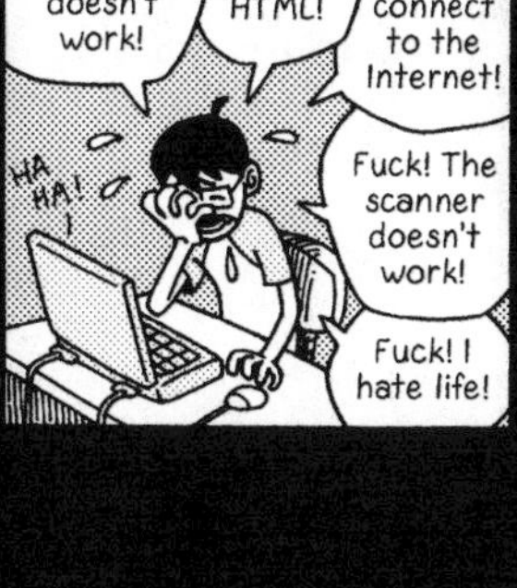
Fuck! The mouse doesn't work!
Fuck! No HTML!
Fuck! It won't connect to the Internet!
Fuck! The scanner doesn't work!
Fuck! I hate life!
HA HA!

This is really awful because I rely on the computer to pay my bills. Currently, I'm having this reoccurring wet dream...

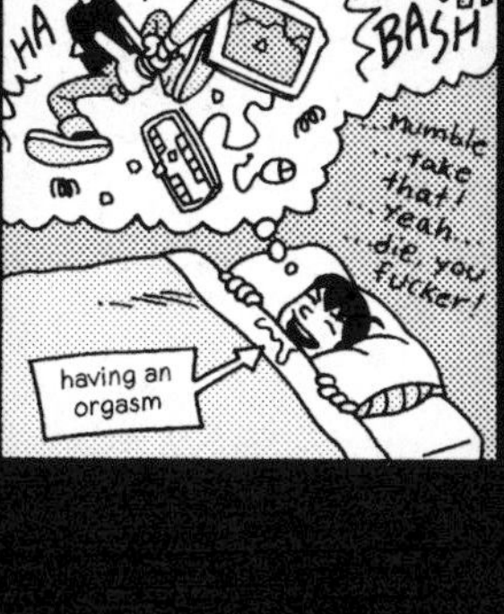
HA HA
HA
SMASH
BASH
...Mumble ...take that! Yeah.. die, you fucker!
having an orgasm

Speaking of jobs, though, one of my cash cows--this newspaper I used to draw for--dropped me like a hot potato once they found out I was moving to Korea.

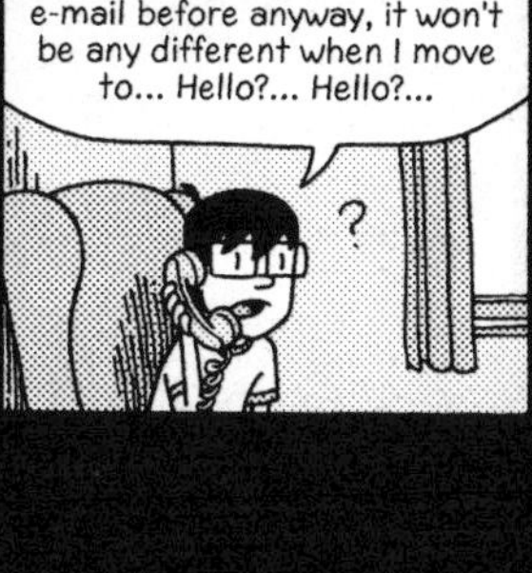
...Yeah, so since I did all my work for you guys through e-mail before anyway, it won't be any different when I move to... Hello?... Hello?...
?

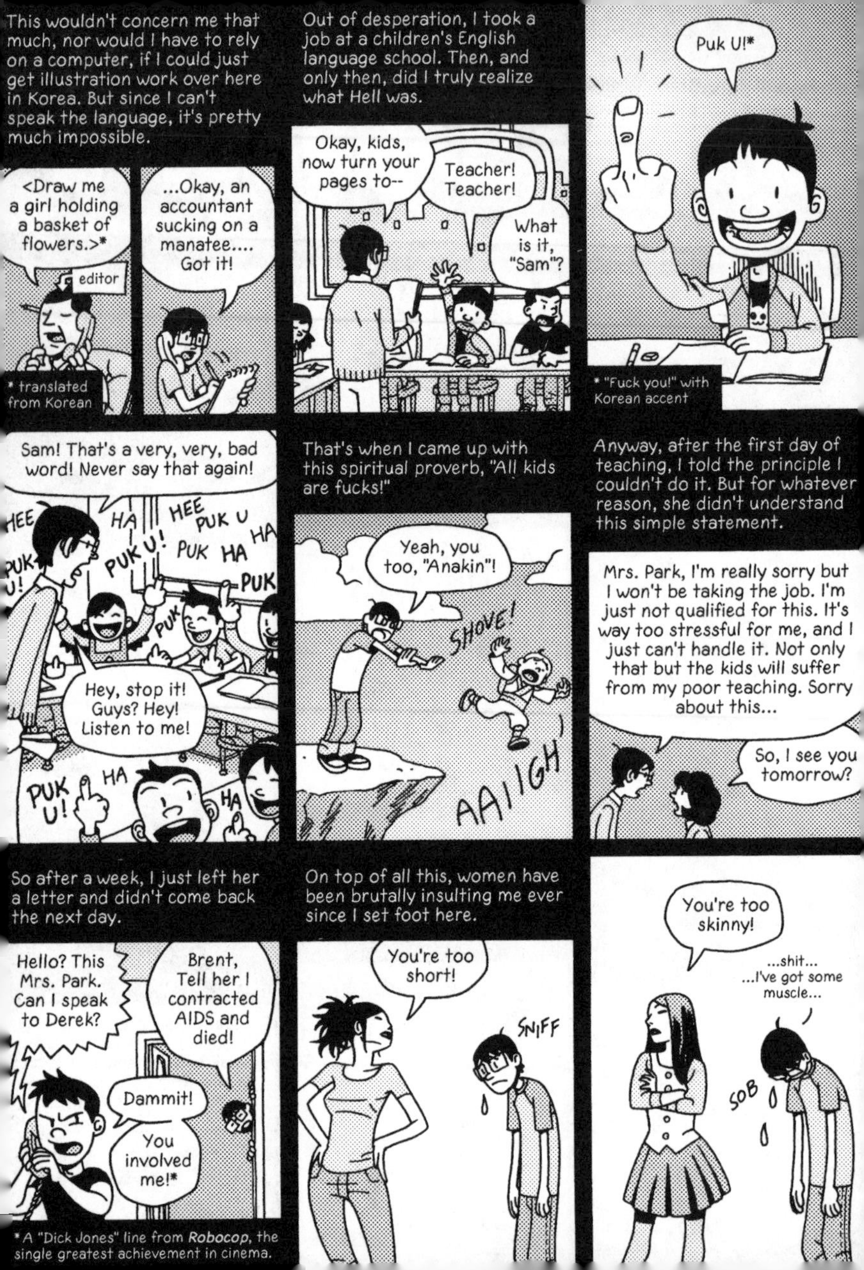
This wouldn't concern me that much, nor would I have to rely on a computer, if I could just get illustration work over here in Korea. But since I can't speak the language, it's pretty much impossible.
<Draw me a girl holding a basket of flowers.>*
editor
* translated from Korean
...Okay, an accountant sucking on a manatee.... Got it!
Out of desperation, I took a job at a children's English language school. Then, and only then, did I truly realize what Hell was.
Okay, kids, now turn your pages to--
Teacher! Teacher!
What is it, "Sam"?
Puk U!*
* "Fuck you!" with Korean accent
Sam! That's a very, very, bad word! Never say that again!
HEE HA HEE PUK U HA PUK U! PUK U! PUK HA PUK PUK
Hey, stop it! Guys? Hey! Listen to me!
PUK U! HA HA
That's when I came up with this spiritual proverb, "All kids are fucks!"
Yeah, you too, "Anakin"!
SHOVE!
AAIIGH
Anyway, after the first day of teaching, I told the principle I couldn't do it. But for whatever reason, she didn't understand this simple statement.
Mrs. Park, I'm really sorry but I won't be taking the job. I'm just not qualified for this. It's way too stressful for me, and I just can't handle it. Not only that but the kids will suffer from my poor teaching. Sorry about this...
So, I see you tomorrow?
So after a week, I just left her a letter and didn't come back the next day.
Hello? This Mrs. Park. Can I speak to Derek?
Brent, Tell her I contracted AIDS and died!
Dammit!
You involved me!*
*A "Dick Jones" line from Robocop, the single greatest achievement in cinema.
On top of all this, women have been brutally insulting me ever since I set foot here.
You're too short!
SNIFF
You're too skinny!
...shit... ...I've got some muscle...
SOB

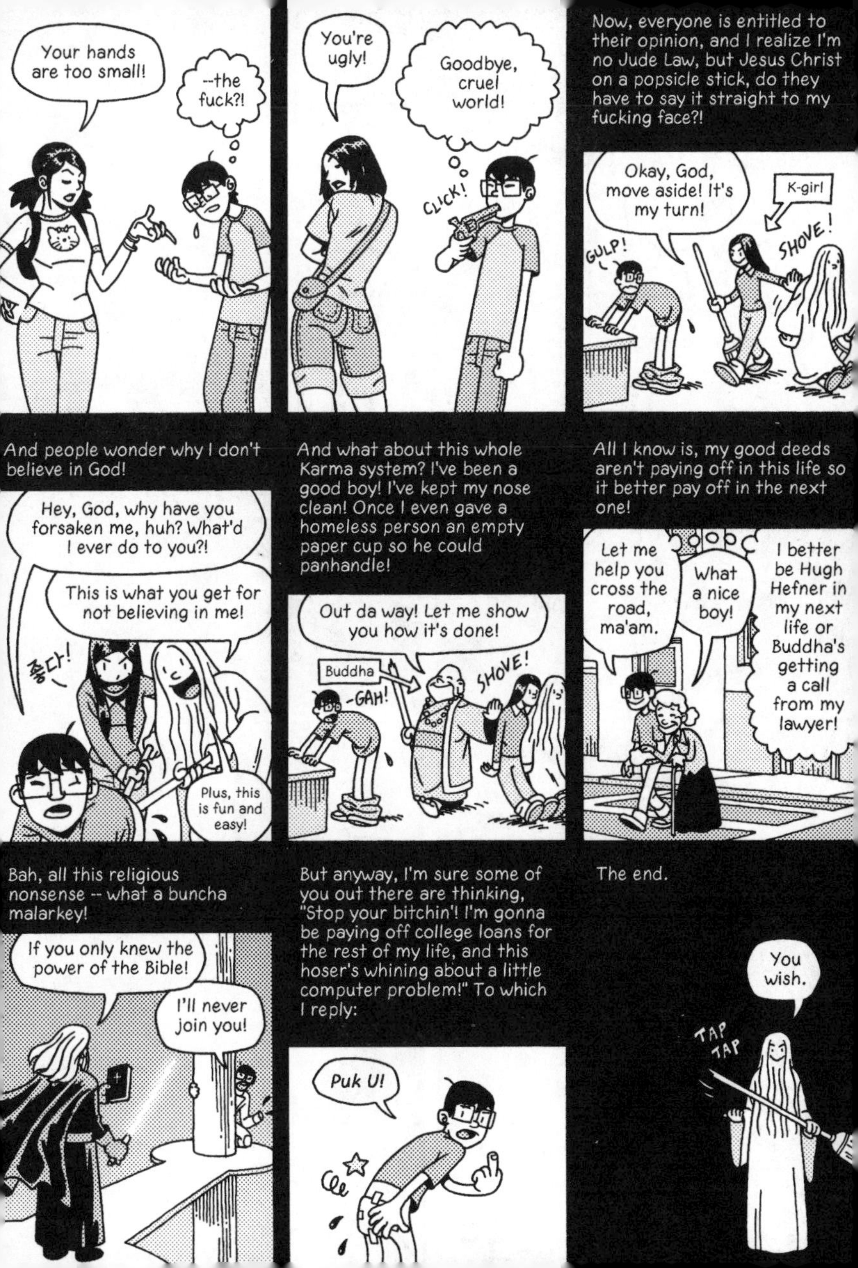
Your hands are too small!
--the fuck?!
You're ugly!
Goodbye, cruel world!
CLICK!
Now, everyone is entitled to their opinion, and I realize I'm no Jude Law, but Jesus Christ on a popsicle stick, do they have to say it straight to my fucking face?!
Okay, God, move aside! It's my turn!
K-girl
GULP!
SHOVE!
And people wonder why I don't believe in God!
Hey, God, why have you forsaken me, huh? What'd I ever do to you?!
This is what you get for not believing in me!
좋다!
Plus, this is fun and easy!
And what about this whole Karma system? I've been a good boy! I've kept my nose clean! Once I even gave a homeless person an empty paper cup so he could panhandle!
Out da way! Let me show you how it's done!
Buddha
-GAH!
SHOVE!
All I know is, my good deeds aren't paying off in this life so it better pay off in the next one!
Let me help you cross the road, ma'am.
What a nice boy!
I better be Hugh Hefner in my next life or Buddha's getting a call from my lawyer!
Bah, all this religious nonsense -- what a buncha malarkey!
If you only knew the power of the Bible!
I'll never join you!
But anyway, I'm sure some of you out there are thinking, "Stop your bitchin'! I'm gonna be paying off college loans for the rest of my life, and this hoser's whining about a little computer problem!" To which I reply:
Puk U!
The end.
You wish.
TAP TAP

Ungrateful Appreciation

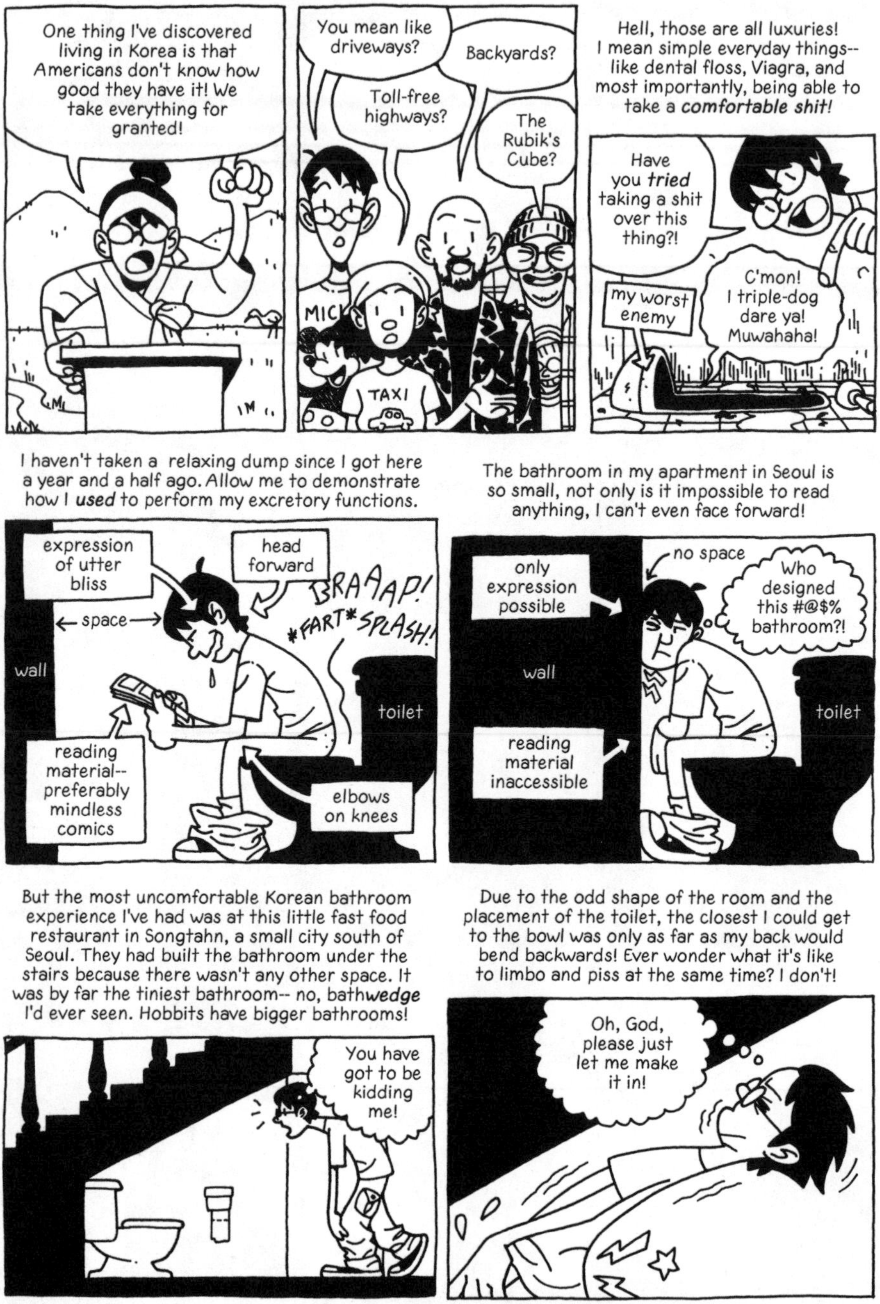

One thing I've discovered living in Korea is that Americans don't know how good they have it! We take everything for granted!
You mean like driveways?
Backyards?
Toll-free highways?
The Rubik's Cube?
TAXI
Hell, those are all luxuries! I mean simple everyday things-- like dental floss, Viagra, and most importantly, being able to take a ***comfortable shit!***
Have you *tried* taking a shit over this thing?!
my worst enemy
C'mon! I triple-dog dare ya! Muwahaha!
I haven't taken a relaxing dump since I got here a year and a half ago. Allow me to demonstrate how I *used* to perform my excretory functions.
expression of utter bliss
head forward
space
BRAAAP!
FART
SPLASH!
wall
toilet
reading material-- preferably mindless comics
elbows on knees
The bathroom in my apartment in Seoul is so small, not only is it impossible to read anything, I can't even face forward!
no space
only expression possible
Who designed this #@$% bathroom?!
wall
toilet
reading material inaccessible
But the most uncomfortable Korean bathroom experience I've had was at this little fast food restaurant in Songtahn, a small city south of Seoul. They had built the bathroom under the stairs because there wasn't any other space. It was by far the tiniest bathroom-- no, bath*wedge* I'd ever seen. Hobbits have bigger bathrooms!
You have got to be kidding me!
Due to the odd shape of the room and the placement of the toilet, the closest I could get to the bowl was only as far as my back would bend backwards! Ever wonder what it's like to limbo and piss at the same time? I don't!
Oh, God, please just let me make it in!

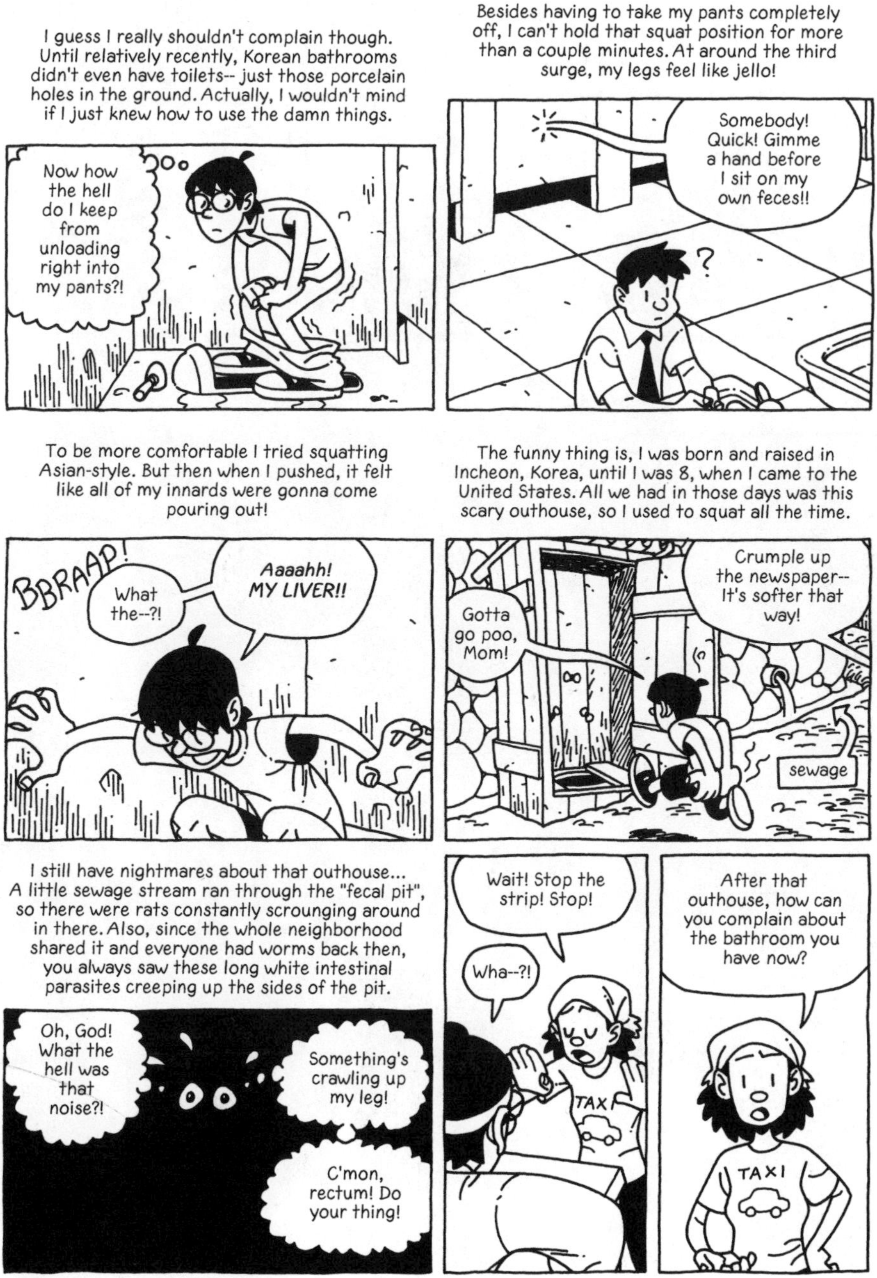
I guess I really shouldn't complain though. Until relatively recently, Korean bathrooms didn't even have toilets-- just those porcelain holes in the ground. Actually, I wouldn't mind if I just knew how to use the damn things.
Now how the hell do I keep from unloading right into my pants?!
Besides having to take my pants completely off, I can't hold that squat position for more than a couple minutes. At around the third surge, my legs feel like jello!
Somebody! Quick! Gimme a hand before I sit on my own feces!!
?
To be more comfortable I tried squatting Asian-style. But then when I pushed, it felt like all of my innards were gonna come pouring out!
BBRAAP!
What the--?!
Aaaahh! MY LIVER!!
The funny thing is, I was born and raised in Incheon, Korea, until I was 8, when I came to the United States. All we had in those days was this scary outhouse, so I used to squat all the time.
Gotta go poo, Mom!
Crumple up the newspaper-- It's softer that way!
sewage
I still have nightmares about that outhouse... A little sewage stream ran through the "fecal pit", so there were rats constantly scrounging around in there. Also, since the whole neighborhood shared it and everyone had worms back then, you always saw these long white intestinal parasites creeping up the sides of the pit.
Oh, God! What the hell was that noise?!
Something's crawling up my leg!
C'mon, rectum! Do your thing!
Wait! Stop the strip! Stop!
Wha--?!
TAXI
After that outhouse, how can you complain about the bathroom you have now?
TAXI

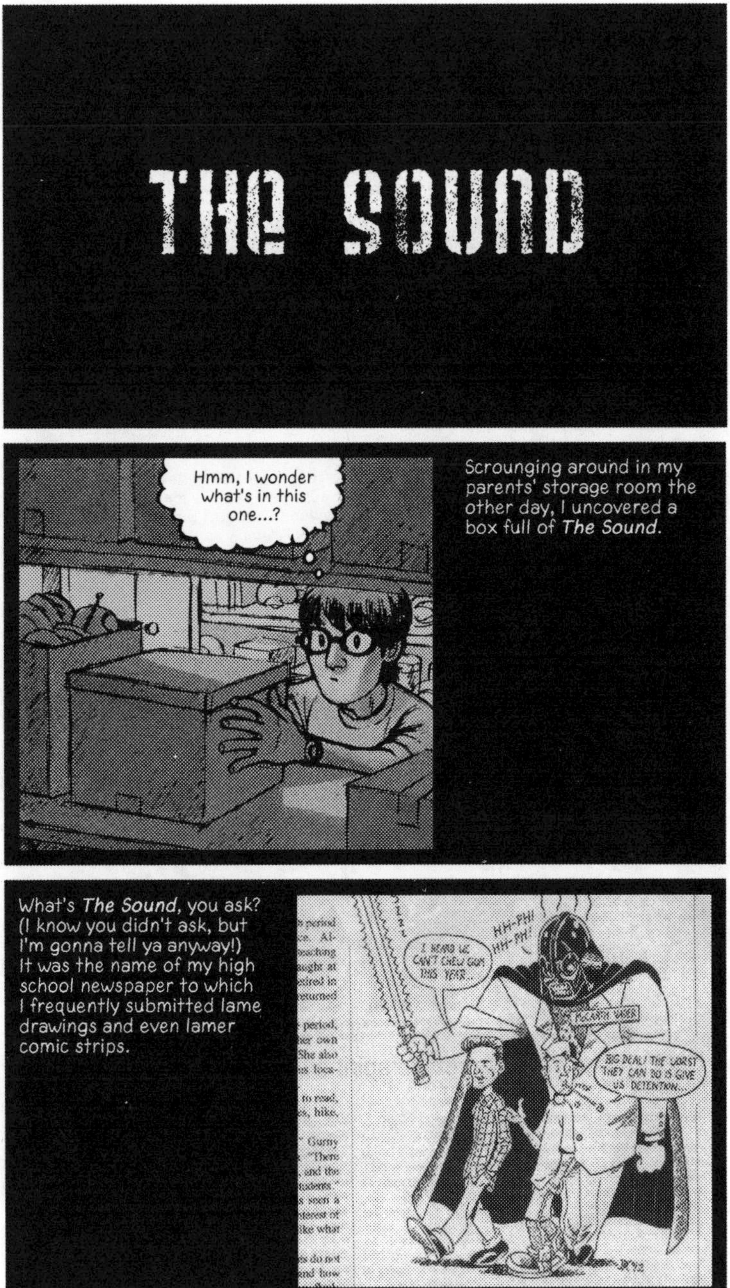
THE SOUND
Hmm, I wonder what's in this one...?
Scrounging around in my parents' storage room the other day, I uncovered a box full of *The Sound*.
What's *The Sound*, you ask? (I know you didn't ask, but I'm gonna tell ya anyway!) It was the name of my high school newspaper to which I frequently submitted lame drawings and even lamer comic strips.
I HEARD WE CAN'T CHEW GUM THIS YEAR...
HH-PH! HH-PH!
BIG DEAL! THE WORST THEY CAN DO IS GIVE US DETENTION...

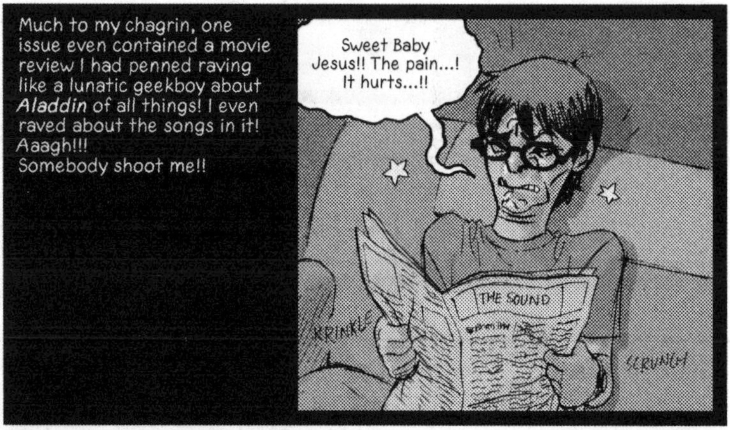
Much to my chagrin, one issue even contained a movie review I had penned raving like a lunatic geekboy about *Aladdin* of all things! I even raved about the songs in it! Aaagh!!! Somebody shoot me!!
Sweet Baby Jesus!! The pain...! It hurts...!!
THE SOUND
KRINKLE
CRUNCH

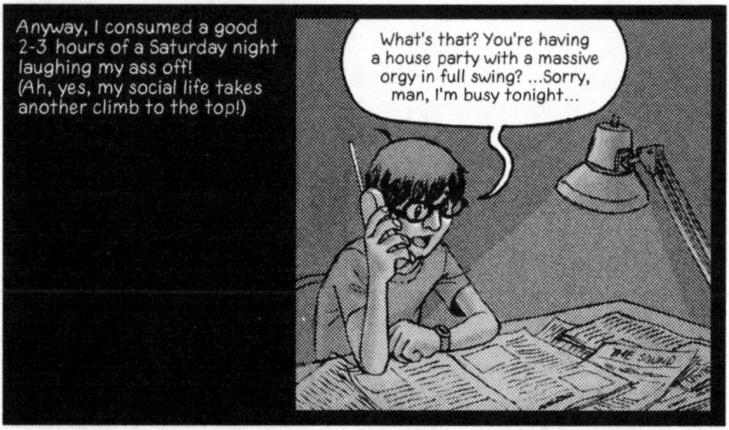
Anyway, I consumed a good 2-3 hours of a Saturday night laughing my ass off! (Ah, yes, my social life takes another climb to the top!)
What's that? You're having a house party with a massive orgy in full swing? ...Sorry, man, I'm busy tonight...
THE SOUND

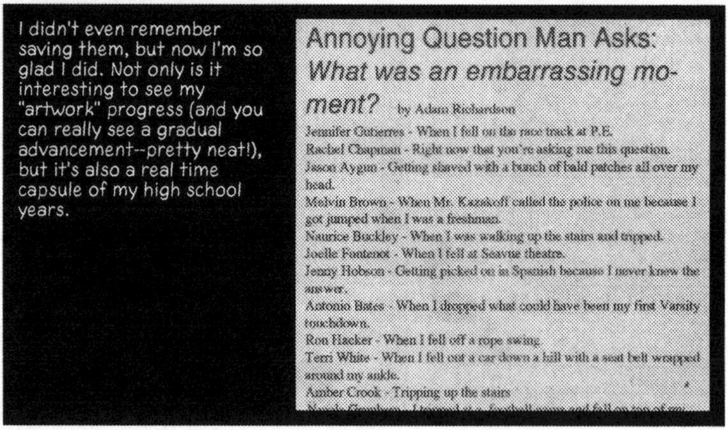
I didn't even remember saving them, but now I'm so glad I did. Not only is it interesting to see my "artwork" progress (and you can really see a gradual advancement--pretty neat!), but it's also a real time capsule of my high school years.

Annoying Question Man Asks:
What was an embarrassing moment? by Adam Richardson

Jennifer Gutierres - When I fell on the race track at P.E.
Rachel Chapman - Right now that you're asking me this question.
Jason Aygun - Getting shaved with a bunch of bald patches all over my head.
Melvin Brown - When Mr. Kazakoff called the police on me because I got jumped when I was a freshman.
Naurice Buckley - When I was walking up the stairs and tripped.
Joelle Fontenot - When I fell at Seavue theatre.
Jenny Hobson - Getting picked on in Spanish because I never knew the answer.
Antonio Bates - When I dropped what could have been my first Varsity touchdown.
Ron Hacker - When I fell off a rope swing.
Terri White - When I fell out a car down a hill with a seat belt wrapped around my ankle.
Amber Crook - Tripping up the stairs

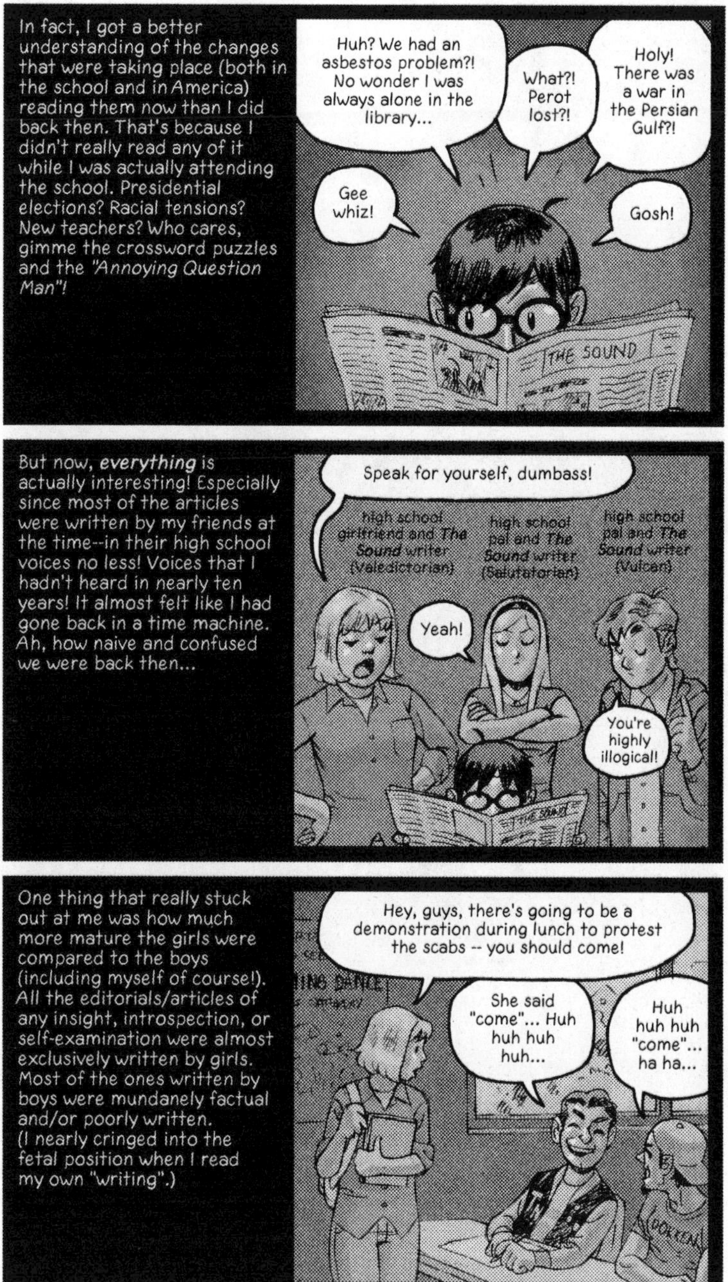
In fact, I got a better understanding of the changes that were taking place (both in the school and in America) reading them now than I did back then. That's because I didn't really read any of it while I was actually attending the school. Presidential elections? Racial tensions? New teachers? Who cares, gimme the crossword puzzles and the *"Annoying Question Man"*!
Huh? We had an asbestos problem?! No wonder I was always alone in the library...
What?! Perot lost?!
Holy! There was a war in the Persian Gulf?!
Gee whiz!
Gosh!
THE SOUND
But now, ***everything*** is actually interesting! Especially since most of the articles were written by my friends at the time--in their high school voices no less! Voices that I hadn't heard in nearly ten years! It almost felt like I had gone back in a time machine. Ah, how naive and confused we were back then...
Speak for yourself, dumbass!
high school girlfriend and *The Sound* writer (Valedictorian)
high school pal and *The Sound* writer (Salutatorian)
high school pal and *The Sound* writer (Vulcan)
Yeah!
You're highly illogical!
One thing that really stuck out at me was how much more mature the girls were compared to the boys (including myself of course!). All the editorials/articles of any insight, introspection, or self-examination were almost exclusively written by girls. Most of the ones written by boys were mundanely factual and/or poorly written. (I nearly cringed into the fetal position when I read my own "writing".)
Hey, guys, there's going to be a demonstration during lunch to protest the scabs -- you should come!
She said "come"... Huh huh huh huh...
Huh huh huh "come"... ha ha...
DOKKEN

Don't believe me? Go dig out your old high school newpapers and see for yourself. Anyway, this major imbalance in maturity between the genders is so glaringly obvious now, but it never even occurred to me back then. No wonder so many high school girls don't want to date their male counterparts. We're slobbering amoebas at that stage! (Ten years later we evolve into slobbering ***Neanderthals.***)

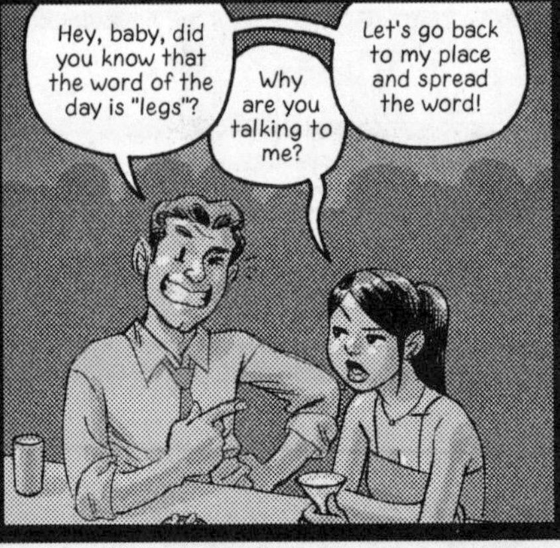
Hey, baby, did you know that the word of the day is "legs"?
Why are you talking to me?
Let's go back to my place and spread the word!

This particular article really moved me:

What I Really Got Out of High School
by Rebecca XXXXX

For my piece in the paper I was going to write about the budget cuts imposed on the school, however when I asked myself what I wanted to write about, budget cuts wasn't high up there. What came to mind was that I should write on what I really thought I got out of high school. Contrary to popular belief it wasn't really education, and it wasn't four uneventful years of hell. I believe it was an understanding of myself and other people. High school gave me an opportunity to find out what life was about and what the world would let me get away with.

I think now that I'm a senior I can safely look back and say I probably would have never again done some of the things I did (but I'm glad I did, I did them anyway). There were those years of experimentation which I think (hope) are mostly behind me. There were the parties where I had more than my fair share of what was available. There were the guys whose names I can't remember and the people whose faces I can not erase.

Throughout high school there were a lot of good and bad times, both taught me what it was like to be alive. How I made it through the bad times is a mystery to me. All I know is that friends, if they are true, will always have an open mind and a shoulder to cry on. God knows I've cried my ocean of tears and I know now that I've also been the cause for many of them. From that I learned that it's not fair of me to think I don't affect other people with my words or actions.

My teenage years are going to be the largest influence on the rest of my life because they are the stepping stones of my self discovery. I know things now about myself I never would have guessed at four years ago. I've teetered several times along the edge of sanity trying to discover who I was. What did I come up with? Something astounding, that even I, in my infinite wisdom, have faults, and limits, and do not always make the right decisions.

Out of my whole experience however, there will always be one thing that will stand out in my high school memories, and that one thing is what I hold more dear in all the world, friendship. There is nothing more wonderful in life than having others with whom you can make and share experiences. After all, what is life if you have no one to share it with. I know that I've put my friends though a lot, but we've always come out together and we've never really forgotten who we were, or why we were drawn toward each other. The only regret I will ever have is that I could never spend enough time with them, which is something that troubles me now that I know we may not always be together. I realize, though, that even if I were never to see them again, I'd still be content, because I know they loved me and I, at the least, will have them in memory throughout my life.

Why wasn't I ever this reflective and focused? (And if I was, why couldn't I express myself? Why couldn't I put it into words?) And why didn't I read this at the time? Most importantly, why didn't I get to know this person better?? While my nose was buried in Spider-Man's marital problems and Piers Anthony's horse-sex fetish, real life, real people were passing me by.

What a fool I was.

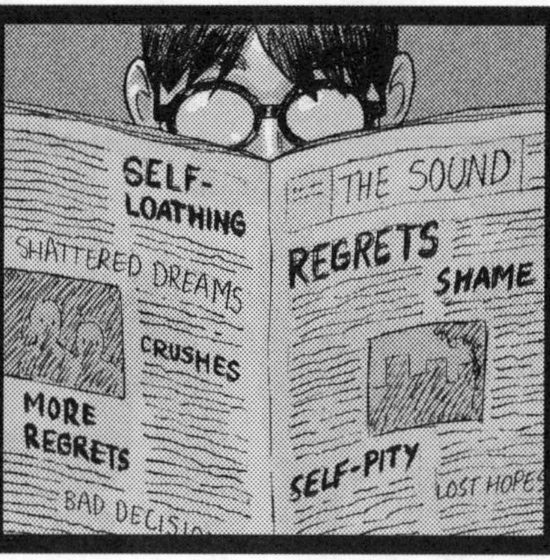
SELF-LOATHING
THE SOUND
REGRETS
SHAME
SHATTERED DREAMS
CRUSHES
MORE REGRETS
SELF-PITY
LOST HOPES

island

A couple of days ago, I went and saw *About A Boy* with Anne, one of my favorite friends from the traditonal Korean drumming group I'm a part of. As we headed to our cars after the film, we got into a discussion about one of the major themes of the story.

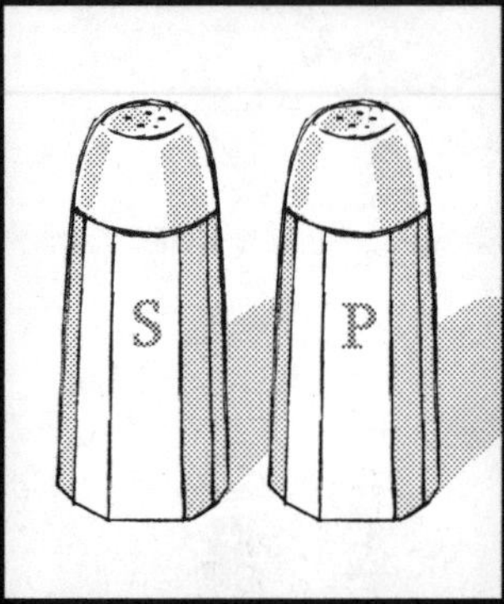
S
P

The movie was harping on about how "no man is an island". How life can be empty and meaningless without people to share it with. It served the story well. And Anne pretty much agreed with the sentiment, as I'm sure most people would.

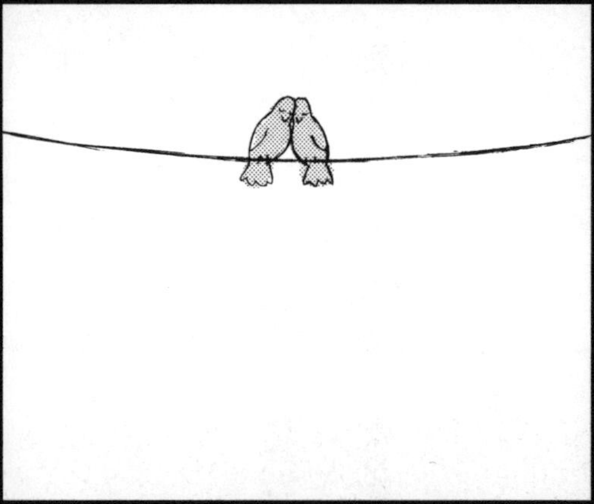

I'm nearly thirty now and I don't have a wife or kids, and have been girlfriendless for 99.9% of my life. Also, I've lived alone much of my adult life and wished to hell I *was* living alone whenever I had a housemate. Yet I have a full, textured life that I feel very satisfied with. And frankly, I *like* being by myself most of the time. What's so terrible about being alone? You don't have to worry about getting hurt or hurting someone else, and you can fart under the sheets without a thought.

Don't get me wrong, I'm very sociable and happy to "hang out" when the occasion arises, but so many of the things that I love to do most are activities that are best done alone. (Yeah, yeah, insert your masturbation joke here and get it over with!)

But sometimes I wonder. I wonder if I'm just fooling myself. Am I tricking myself into thinking this way to keep from becoming unhappy?

I don't know
...because I can't tell the difference.

NOTES

Most of the stories in this collection were originally serialized at my website, lowbright.com, from 2000-2003. I will continue to debut and serialize my stories there, hopefully for many years to come. Also, many of the stories in this book are actually in color on the website.

CHRONOLOGY

Much to my frustration, I've always been very careless about dating my work. Coupled with a memory bordering on Alzheimer's Disease, it's nearly impossible for me to recall the dates of when I wrote and drew the stories in this collection. But I do have a vague idea of the order in which I did them, and I will attempt to list it here.

Pulling - (1997-98) First short story I ever completed in comics form. Debuted in a xeroxed mini-comic called, *Small Stories: Boys,* published in February 1998.

Super Unleaded - (1997-98) Also debuted in *Small Stories: Boys.*

The Shaft - (2000, around April) I lived in South Korea from February 2000 to December 2001, just shy of two years. This was the first story to spill onto paper after a two-year writer's block. Moving to Korea triggered a new period of creativity for me.

Same Difference - (2000-2003) The actual pages didn't debut on the site until a few stories later, but the writing and drawing began shortly after *The Shaft.*

My Sistine Chapel - (2000, maybe 2001) From here it gets really fuzzy. I know this one was done fairly early on, but I can't remember between which stories.

Hurdles - (2000) First published in *Smart Mouth,* a WritersCorp publication of poetry and prose.

Oliver Pikk - (2000-02) Each strip was done sporadically between other stories. I may have started Oliver Pikk in 2001, and not 2000, I'm not sure.

Ungrateful Appreciation - (2001)

Interview With A Human - (September, 2001) I wrote and drew this one on the night after 9/11 in a fit of anger, frustration, and sadness.

Emo Rock Hyung - (late 2001) A guest strip for dieselsweeties.com.

Valentine's Day - (February, 2002)

The Sound - (May, 2002)

Island - (July, 2002)

GUSHING THANKS

Omma and Dad - whose unending love and support made the finishing of this book possible.

Helen Kim - for being the best friend and inspiration a person could ever ask for.

Gene Yang - for always making me want to be a better person.

Scott McCloud - who instills hope in me every day.

Joey Manley - whose generous heart rescued my little website.

Jeff Mason - for unending help and enthusiasm.

John Pham - whose computer expertise, and patience for the computer-retarded made the formatting of this book possible.

Fred Chung - for stepping in at the last minute to do the thankless, selfless chore of proofreading.

Brett Warnock and Chris Staros - for taking chance on this book, and just being two of the nicest publishers in comics.

Also special thanks, hugs, and apologies to: Brent Kirk, all my extended family on Omma's side (Thanks, Kev!), Peggy Lee, Shaenon K. Garrity, Andrew Farago, Julie Kim, Raina Lee, Martin Cendreda, Jenny Suh, Jason Shiga, Jesse Hamm, Amanda Lovell, (Estro)Jen Yin, Vera Brosgol, Jen Wang, Bill Mudron, Dylan Meconis, Erica Moen, Kevin Hanna, Lark Pien, Thien Pham, Amber Heaton, Scott Louie, Bill Poon, Jessica Gao, Hana Kim, Grace Lim, Geoffrey Pay, Drew Weing, Tracy White, KYCC, Jing Mei Lee Bentley, everyone at Modern Tales, Alex Robinson, Jason Little, Hellen Jo, R. Stevens, Kathleen Kim, Paul Hornschemeier, David Choe, Peter Bagge, Eric Nakamura, Tabasco Sauce, and last, but definitely not least, all the wonderfully open-minded readers who gave me a chance online.